The Chinese Wine Renaissance

The Chinese Wine Renaissance

A wine lover's companion

JANET Z. WANG

EBURY
PRESS

3 5 7 9 10 8 6 4 2

Published in 2019 by Ebury Press an imprint of Ebury Publishing,
20 Vauxhall Bridge Road,
London SW1V 2SA

Ebury Press is part of the Penguin Random House group of companies
whose addresses can be found at global.penguinrandomhouse.com

Penguin
Random House
UK

This edition published by Ebury Press in 2019

www.penguin.co.uk

A CIP catalogue record for this book is available from the British Library

ISBN 9781529103601

Please go to winepeek.com to access special reader offers on Chinese wines, author's
updates and additional material

Picture credits:
Attribution-ShareAlike 2.0 Generic: 173
Château Changyu Moser XV: 27; first colour section 6
Chengdu Youyuanfang Spirits Co. Ltd: 36, 40, 170; first colour section: 11, 12
Fang Ruozhou: 111, 113, 142,149, 158, 168, 172, 180, 181, 185, 193, 205: first colour
section: 13, 14, 15, 16
Lu Kuangsheng: 72, 85, 86, 88; endpapers
Li Demei: 34; first colour section: 2, 7, 8, 9, 10
Moët Hennessy, Jean Penninck: first colour section: 1(*top and bottom*)
Rong Jian: first colour section: 4, 5
Skyline of Gobi Vineyard: first colour section: 3
Wellcome Collection: 107, 141, 207, 212; second colour section: 14, 16

Other images are by courtesy of the museums noted in captions
Text design: Peter Ward

Every effort has been made to secure permissions and credits where necessary;
the author and publishers would be happy to hear of any oversight

Titles of the interviewees are as they were at the time of the interview

Typeset in India by Integra Software Services Pvt. Ltd, Pondicherry

Printed and bound in Great Britain by Clays Ltd, Elcograf S.p.A.

CONTENTS

A VERTICAL TASTING
OF HISTORY

117

APPENDICES

Foreword
by Oz Clarke

I've been visiting China for over 30 years on trips to do with food, tea, music and culture, even railways, yet rarely with wine as my prime objective. But I learned quickly enough about *jiu* – a word that seems to encompass pretty much every alcoholic beverage in China, from the fieriest white spirit to the fascinating, mellow, ancient world of rice-based wines, and now to the pulsating, rapidly changing, constantly evolving world of wines made from the grape. I also revelled in the eating and drinking culture that so many different regions of China boast in all their glorious individuality. But I never really got to the heart of what turns out to be a truly astonishing culture of wine in China, reaching back thousands of years, and now racing forwards faster than any wine culture in the world.

Janet Wang could not have come into my life at a more propitious time. I first met her at a tasting of Swiss wines, and she immediately impressed me with her enthusiasm, her determination to understand and experience every different flavour and style, and also with her open-mindedness. When I said I'd like to understand the world of Chinese wine better, she just said, 'Give me time and you will.'

This indispensable new book shows that Janet has spent her time well. She has managed to bend her extremely focused, business-like mind to this complex world and explain it to Western readers in such a reasoned and clear-eyed way that the challenges of understanding China and its relationship with wine turn into intriguing mysteries, which she unravels on the page, and often illustrates with the counterpoint of Chinese poetry.

The Chinese Wine Renaissance is not just about Chinese wine, though. It is about China *and* wine – what part wine has played in Chinese life, how this changed dramatically in the early part of the twenty-first century, and where wine in China is now headed.

This book takes me into the Chinese mind, for better and for worse, and has transformed my ability to enjoy the rich tradition of all forms of Chinese wine, from the misty distant past of ancient rice harvests to the glaring spotlight of the latest Cabernet Sauvignon. It also explains very punchily and lucidly the current Chinese attitudes to wine, and the ambitions the Chinese quite unashamedly harbour for the future. Thank you, Janet. I am sure your book will find the audience it deserves.

A note on spellings

In this book, and in most modern texts on China, Chinese words are generally spelled using the pinyin system, which is the standardised phonetic transliteration of Mandarin Chinese words using the Roman alphabet, a system devised in the 1950s and gradually adopted internationally.

Pinyin spellings are used here unless certain words are much better known in their Romanised or Wade–Giles forms (the legacy European transcription systems), in which case the most familiar convention will be used alongside, or instead of, the pinyin version. For example, the Romanised name Confucius is better known than the pinyin version, Kong Fu Zi. Similarly, the Wade–Giles spelling of Canton over Guangdong is more recognisable in English. In other cases, such as several Chinese wine brands, the pinyin and Wade–Giles versions are evenly matched, and interchangeable in common usage. The pinyin versions tend to be more recognisable to a Chinese audience while, globally, the brand has often adopted Wade–Giles spellings, such as in the case of Tsingtao (Wade–Giles)/Qingdao (pinyin), Changyu (Wade–Giles)/Zhangyu (pinyin) and Kweichow Moutai (Wade–Giles)/Guizhou Maotai (pinyin).

In addition, since Chinese words are made up of one or more mono-syllabic characters, pinyin spellings may include a space between each syllable corresponding to each Chinese character, or may be joined up much like an English word. For example, 'pinyin' is sometimes written as 'pin yin' to correspond to the two Chinese characters '拼音'. Currently there is no standardisation, although syllables tend to be closed up as a word becomes familiar: thus 'Beijing' rather than 'Bei Jing', in the same vein that 'wine making' may be written as 'winemaking'. Western writing tends to have spacing by word because it is more relatable to the way in which letters are clustered. For example, the pinyin spelling of the ancient city Xi An is sometimes Xi'an – an apostrophe is required here in the 'spacing by word' system, where two vowels are adjacent to each other, in order to disambiguate the two distinct syllables 'xi' and 'an'. In this book, there will be a mixture of pinyin spellings, depending on convention and ease of reading. The main point to bear in mind is that variations will inevitably arise.

Things become yet more complicated with names of people, dynasties and places. A sovereign may be referred to by their birth name, the name they were known by as a ruler, their posthumous name or temple name; men of letters, such as writers and poets, often adopted a style name in addition to their birth name; even dynasties may have different names depending on one's political stance or for ease of chronology. There are also instances where names are more recognisable or meaningful to the Western reader in their literal form, such as the Yellow River rather than Huang He. I have opted for the versions that will seem most familiar to the modern audience.

The reader should also bear in mind that a particular Romanised spelling could correspond to a multitude of different Chinese characters with different meanings (and possibly different intonations), such as the Zhou dynasty, which overthrew a tyrant king named Zhou. Luckily, the context is usually sufficient to differentiate the two.

Unfamiliar sounds and inconsistent conventions notwithstanding, I generally feel that it is less important to remember names than to know the story. If it is any consolation, spare a thought for the Chinese drinker who gives up on Château Pichon-Longueville Comtesse de Lalande just because the wine name is too taxing!

A basic guide to pinyin pronunciations

Letter	Sounds like
A	*a* in 'apple'
B	*b* in 'ball'
C	*ts* in 'tents'
D	*d* in 'dirt'
E	*ur* in 'fur'
F	*f* in 'fort'
G	*g* in 'girl'
H	*h* in 'herd'
I	*ee* in 'bee'
J	*j* in 'jeep'
K	*k* in 'kirk'
L	*l* in 'lurk'
M	*m* in 'more'
N	*n* in 'nerve'
O	*o* in 'oat'
P	*p* in 'pour'
Q	*ch* in 'cheek' (approximately)
R	*r* in 'red'
S	*s* in 'sir'
T	*t* in 'turf'
U	*oo* in 'roof'
Ü	*ew* in 'pewter'
V	not applicable
W	*w* in 'wall'
X	*sh* in 'share' (approximately)
Y	*ee* in 'bee'
Z	*ds* in 'woods'

Letter combination (not exhaustive)	Sounds like
ch	*ch* in 'chair'
sh	*sh* in 'shirt'
zh	*j* in 'jam'; *dg* in 'fudge'
ai	*ai* in 'Thai'
ao	*ow* in 'cow'
ei	*ay* in 'bay'
ie	*ye* in 'yet'
iu/yu	*ewe* in 'ewe'
ui	*wei* in 'weigh'
ou	*o* in 'go'; *oa* in 'goat'

To warm up, here is a wine-themed Chinese tongue-twister to challenge your friends with, and then impress them with your rendition:

Jiu jiu chi jiu, jiu zui jiu jiu qiu jiu.

The uncle drank wine, drunk on wine, the uncle begged for help.

Preface

Pray do not decline my first toast of wine;
Pray do not doubt my second toast;
Pray on the third you will begin to know my heart.

Bai Juyi (772–846)

These three simple lines reveal much about the Chinese psyche: three rounds of wine represent the Confucian decorum that still resonates to this day. Through the act of toasting, the poet indicates the desire to establish rapport, sincerity and trust – the foundations of any relationship – between the host and guest. These sentiments ring true down the ages and across the world. So an appreciation of culture through wine can open doors and hearts, both in business and personal affairs.

This is the sort of snippet I serve up to my Western friends when they ask for an executive summary of Chinese etiquette or for ice-breaking tips before dining with a Chinese delegation. As a British-Chinese, I was fortunate to grow up in both countries, and have been able to assimilate a part of both cultures within myself. Thanks to this dual perspective, I am in turns enlightened by different points of view, inspired by alternative approaches, amused by eccentricities, infuriated by stereotypes and intrigued to find similarities between cultures. A Chinese idiom goes, 'the eastern and western halves complete the round jade', and it is my hope to convey the best of both East and West.

I grew up in China, a child of the 1980s, in the bold new era of 'Reform and Opening Up' that saw China adopt capitalist economic models with increasing confidence and clout on the international stage. My generation came of age amid a sense of vibrancy and optimism. I also had the good fortune to complete my education in the UK among friendly peers who embraced my cultural background with great interest.

I am passionate about Chinese history and literature, especially poetry (thanks to an extracurricular regime from a 'tiger mother' since my early years). As I recall from the poems I stuffed into my memory bank as a child, wine was a very popular theme. Wine, it seemed, was something wondrous in the adult world, and wielded great powers over humanity – it could somehow induce elation and joy; it could offer comfort and solace; it could kindle love and friendship; or destroy lives and dynasties. Wine, too, flowed continuously through the endless dramas in the history books in whose riveting stories I liked to get lost. And so, long before my first physical experience of wine, it was clear to me that China was a culture with a rich wine heritage, and locked in the back of my mind were hazy notions of familiarity with the allure of wine.

It was only a matter of time before these feelings were uncorked and poured. During my time at university I had my first encounters with fine wine at dinners, complete with gowns and college clarets, that featured frequently in the social calendar. After graduation, a happy side-effect of my career as a commodities trader, dealing mostly with French, Italian and Spanish counterparts, was the opportunity to taste many exquisite wines. It seemed all along that I was destined to fall in love with wine. My fate was sealed after a visit to Bordeaux, where I was smitten by the picturesque vineyards and fairy-tale châteaux, the delights of great food and delicious wine enjoyed with friends, immersed in nature's inimitable beauty. Yet here was the real twist in my story: my innate appreciation of wine, which stemmed from a Chinese upbringing, was made real and vivid by my experience of Western wines. For me, the Chinese poems could have waxed lyrical about *l'art de vivre* of claret just as much as the bottle of Chinese traditional 'Old Well Tribute' wine my parents sealed away at my birth. The emotive language of wine transcends space and time.

After my first trip to Bordeaux, the majority of my subsequent holidays were wine themed. Intriguingly, I found myself rather popular with local proprietors on these wine trips. I recall Bordeaux in particular lingering in the glow of those dream years – the 2009 and 2010 'vintages of the century' – while Chinese customers responded fervently, buying up the finest labels in bulk as if their thirst was unquenchable. My popularity, it seemed, owed at least something to my Chinese appearance!

Of course, I felt a sense of pride at the economic prowess China enjoyed at this time, but it was tinged with a touch of dismay at stories of excessive flaunting of wealth. I began to talk to winemakers, merchants and marketers about the Chinese buyers and they painted an intriguing picture of the Chinese wine market. On the one hand, there were anecdotes about herd buying of trophy brands and speculation to make a quick fortune, of indifference to the wine and its heritage, even horror stories about people mixing prized vintages with Coca-Cola. On the other hand, there was admiration of how readily the Chinese can take on new knowledge, and their quick appreciation of nuanced wine concepts such as tannins, balance, structure and terroir.

Everyone agreed, however, that the Chinese market was extremely important for the future of the global wine industry because of its sheer size, its increasing wealth and its newfound fervour for wine. Engaging the Chinese in a cultural exchange about wine is therefore high on the Western wine industry's agenda, to ensure that demand is driven by drinking and learning and not reliant on monetary speculation or fashionable posturing. This could not be more relevant now, as the frenzied Chinese buying of high-end wines ran out of steam by 2011. The ability to grow a stable fan base of genuine wine drinkers with consistent spending power is the key to a sustainable future for wine in the Chinese market. The increasing presence of Chinese wine lovers in the international arena has started new conversations. In tasting rooms and wine cellars around the globe, people are beginning to talk about new grape varieties, new tastes and drawing new comparisons, such as 'I learned about a *Vitis quinquangularis Rehd* that's indigenous to Guangxi province and could enhance a blend in acidity and colour' or 'I smell the aroma of loquat in Sauternes and it takes me back to my childhood in Hong Kong.'

Around the harvest time of the 2011 vintage I began to harbour the idea of writing a book about Chinese wine culture, harnessing my experience and understanding of East and West. By this point, I'd had experience of consulting business owners and wine merchants about doing business in China, and talking to them about Chinese wine culture. I had also explored the viability of electronic wine trading platforms and of commoditising wine trading and settlement with several entrepreneurs and investors, with a view to tracking provenance and tackling the fake wine epidemic in China. Through my research and interaction with the wine industry over the years, I was convinced that wine drinking in China would experience a genuine renaissance, and was not just a fashion for the elite, set to last just a few seasons. The Chinese have earned a reputation for acquiring breadth and depth of wine knowledge quickly and intuitively, perhaps because their cultural DNA underpins such abilities: as the book will show you, wine is an old and familiar friend to the Chinese.

While the desire to understand Western wine is rapidly growing in China, the reverse flow of knowledge is lacklustre by comparison, especially when compared to the interest in Chinese food. But Chinese wine culture is no less fascinating, so why should this be? It cannot be due to a lack of desire to understand China, yet the mindset of the wider world is often Western-centric. Within the wine trade many people, including the Chinese, tend to believe that the aim of a greater understanding of Chinese culture would ultimately be to transmit Western winemaking concepts to the Chinese, rather than to acquire useful insights. The fledgling Chinese domestic wine production industry is an example of how this does not have to be the case. There, exchanges and learning are mutual and China's terroirs pose both opportunities and challenges for international collaborations, notably the challenge of extremely cold winters that require most vines to be buried in winter and dug out again in spring. Local grape varieties and new mixed varieties are being experimented with to improve the robustness, yield, quality and style of China's own wines, and this is enriching the international language of wine in the process.

Typically, though, if the topic of wine culture in China arises at all in conversation, even among wine professionals, terms such as 'lacking', 'new' and 'foreign' are often used. This could, perhaps, be due to translation: in China, the closest word for 'wine', *jiu*, can refer to alcoholic drinks in general, including grain-based wines and distilled liquors that are more characteristically Chinese, to the extent that many people do not realise that grape wine, too, has enjoyed a long history in China. Another reason could be wine's shared fate with China's social, economic and political health. Throughout Chinese history, time and again there were cycles of harmony and discord, of power and peril, of wealth and hardship accompanied by the boom and bust of wine culture. During periods of political confidence, economic prosperity and social stability, wine culture flourished and greatly enriched every aspect of life. Yet during periods of political peril, economic woe, natural or social disasters, wine was widely prohibited, labelled as non-essential, wasteful of resources and a facilitator for social unrest. In the past century, wine culture in China had greatly suffered as a result of political turmoil and social fragility. It is quite understandable that, within living memory, wine culture appeared lacklustre in China, in the same way that most Westerners perceive China as a newly emerging market, while the Chinese themselves, with a keen sense of their country's long civilisation and history, consider superpower status as a return to order and normality. Now, as the second-largest world economy, a new lease of life has emerged in an ancient wine culture, this time embracing globalisation but also asserting its own characteristics. The love affair with wine is blossoming once more. To the Chinese, wine needs no introduction – it is experiencing a renaissance.

> *The wild fire could not exterminate it all;*
> *The spring breeze will breathe in life once more.*

Bai Juyi (772–846)

I believe the whole world will take note of China's wine renaissance. It will bring both opportunities and threats (depending on one's perspective). It calls for a willingness to understand and readiness to embrace a new phenomenon. As I hope to make clear in this book, the current revival is merely the latest iteration of an ancient Chinese culture in which wine is very much part of the nation's identity. Wine is woven into the fabric of life and features throughout the history books: it assumes prominent roles in religion, rites, politics, philosophy, diplomacy, technology, science, medicine, art, poetry, calligraphy, music and games. Wine culture has much to tell about China's past, present and future, and much to add to our collective wisdom.

Wine culture guides everyday situations, too. For example, a wine merchant new to China may be surprised to face frequent questions about the relative health benefits of various wines; a business executive may feel at a loss due to the numerous rounds of wine toasts at a Chinese banquet; an exchange student in China may wonder whether a bottle of wine would be a suitable meeting gift for the host family. The clues to such questions can be gleaned from Chinese wine's historic connection with Chinese medicine, and its irreplaceable function in Confucian honorary rites, which mean that wine is often used as a gesture of respect and goodwill. These practices, steeped in ancient traditions, still shape thinking and behaviour today. They are also finding modern relevance in many fields: wine merchants and medical researchers alike are paying attention to the possible health-related benefits of wine, and even the lucrative beauty industry is taking note with wine-derived lotions and potions.

This book is, in part, my attempt to remedy some misconceptions about Chinese culture and fill in some key knowledge gaps. As wine lovers know, discussions of world history, culture, arts and customs among people from different backgrounds become stimulating and bring people closer with a glass of wine in hand. By looking at China through a wine glass, I offer a wide perspective that encompasses China's past in order to understand its present and look to the future.

Part I, by way of an aperitif, will introduce you to China's wine industry, its major wine-producing regions and the evolution of grape wine among the various types of alcoholic beverage that make up China's wide repertoire. Part II is a mixed case in which we look at enduring wine themes in the context of China and explore the distinctive fusion of cultures in wine and beyond. Part III is a vertical tasting of the dynastic history of China, illustrating the evolution of wine alongside the evolution of a civilisation.

This book is not solely for wine lovers and professionals. It is also a story for anyone interested in Chinese culture and history, with wine as the protagonist. I hope it appeals not only to Western readers curious about Chinese wine, but also to inquisitive Chinese people who are increasingly aware of, and seeking different perspectives to reflect on, their own culture. I aim to speak even-handedly without excessive fervour or cynicism, but with the unrepentantly healthy dose of pride of the native talking about her motherland. I think it is helpful for Western audiences to understand how the Chinese perceive their culture and history, just as it is for the Chinese to reconnect with their own heritage, in a way that is aware of a global context.

So here it is, a taste of China through a wine journey. What a delightful way to explore a culture! With thousands of years of stories and wine drinking, China's tales have not yet all been savoured. With this book I hope to bring life, colour, knowledge and ultimately a greater understanding of China, to everyone. To ardent and prospective wine lovers alike – cheers, *ganbei*!

Janet Z. Wang

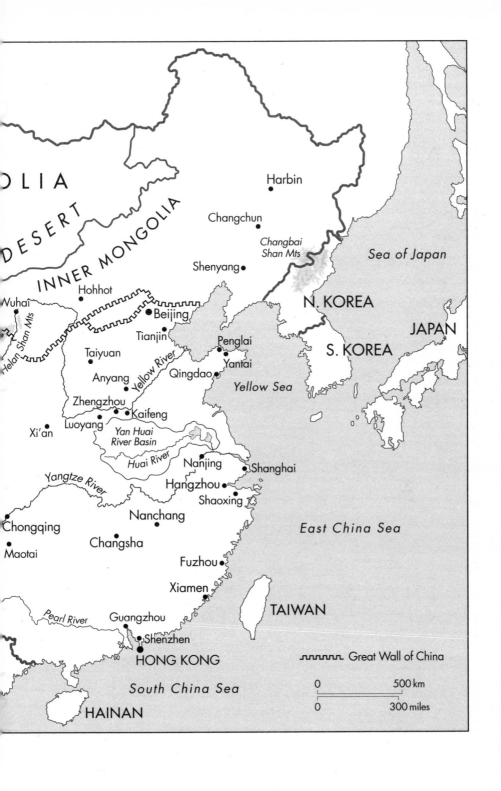

Harbin

Changchun

Changbai
Shan Mts

Shenyang

Sea of Japan

N. KOREA

S. KOREA

JAPAN

OLIA

DESERT

INNER MONGOLIA

Wuhai

Helan Shan Mts

Hohhot

Beijing

Tianjin

Taiyuan

Anyang

Yellow River

Penglai

Yantai

Qingdao

Yellow Sea

Zhengzhou

Kaifeng

Xi'an

Luoyang

Yan Huai
River Basin

Huai River

Nanjing

Shanghai

Hangzhou

Shaoxing

East China Sea

Chongqing

Yangtze River

Nanchang

Changsha

Maotai

Fuzhou

Xiamen

TAIWAN

Pearl River

Guangzhou

Shenzhen

HONG KONG

South China Sea

HAINAN

⎍⎍⎍⎍⎍ Great Wall of China

0   500 km

0   300 miles

APERITIF

Wine predates humanity's record keeping. Currently the earliest archaeological finding of a fermented beverage was in China and dates back some 9,000 years. It was possibly made from rice, honey and wild grapes or hawthorn. Since the infancy of humanity, wine has accompanied the making of civilisations. This is compellingly so for Chinese civilisation: over thousands of years, wine has survived, though dynasties have risen and fallen and the Middle Kingdom has seen cycles of unity and discord. Wine culture, then, is a potent indicator of China's social, economic and political health. Wine's epic history is full of intrigue, drama and lessons in humanity: it has bonded armies on the eve of epic battles; played accomplice in power struggles and palace intrigues; engaged philosophers in debates and books; and inspired artists, poets and calligraphers to unleash their masterpieces. Wine is the concentrated wisdom of a culture, and the liquid mirror to the heart and soul of a people.

The Chinese word *jiu* is often translated as 'wine', but in fact refers broadly to alcoholic beverages. 'Wine' seems a more fitting translation than, say, 'alcohol' or 'liquor' because of its nuanced association with culture. Chinese *jiu*, which counts fermented grape juice among its repertoire, holds the positive cultural cachet bestowed on the word 'wine' that is lacking in other terms. In this book, 'wine' usually refers to Western-style grape wine, while in a historical context it applies to traditional Chinese wines that could be made from various ingredients. Distinctions about types of wines are made when necessary or for emphasis.

Chinese winemaking ranges from the familiar – naturally fermented, distilled and blended – to the distinctive Chinese innovation of using fermentation inducers: a mixture of cultured moulds, yeasts and grains to induce and control fermentation and add character to the wine. *Huang jiu* (literally: yellow wine) is the generic name for grain-based Chinese wines; *bai jiu* (literally: white wine) usually refers to highly alcoholic distilled liquor; *hong jiu* (literally: red wine) traditionally refers to yellow wine produced with the addition of a red-coloured fermentation inducer, but in modern usage tends to mean Western-style grape wine of any colour. Wine names may highlight their origin: for example, *Shaoxing jiu* is traditionally made in the Shaoxing region, in the eastern province of Zhejiang. Some names play up the wine's character: for example, Zhu Ye Qing (Bamboo Green), which contains bamboo leaves among its herbal ingredients. Others may opt for a poetic or auspicious name, such as Gu Jing Gong (Old Well Tribute), which suggests its heritage and superior quality as a tribute wine gifted to the emperor.

In the grape-wine category, China is on its way to becoming the world's largest producer within half a century. It is already a top-ten producer by volume and has the largest planting area of Cabernet Sauvignon vines in the world. At present, however, Chinese wines are mostly consumed domestically. International appetite for Chinese wine remains limited, partly due to a lack of awareness. The quality-to-price ratio of Chinese wines is a challenge in the global marketplace, for although labour is relatively cheap and abundant in China, viticulture on the whole is highly manual, with deeply entrenched inefficiencies and climatic challenges that are costly to overcome, such as the need to bury vines over winter in many northern vineyards. There will no doubt be a period of systematic efficiency gains, changes in local farming habits and mentalities, and market- and policy-driven adaptations that will in time create a satisfactory ecosystem for viticulture. The current moment is nonetheless a fascinating and pioneering phase in China's modern wine industry, and its impact on the global consumer market could filter through sooner than many may expect.

Despite China's reputation for rapid growth in many arenas, wine consumption remains under-exploited, even when we account for the steady growth since the 1990s and the remarkable acceleration after the turn of the new millennium. China is expected to become the second-largest wine market in sales value by 2020, trailing only the United States. Per capita wine consumption in China, however, is barely two bottles per annum (compared to around 14 bottles in the USA, 28 in the UK and 58 in France). This points to considerable headroom for growth in a country experiencing rapid expansion in its urban middle-class population, which is estimated at around 400 million in 2018 and expected to rise above 700 million by 2030.

For wine drinkers across the world, the emergence of China brings novel wine styles and tasting opportunities. For winemakers, China opens up new frontiers and challenges for collaboration and learning. For wine distributors, an understanding of China's wine culture and heritage is key to communication and relationship-building. The most successful players in the Chinese market are attuned to regional customs and attitudes, and impart wine knowledge in a localised context. Genuine interest in incumbent culture and a display of reciprocity in learning would not only impress but also earn respect, forge trust and open doors.

The rise of grape wine in modern China

To me, the two most fascinating phenomena of our time are the rise of the internet age and China's economic transformation since 'Reform and Opening Up'. Born from humble beginnings these have become epoch-changing chapters in human history. Both are still playing out before our eyes, creating frenzies, opportunities, myths, legends and abysses unlike any gold rush that has come before.

While the digital revolution and China's meteoric rise are keenly felt by all of us, have you noticed the other renaissance they are bringing about, and which will be on everyone's lips soon – quite literally – in the form of wine? Within the trade, China's prominence as the world's fastest-growing wine market since the turn of the millennium is alluring. China is now a leading nation for red wine consumption, the fourth largest global importer of grape wines and among the top wine producers.

China's online and mobile-led e-commerce is sophisticated and flamboyant. Digital giants such as Alibaba, Tencent and JD.com have incredible reach to millions of new and young Chinese consumers. Yet more compelling is the fact that the Chinese wine market, both online and offline, is young and unevenly distributed, with plenty of opportunity for expansion.

For wine enthusiasts, China is the dark horse to watch as a wine-producing nation, and has made bold moves to improve quality through domestic and international collaborative efforts. With vineyards spreading across diverse terrains, China will offer some characterful wine styles and enrich the international vocabulary of wine tasting in the years to come: from the foothills of the Tibetan Plateau to the Yellow River valley, from extreme altitudes of 3,000m above sea level to extreme winter temperatures of –25°C, winemakers embrace the awesome terroirs that China offers. At the 2017 Vinexpo, the world's most prestigious wine fair, China's first official appellation, Ningxia Helan Mountain, was among the most discussed exhibitors. The appellation is a multi-billion dollar project on the border of the Gobi Desert some 800km west of Beijing. The region shot to international fame in 2011 when the Helan Qingxue winery's Jia Bei Lan 2009, a Bordeaux-style red wine, won the most coveted international trophy at the *Decanter* World Wine Awards – a new benchmark for Chinese producers at international level, and a sign of things to come.

The turn of the new millennium saw a gold rush of a different kind. Chinese buyers became a colossal speculative force in the Bordeaux fine-wine market and led to an unsustainable price bubble (*see* pages 49–62). Prices stabilised in 2011 and the growth outlook has markedly improved again since 2015, this time with more drinkers than speculators steering the market. Demand for wine education has also enjoyed strong growth in recent years, both as a desirable profession and among the general public. This supports the promise of a more sustainable future for wine in China.

A brief history of grape wine in China

What may surprise many people, both inside and outside China, is that grape wine has enjoyed a very long history there. Fossil records of 26 million year-old wild grapes called *qiu pu tao* (literally autumn grape, *Vitis romanetii Roman. du Caill. ex Planch.*) were found in the eastern coastal province of Shandong. Sediments found in seventh-millennium BC Neolithic pottery at the Jiahu site in the central Yellow River plain suggest that wild grapes may have been used to produce wine since antiquity.

The earliest surviving collection of Chinese poetry, the *Shi Jing*, which was compiled between the eleventh and sixth centuries BC, noted that grapes were eaten in the 'sixth month' (equivalent to August in the Gregorian calendar), while the *Shi Ji* (*Records of the Grand Historian*), completed in the first century BC during the reign of Emperor Han Wudi, records cultivated grape varieties being introduced to China from the Western Regions (parts of today's north-western province of Xinjiang and Central Asia). This is thanks to envoy Zhang Qian's westward explorations at the request of the emperor, which resulted in the trade route we now know as the Silk Road. Emperor Han Wudi was very interested in cultivating vineyards within China's Central Plain region, and even brought in winemakers from the Western Regions.

Lady-in-waiting holding a pitcher and wine glass, wall mural from the tomb of Princess Fangling (619–73), Tang dynasty. Height 182cm, width 90cm. Currently housed in Shaanxi History Museum

Han Wudi and the Silk Road thus marked a watershed moment in the history of viticulture in China.

By the Tang dynasty (AD 618–907), increased cultural and trade interactions with the Western Regions propelled viticulture to an unprecedented height in China, and grape wine was now much more accessible. It was relished by the elite, the learned and frontier soldiers, and was even used as a dowry for young brides from wealthy families. Wine-inspired poetry was prolific and became a lasting legacy of the dynasty.

During the enlightened Song dynasty (960–1279), grape wine continued to be revered. *Garagiste*-style homemade wines were in vogue, often gifted and drunk with much discernment among the literati, and wine-tasting notes were written in poetry form.

The Mongol-ruled Yuan dynasty (1279–1368) endorsed grape wine and *kumis* (fermented horse's milk) as imperial state wines. With the expansion of the Mongol empire, the wine-producing region continued to grow, and tribute wines travelled from west and Central Asia to Dadu – the 'Great Capital' that is now Beijing. By this time, grape wine was widely available and had become popular across all social classes.

During the Ming dynasty (1368–1644), the level of discernment remained fairly high. Ming connoisseurs were appreciative of the colour, nose, taste and cultural values of grape wine, as the political class attempted to restore Confucian values, which extended to etiquettes related to wine appreciation. Grape wine eventually fell out of royal favour, however, owing to its costly logistics as an imperial tribute, which meant it had to travel from distant areas to the capital. Grape wine production and consumption gradually declined across the realm.

During the Qing dynasty (1644–1912), imported European wines – the sort we could more readily identify with today – made their way across the oceans to China in significant quantities, and were held in great esteem by the Qing court. In 1892, Changyu (alternatively spelled Zhangyu) winery was founded in Yantai, Shandong province. It was the first Chinese commercial winery for European-style wines on an industrial scale. By this time, the Qing government was in crisis and, amid heightened nationalist calls to modernise China, Changyu winery's founder, Zhang Bishi, found his calling in wine against this historical backdrop. Changyu is credited with developing the grape variety Cabernet Gernischt (the old-world Carménère) in China. In fact, Zhang Bishi introduced no fewer than 120 European grape varieties to his vineyards.

For a brief overview of the imperial dynasties of China and a historical timeline, please see pages 230 and 237 respectively.

With the fall of the last dynasty in 1912 and the turbulence that ensued well into the twentieth century, the wine industry entered a period of general decline in China. During the semi-colonisation period (1840–1949), several overseas-owned wine companies emerged. These wineries served the demands of their German, French or Japanese owners and collaborators and the local expatriate communities. Some of these wineries are still operating today, for example the Beiping Shangyi Winery, founded in 1910 by French missionaries in western Beijing and operating today as the Beijing Dragon Seal Winery; the Shandong Melco Winery, established in Qingdao by the German occupiers in 1930 and operating today as the Qingdao Huadong Winery; the Changbai Shan Wine Company and the Tonghua Wine Company, founded in 1936 and 1937 respectively by the Japanese in Jilin province, are still operating today under the same names.

Following the establishment of 'New China' in 1949 when the People's Republic of China was founded, wine began its comeback. Even during the politically unstable period of the 1950s to the 1970s, significant progress was made in research and breeding programmes of grape varieties, notably the cross-breeding of native Chinese varieties with European varieties to find species suited to regional climatic and soil conditions. As early as 1951, the Jilin Institute of Pomology produced a Muscat Hamburg and *Vitis amurensis* hybrid named Gong Niang No. 1 that can resist freezing temperatures of -22°C. Similar efforts in various parts of the country over the decades have produced other hybrids that can overwinter safely at -29°C, with additional advantages such as disease and rot resistance, high yields and sweeter grapes. Research aside, however, production quality and general consumption were low. Much of the domestically produced wine of this period was mixed with juices, water or other ingredients to lower costs, a practice known as 'half juice' that was eventually phased out and abolished in 2004.

The 1980s heralded the 'Reform and Opening Up' economic policies that set China on an unparalleled growth trajectory. During this period, foreign investments and joint ventures poured into China, while wine imports also began to flourish. From this era, the brands Great Wall and Dynasty joined Changyu as household names of Western-style wines, making Bordeaux-blend reds and dry whites. Since the 1990s, wine import, consumption and domestic production have all gathered pace, and since 2000 China has become one of the most important and influential wine markets in the international arena. Thirst for wine knowledge has exploded in recent years and wine tourism, both internationally and domestically, is gaining popularity. Continued investments and international joint ventures are propelling China to emerge as a serious contender for fine winemaking.

The main winemaking and production regions

The Yellow River and Yangtze River are the lifelines of China, roughly dividing two large agricultural plains. The Yellow River in the north sustains a colder and drier region, where wheat, sorghum and millet are suitable crops, The Yangtze in the south drains warmer, wetter and fertile lands where rice cultivation thrives. Most of China's vineyards are located north of the Yangtze River.

Beyond these river basins, China is protected by mountain ranges to the west, jungles to the south and the sea to the east. The north-western deserts and northern steppes (grasslands), however, have traditionally been the weak link in China's defences. To compensate for the lack of natural protection along the northern frontiers, the Chinese began to build defensive walls over 2,000 years ago, and the collective efforts down the dynasties became what is known as the Great Wall. There still persists an urban myth that the Great Wall of China is the only man-made structure visible from outer space – fantastic, yet sadly untrue, just like a new wine myth that shocked the French in recent years: that China has more winegrowing land area than France. This is not correct, for now at least. At present, China has the second largest area under vine at around 847,000 hectares, behind Spain but ahead of France, but only about 140,000 hectares are for wine grapes. The rest are for table grapes. So China's planting and output for winemaking have not yet surpassed the traditional top producers such as France. This 'vineyard area' figure is widely misinterpreted, which reflects the perceived pace of China's growth and the fantastical nature of statistics on China. Sources and accuracy are often difficult to validate or prone to being misread, and often outdated by the time they are compiled, so much so that any astronomical number or rate of growth attached to China sounds plausible. In this book, while care has been taken to present current and reliable sources of information, it is inevitable that some information will change, so the figures perform an illustrative function.

The taxonomy of Chinese wild grapes can be traced to the eighteenth century. Modern research in this field since the 1950s, however, has revealed that China is one of the major gene pools for grape vine species. The *Vitis* genus contains over 70 species, of which the *Vitis vinifera*, known as the European species or the common grape vine, is the most widely used for winemaking and comprises the most familiar grape varieties. China is home to 40 *Vitis* species, one sub-species and 13 varieties. These numbers are subject to change, as research is ongoing and increasingly collaborative. The study, classification and breeding of these so-called Chinese wild grapes are a boon for viticulture worldwide. Chinese native *Vitis* species often have useful qualities such as resistance to cold and diseases such as powdery mildew and rot, notably the *Vitis amurensis*, which is an excellent cold-resistant parent for breeding other cold-resistant varieties. Experiments in cross-breeding could guide the future direction of Chinese wine production, with new species even better suited to the climates and growing conditions of China.

Thus far, Chinese vineyards have mostly opted for Bordeaux varieties, with around 80 per cent dedicated to red varieties. Of these,

Cabernet Sauvignon is the predominant grape, accounting for about 60 per cent, while Cabernet Gernischt (Carménère) and Merlot roughly account for 10 per cent each. Other red varieties include Cabernet Franc, Petit Verdot, Syrah (Shiraz), Pinot Noir, Muscat Hamburg and Marselan. Marselan, in particular, is emerging as a star variety that is adapting well to Chinese conditions and displaying quality potential. It is a cross between Cabernet Sauvignon and Grenache, created in 1961 for the French Languedoc region and named after the coastal commune of Marseillan. Marselan was created to combine desirable qualities such as higher yields, flavourful grapes and high resistance to diseases.

Of the white varieties planted in China, Chardonnay dominates, followed by Riesling (although mostly Welschriesling/Italian Riesling) and other familiar varieties including Sauvignon Blanc, Chenin Blanc and Gewürztraminer. Less well-known varieties, mostly from the ex-Soviet Union blocs of Eastern Europe, for example Rkatsiteli and Saperavi, can still be found in some Chinese vineyards, a reminder of China's strong ties with the Soviet Union during the 1950s.

Today, however, making Bordeaux-style dry red is the holy grail for many Chinese wineries. They have experienced varying degrees of success, not least due to the challenges of cultivating European varieties in often unsuitable conditions. For example, the East Asian monsoon system that affects large parts of China means that summers tend to be quite wet, which restricts sunshine hours and makes vines prone to disease and rot, while the cold and dry winters in northern China mean most vineyards there bury their vines prior to the winter months to help them survive the harsh, freezing and dehydrating conditions (around -17°C is the threshold temperature for burying). The vines then need to be dug out again in spring. All this, of course, is incredibly labour intensive and costly (accounting for roughly one-third of the vineyard running costs). Due to such obvious natural disadvantages as compared with, say, the temperate Mediterranean, Chinese winemaking tends to require more technical intervention and precision, and the steep learning curve is valuable. Experiments in producing hybrids, particularly crosses between Chinese and European varieties, which result in high resistance to frost and diseases, could open up new possibilities. China could become much

Château Changyu Moser XV in Ningxia is built in a grand European style

more assertive and creative over time, with its native varieties and hybrids playing up rather than subduing differences of their terroirs from those of other wine regions of the world.

Cooperation and knowledge transfer between winemakers are becoming increasingly two-way. Many vineyards in China have foreign interests in investment, technology and directorships, with imported expertise, facilities and even European-style castles (dubbed the 'château movement'), and some internationally respected experts are emerging from China with plenty to say about China's position in the wine industry.

Shandong province

This historical winemaking region is a flat peninsula with some hills in the centre, and has a maritime climate with mild winters but cool and wet summers. These increase the risk of fungal disease on vines, but the mild winters mean that vines can survive without burying. The notable wine-producing areas are Yantai, Penglai and Qingdao, and the main grape varieties grown here are Cabernet Gernischt (Carménère),

Riesling, Chardonnay and Bordeaux varieties such as Cabernet Sauvignon. Notable producers in this region include Changyu, Castel and Barons de Rothschild.

WINES TO TRY

Château Nine Peaks 九顶庄园: try a reserve Cabernet Sauvignon or Bordeaux blend, such as the 2005 or 2012 examples with ripe and expressive dark berry notes and firm tannins; or a Chardonnay that offers easy drinking with bright acidity and ripe tropical fruity notes.

Changyu 张裕: try their premium dry red made with Cabernet Gernischt, which is a sophisticated, well-balanced wine with red berry aromas mixed with savoury, earthy mushroom notes and fine tannins. Alternatively, both the entry level Noble Dragon Cabernet Gernischt and Riesling make good dinner-party gifts and conversation starters.

Hebei province

Hebei province has hot, humid summers and cold, dry winters. It is mountainous in the north (where some vineyards are located over 1,000m above sea level) and has flat floodplains in the south.

The region has a long history of winemaking, its proximity to Beijing enhancing demand and providing good marketing and sales channels.

The main wine-producing areas are the coastal Changli county and the hilly Huailai county (with Shacheng and the Yan Huai River Valley becoming rising-star regions). Some of the grape varieties grown here are Cabernet Sauvignon, Chardonnay, Merlot, Marselan and Riesling. Key producers include COFCO Great Wall and the Chinese-French Demonstration Vineyard (Domaine Franco-Chinois).

As in the Shandong peninsula, there is a high risk of fungal vine diseases in Hebei province due to the rainy summers. Vines in Changli require manual burying in winter to insulate them from the freezing temperatures and Siberian winds.

WINES TO TRY

Château Martin 马丁酒庄: for something distinctive, try a wine made from the Longyan (dragon eye) grape. This belongs to the *Vitis vinifera* family and has been planted in China for hundreds of years. It is not to be confused with the longyan (or long'an) fruit, which belongs to the same family as the lychee and rambutan fruits. Martin Longyan White or Rosé will lift your spirits with fresh and delicate notes of peaches, lychee and citrus.

COFCO Great Wall 中粮长城: Great Wall was the pioneer brand that used the Longyan grape to make China's first dry white wine in 1979. Its Bai Nian Lao Shu is quite special – the name literally means 'hundred-year-old tree', highlighting the remarkable age of the Longyan vines. The result is a mellow mouthfeel but the wine is still lively, with fresh fruit aromas of peaches and plums.

Great Wall Huaxia Bordeaux Blends are also signature wines: serious attempts at the Bordeaux dry red style, packed with plums and blackcurrant notes and firm tannins – the vintage 2005 is a successful example. For another change of style, seek out the Vindiche VSOP Brandy, which is fairly well balanced with just the right amount of oak and aromas of oranges and maple syrup.

Domaine Franco-Chinois 中法庄园: try a Marselan Reserve here, as this is the first Chinese vineyard to experiment with the Marselan grape. The 2011 and 2012 vintages are exquisite, with generous fresh fruits of blueberries and plums and hints of dark chocolate.

Château Nubes 瑞云酒庄: try the Reserve Syrah, which shows a delightful combination of blackcurrants, mulberries with hints of truffles, liquorice and pepper. Also look out for China's first biodynamic wines from this estate.

Shanxi province

The continental climate and higher altitude here allows for longer sunshine hours and high variation between day- and night-time temperatures, which can lead to high-quality, balanced wines, as the grapes can ripen well during the warm day and retain acidity during the cool nights. The notable wine-producing areas are Taiyuan and the Loess Plateau, where Cabernet Sauvignon, Muscat, Chardonnay and Merlot are grown by producers including Grace Vineyard and Château Rongzi. The favourable and varied terroirs lead to high-quality and characterful wines, but inconsistent annual rainfall brings greater uncertainty from vintage to vintage in terms of vine health, yield and wine quality. Vines require manual burying in the winter to survive.

WINES TO TRY

Grace Vineyard 怡园酒庄: a top boutique winery that flies the flag for premium winemaking in China. The Tasya's Reserve Marselan 2012 is an excellent example of its appeal and potential as a Chinese star grape variety, with juicy dark berries, plenty of freshness, bright acidity and structured tannins.

Château Rongzi 戎子酒庄: another winery that makes quality dry reds, typically well balanced and approachable, with fresh ripe berries and lively acidity.

Ningxia autonomous region

Ningxia is emerging as a star region for China's modern wine industry and wine is the key economic driver for the area. This expanse of land in north-western China borders the Gobi desert. A cold arid and semi-arid climate offers plenty of warmth, light and low rainfall, but also extremely low temperatures in the winter. High-quality winemaking conditions are made possible by the Helan Mountains, which shield the foothills from cold winds, and a well-irrigated valley thanks to the Yellow River. The soil is stony and well drained. Most wineries are built around the eastern foothills of the Helan Mountain range, including large stakeholders such as Pernod Ricard (Helan Mountain), Château Changyu (Moser XV) and Moët Hennessy (Chandon China), as well as boutiques such as Silver Heights and Kanaan Winery. Cabernet Sauvignon and Merlot are the most planted varieties here, along with Cabernet Gernischt, Syrah, Marselan,

Chardonnay and Riesling. There are great conditions – the dry climate means low threat of fungus or rot – as well as challenges for viticulture. The high temperature contrast between day and night leads to balanced ripeness and acidity in the grapes, and the well-drained and stony soil encourages the vine to preserve nutrients for growing the grapes, leading to smaller yields of more flavoursome berries. On the negative side, the winter is long and harsh and vines need to be buried in order to survive. Slower ripening Cabernet Sauvignon may not be the most suitable variety for this region, as the summer is relatively short, although rather successful Bordeaux blends are produced here, typically lighter and less concentrated in style with softer tannins and a herbaceous character. The Ningxia government is very supportive of the wine industry because it helps alleviate regional poverty, and vine planting reduces land desertification. Wines from this area have won prestigious international awards, and attracted investments and tourism to the province.

WINES TO TRY

Helan Qingxue 贺兰晴雪酒庄: one of the most high-profile wineries, which sets the bar in fine winemaking in China, made famous by its Jia Bei Lan Bordeaux-style red wine. The 2009 vintage of Jia Bei Lan Cabernet Blend won the most coveted 'Red Bordeaux Varietal over £10 International Trophy' at the *Decanter* World Wine Awards in 2011, beating entries from Bordeaux itself and other premium wine regions, and firmly announcing the arrival of serious winemaking in China to an international professional audience. Judges remarked that the wine was 'supple, graceful and ripe but not flashy' and praised its 'excellent length and four-square tannins'. The estate also produces excellent white wines such as its Jia Bei Lan Chardonnay, with elegant floral bouquets, round mouthfeel and good minerality.

Kanaan Winery 咖南美地: a distinctive image of a horse adorns Kanaan's wine labels. Try the Kanaan Pretty Pony, a full-bodied, juicy, fruity, dry red Bordeaux blend. Their Riesling and Semi-sweet White Wine (a Riesling and Chardonnay blend) are well balanced and clean with bright acidity and fresh citrus and floral notes.

Pernod Ricard Helan Mountain 贺兰山: Helan Mountain Special Reserve Chardonnay is a well-made example of Chinese Chardonnay with the right amount of oak to balance the fruitiness.

Lux Regis 类人首酒庄: Lux Regis Winery Reserve S is a Cabernet Sauvignon and Merlot blend that is quite typical of a Ningxia Bordeaux blend, with fresh cassis, well-balanced oak and a herbal note of bay leaf.

Silver Heights 银色高地: a rare gem of family-owned fine-wine producer in China. 'Emma's Reserve' 100% Cabernet Sauvignon is the namesake wine of the owner and producer Emma Gao. Try the 2009 and 2011, which are noted for their velvety mouthfeel and opulent dark, juicy fruits. Also look out for The Summit Bordeaux blend; the 2013 vintage is a typically balanced and clean-tasting dry red, with plenty of ripe berries and a hint of toast from good use of oak.

Xi Xia King 西夏王: try single varietal wines to sample the Ningxia characters of certain grapes, for example the 1950 Chardonnay, Envoy Dry White Wine (Italian Riesling) or the Envoy Dry Red Wine (Merlot).

Chandon 夏桐: compare the Chandon Brut – Ningxia's answer to sparkling wine – with its international superstar sibling Moët & Chandon champagne. You might be pleasantly surprised by its fine and long-lasting bubbles, zesty citrus and fragrant apricots, and the overall lively, refreshing taste.

Château Changyu Moser XV 张裕摩塞尔十五世: the Moser XV wines from China's oldest and largest wine brand in consultation with Austrian winemaker Laurenz Moser are making inroads for Chinese wine in the international market. Try the Grand Vin Cabernet Sauvignon 2013 for a fine example of Ningxia-style dry red – intense colour, abundance of fruit with a hint of mint and spice. For something unusual and a great conversation starter, try the 'blanc de noirs' white Cabernet – a white wine made from Cabernet Sauvignon, which serves up bright acidity and luscious peach with plenty of floral and exotic fruit aromas.

Xinjiang autonomous region

This historical wine-producing region formed part of the Western Regions in Chinese historical records. It consists of massive expanses of desert and the Tianshan mountain ranges, covering an area of 1.6 million km². It is the largest wine-producing region of China, traditionally famous for high-quality raisins. Its remoteness, however, brings logistical and transportation challenges. It has a continental/semi-arid climate with very hot, dry summers and extremely cold winters, which means vines require burying for protection.

Cabernet Sauvignon, Merlot and Chardonnay are grown in the regions of Turpan, Tianshan Manas Basin and Yanqi Basin. Representative producers here include Château Zhong Fei and Skyline of Gobi.

WINES TO TRY

Château Zhong Fei 中菲酒庄: Zhong Fei Barrel-Aged Shiraz displays good use of oak and structural complexity. Jammy blackberries with coffee and dark chocolate notes accompany a soft and supple mouthfeel.

Skyline of Gobi 天塞酒庄: Skyline of Gobi Reserve Chardonnay – at its best this is beautifully balanced, with a complex interweaving of fresh citrus fruits and toasty notes from a well-judged use of oak.

Yunnan province

This far south-western province has a long history of producing wine, with a hardy local hybrid variety and the Rose Honey grape, which is believed to have been lost in Europe during the phylloxera epidemic of the nineteenth century. This grape was a legacy of Catholic missionaries, and was preserved in a churchyard in Cizhong village, Deqen County – a small village by the Lancang River (the upper reach of the Mekong) near the Tibetan Plateau. In the vicinity of Cizhong, the low latitude, combined with high-altitude mountainous terrains, gives rise to more favourable vine-growing conditions similar to that of a continental climate, with ample exposure to sunshine and cool nights that give concentration, flavour and good acidity to the grapes, and a mild winter. The soil here is mineral-rich and imparts unique characters to the wine. The logistically challenging terrains, however, do not lend themselves to large-scale production, but are more suited to small parcels of enterprises. The scattered plots are mostly planted with Cabernet Sauvignon, and also some Merlot, Cabernet Franc and Chardonnay. LVMH Moët Hennessy Louis Vuitton is producing premium wine at the Shangri-La Winery, at the foot of the sacred Meili Mountain.

WINES TO TRY

Shangri-La Ao Yun 香格里拉 傲云: if money is no object, then this £200-a-bottle 'lofty clouds' red wine is a taste of history in the making: its inaugural 2013 vintage is a 90 per cent Cabernet Sauvignon and 10 per cent Cabernet Franc blend that is a truly premium Chinese red wine – the most costly wine produced by the luxury group LVMH due to its high altitude of up to 2,600m above sea level, which makes vine maintenance labour-intensive in villages where electricity is frequently unavailable. The colour is saturated and bold, which is typical of high-altitude wines where the grape skins are thick. It is ripe, pure and fresh, with silky-smooth tannins, sweet berries interweaved with subtle spices and cool minerality. Only 2,000 cases of this vintage were made.

A sinicised church and vineyard in Cizhong village, Deqen county,
Yunnan province

Other areas with notable wine industries include Beijing (a main focal point for demand, and close to the high-profile Yan Huai River Valley); Gansu (neighbouring Ningxia, with a similar climate and a long history of winemaking); Jilin (the Chinese wild Amur grape, *Vitis amurensis*, which is highly cold resistant and an excellent candidate for cross breeding, is grown in the Changbai Mountain area); Liaoning (a north-eastern province producing high-quality ice wines, mostly with Vidal); Sichuan (a south-western province famous for its spicy food but with mild winters that allow vines to survive without intervention); and Guangxi (a warm and humid southern province that is showing promise with the indigenous variety *Vitis quinquangularis Rehd*).

China's traditional wines

Let us now turn to Chinese *jiu* in the word's broader sense, which encompasses alcoholic beverages of all types, and look at the ingredients and processes that go into producing China's vast and colourful range of grain-based wines.

Many people in the West know of Japanese saké or Korean soju, yet few realise that their origins are closely intertwined with historical Chinese counterparts. The respective tongues of the three countries reveal this clearly: in Chinese, Japanese and Korean, clear and colourless distilled liquor is known as *shao jiu, shochu* and *soju* respectively, all originating from the Chinese word that literally means 'burned wine': this refers to the high temperature required for the distillation process and its strong alcoholic character. *Shao jiu* is now more commonly known in China as *bai jiu*. The production of saké is similar to that of traditional Chinese rice wines, where a fermentation inducer (a mixture of cultured moulds, yeasts and grains) is added to kick-start fermentation. Fermentation inducers were introduced to Japan via Korea in the sixth century AD, and have counterparts across Asia. Grain-based wines are commonly known as *huang jiu* ('yellow wine') or *mi jiu* ('rice wine') in China. Of course, each culture has made the wine styles their own, but arguably the Japanese and Koreans have held on more tightly to traditional practices than the post-Cultural Revolution Chinese. So perhaps a sip of Japanese *nigorizake* (cloudy saké), still widely available in Japan today, may be rather similar to the *yu jiang* (crème of jade) wine praised by the eighth-century poet Li Bai. A shot of soju might transport you back to an age of empire when the unstoppable Mongols were riding across the Asian steppes. The history and evolution of rice wines and spirits are just as fascinating as the journeys of the grape vine.

Fermentation inducers

Since antiquity, naturally fermented fruit, milk products and grains have created wines that delighted our ancestors. Archaeological clues suggest that wine has existed in China for over 9,000 years, and the earliest form of skilled Chinese winemaking was probably grain-based. The Chinese discovered the use of fermentation inducers, a mixture of cultured moulds, yeasts, bacteria and grains, known as *jiu qu* or simply *qu*, to induce and control the fermentation process and add character to the wine. The process of making *jiu qu* and that of making wine are equally important and quite distinct arts throughout Chinese history. Written records suggest the use of fermentation inducers in the winemaking process was already established by the Shang dynasty in the second millennium BC. In its most primitive form, *jiu qu* is microbiota growth on starchy materials such as grains. Through experimentation, people began to inoculate the current production with a previously successful batch of *jiu qu* to improve consistency. The pro-

cess is usually completed over a fixed period in a warm and humid environment. The finished product is then dried, resulting in a durable and storable mixture of yeasts, microbes and enzyme metabolites

Fermentation inducer bricks

ready with all the essential components to kick-start fermentation when they are rehydrated with wine ingredients and water.

The use of fermentation inducers is a key difference between Chinese grain-based wines and beer. Beer is brewed using sprouted ('malted') grains, which then go through a process called mashing to prepare them for fermentation. The malts are steeped in hot water to activate natural enzymes in the sprouted grains that convert carbohydrates into fermentable sugars. Grains used for Chinese wines, however, do not need to be sprouted and rely on the addition of *jiu qu*, which contains the necessary enzymes and yeasts for the dual purpose of simultaneous catabolism and fermentation. This Chinese method is sometimes called 'mash fermentation' in contrast with beer production, in which mashing and fermenting are separate stages in the brewing process. Furthermore, *jiu qu* can be made with additional ingredients to bring aromatic and textual complexity to the wine, as well as medicinal ingredients for added health benefits.

The development and controlled use of *jiu qu* in ancient Chinese winemaking is essentially biomolecule manufacturing that ventures into the realm of microbial biology. The process has been continuously expanded and refined down the ages and has had a far-reaching impact on winemaking and food cultures throughout eastern Asia. For example, Japanese *koji,* used in the production of saké, is a well-known variant of *jiu qu* across Asia, and soya sauces, bean pastes and some vinegars all use various types of *qu* for fermentation. The presence of 'good bacteria' in *qu* has also been integral to the health and medicinal benefits assigned to wine and fermented foods in China and other Asian cultures.

The ancient practice of using *jiu qu* to control fermentation and wine characteristics has parallels in modern grape winemaking, in which cultured yeast is increasingly used to control fermentation, rather than winemakers relying on the ambient yeasts that naturally exist in the vineyard and winery. Cultured yeast tends to be a single strain selected from ambient yeasts for particular fermentation characteristics. Although this increases the predictability of the fermentation process, it is at the expense of the wider range of flavours and characteristics that comes from the natural variations in ambient yeasts. *Jiu qu*, on the other hand, typically serves the dual function of controlling fermentation and adding desirable and complex characteristics to the wine. Currently there are various international research efforts to formulate mixed-culture blended yeasts that could combine the advantages of cultured and ambient yeasts. Another common stage in grape winemaking, especially of red wine, is the malolactic fermentation, in which harsh-tasting malic acid is converted to mellow-tasting lactic acid. Although this process can occur naturally, it is usually initiated by an inoculation of lactic-acid bacteria.

Yellow wines (*huang jiu*)

The earliest grain-based wines were unfiltered, resulting in a muddy, opaque liquid, but as winemaking methods progressed, filtering techniques achieved clear wine without sediment.

The name 'yellow wine' does not do justice to the range of colours found in grain wines. The various types of grains and range of different *jiu qu* used in making yellow wines result in a wide range of colours, from light yellow to amber, brick orange, brown and maroon, while tastes vary all the way from sweet through to semi-sweet, semi-dry and dry. In fact, some rice wines made with red *jiu qu*, which contain red rice moulds, produce garnet or maroon-coloured wines, which were historically known as *hong jiu* ('red wine'). In modern-day usage, however, *hong jiu* is often interchangeable with the term *pu tao jiu*, meaning grape wine, particularly Western-style grape wine. *Huang jiu* remains the umbrella term for fermented, non-distilled rice wine of any colour. Whether this eliminates or exacerbates the confusion is a matter of opinion!

Huang jiu is still widely made today from a variety of grains. It typically ranges from 12 to 20 per cent alcohol by volume and can age very well. It also has significant nutritional and medicinal values as it contains slow-releasing sugars and is rich in amino acids, vitamins and minerals. *Huang jiu* is often used as a medicinal base or in cooking to enhance aroma and flavour, particularly in poultry and seafood recipes. Well-known dishes such as drunken chicken (*zui ji*), drunken duck (*zui ya*), drunken crab (*zui xie*) and drunken prawns (*zui xia*) are usually drunk on the yellow wine used in their preparation. The most famous group of yellow wines, with over 3,000 years of history, is called *Shaoxing jiu*, named after the wine region in Zhejiang province. The main ingredients are high-quality glutinous rice and water drawn locally from the Mirror Lake (Jian Hu). There are various styles of Shaoxing wine, most notably *zhuang yuan hong* ('scholar red', a dry wine made using a red inducer); *jia fan* ('add rice', semi-dry made with extra rice); and *shan niang* ('well aged', semi-sweet and made by adding aged wines to new batches). There are also lower grade Shaoxing wines commonly used for Chinese cooking, which are widely available in Chinese supermarkets around the world.

Quality *huang jiu* has an elegant yet complex nose: one moment of incense, another of oolong tea, or sometimes pickled olives, or sourdough bread, or honeyed figs. On the palate it is smooth, mellow but well structured and balanced between its acidity, sweetness, bitterness and umami dimensions. The aromas can be ever changing and lingering in the mouth, with hints of ripe grains and herbs. Yellow wines pair well with Chinese food, and can be drunk cold or warm depending on one's constitution, taste preference or the season.

Despite *huang jiu's* undisputed heritage, remarkable artisanship and health-giving properties, it has become a victim of its own cultural and quality standards during the last century. Its production methods used to meticulously account for how far the wine might travel in order to maintain quality standards throughout its distribution network. Since the fall of the last Chinese dynasty in the twentieth century and the ensuing foreign invasions and civil wars, the distribution networks of *huang jiu* were severely disrupted. Even to this day, *huang jiu* consumption remains fairly regional and fragmented to pockets of production areas such as Zhejiang and Jiangsu provinces. *Huang jiu's* cultural identity and terroir appeal strongly in the local area, but is ill-suited to compete nationally in price wars and any 'race to the bottom', as the required cost compression does not suit the quintessence of quality *huang jiu*.

Changes in drinking habits in modern China have affected it too: the *ganbei* ('bottoms up') culture of draining cups in one gulp is not suited to *huang jiu* culture, in which small sips are savoured. This is all changing, however, although quite slowly, as Chinese consumers are becoming more health conscious and interested in reigniting heritage wine culture. A revival of *huang jiu*, and to popularise it internationally, would require collaborative efforts to promote its cultural value and traditional craftsmanship. Arguably, the taste profile of *huang jiu* should be accessible to international wine consumers, as it has a vast range of characters and tastes that could draw comparisons with mead, rosé wine, Oloroso sherry and much more.

Distilled grain spirits (*bai jiu*)

Although *huang jiu* enjoys a much longer history than any other type of wine in China, the spread of distillation techniques during the Middle Ages fundamentally changed drinking preferences and initiated behaviours that persist to this day. What we now call *bai jiu* (also commonly written as *baijiu* or *baiju*) is a clear, distilled, grain-based liquor, which is typically between 40 and 60 per cent alcohol by volume, comparable to whisky (which explains whisky's recent popularity in China). The most common ingredients are sorghum or glutinous rice, although maize, barley, wheat, millet and other grains are also used. The exact date of *bai jiu*'s emergence is the subject of great academic debate, but the product itself has a distinguished history in Chinese wine culture. *Bai jiu* is revered

Sorghum is commonly used in *bai jiu* production

for its intriguing aromas and mouthfeel, and the finest can be extremely nuanced on the nose and the palate, with lingering fragrances and a very long finish. Thus *bai jiu* is often classified by its predominant aroma type. When *bai jiu* is poured, often to accompany a banquet, the aroma immediately fills the air and seems to integrate with and enhance the aromas of the food, hence its wide appeal as the most popular liquor in China.

Bai jiu is the most consumed spirit in the world: over 10 billion litres are drunk every year within China (versus just over 4 billion litres of vodka drunk globally in a year). It remains fairly unknown in the West, however, partly because it is an acquired taste as it can come across as fiery and harsh to the uninitiated palate. High quality *bai jiu* undergo very intricate and artisan processes and tend to be consumed domestically where supply could barely keep up with demand. They command large price premiums to even the most expensive whiskies. Guizhou Maotai, or Kweichow Moutai, China's most famous *bai jiu* brand and producer, overtook Johnnie Walker's owner Diageo as the world's most valuable liquor company in April 2017.

Typical *bai jiu* aromas include:
- 'Sauce' aroma (*jiang xiang*): so called for its savoury dimension reminiscent of fermented bean sauce and soya sauce, accompanied by a velvety mouthfeel and a very long finish. The most typical *bai jiu* of this type is Maotai (or Moutai) from Guizhou. This is the most famous Chinese *bai jiu* production region and home to the Kweichow Moutai brand.
- 'Strong' aroma (*nong xiang*): complex and intriguing fruity, spicy and sweet dimensions with a long finish. This is the most popular aroma group and there are many examples, notably Gu Jing Gong Jiu from Anhui province. Wu Liang Ye, Lu Zhou Lao Jiao, Shui Jing Fang, which is part-owned by Diageo, and boutique artisan brand You Yuan are from Sichuan province, the main production region.
- 'Light' aroma (*qing xiang*): delicate and light fragrance, clean and refreshing on the palate with a lingering finish. A representative of this class is Fen Jiu from Shanxi province.
- 'Rice' aroma (*mi xiang*): as its name suggests, there is the sweetness and fragrance of rice, with a hint of herbs, and the mouthfeel is soft

yet cleansing. A well-known example is San Hua Jiu from Guilin.

- 'Phoenix' aroma (*feng xiang*): light but not bland, elegant and well balanced, fruitiness combined with a hint of earthiness. So named after its most representative example, Xi Feng Jiu (which means 'West Phoenix') from Shaanxi province.
- 'Mixed' aroma (*jian xiang*): this refers to *bai jiu* with such complexity that they belong to two or more predominant aroma groups. As such, they vary greatly in character. One example is Kou Zi Jiao from Anhui province.

Beer

Malt grains were also used for winemaking in ancient China, resulting in a drink called *li*, comparable to a kind of beer. It is low in alcohol, usually less than 4 per cent, rather sweet and, according to Han-dynasty written records, can be made quite easily overnight. It seems to have fallen out of favour over time, however, possibly because its flavour was relatively weak. One theory is that the development and popularity of fermentation inducers, *jiu qu*, gradually replaced the use of malted grains, and *huang jiu* became the predominant grain-based wine because the wine's character can be better controlled by various types of fermentation inducers. Another theory is that, over time, the use of malted grains (through soaking the grains) was simply incorporated into the production method of *jiu qu*, so that by the Han dynasty the distinction between *li* (beer) and *jiu* (wine) was blurred. Beer as we know it today, however, made a return in the twentieth century. The first industrialised brewery was founded in Harbin in 1900, followed by the now internationally recognised brand Tsingtao (Qingdao) in 1903. Beer consumption in China today is second only to *bai jiu* in terms of total alcoholic beverage consumption.

Other ingredients in grain-based wines

Fruit, flowers, wood and herbs are all widely used in Chinese winemaking, often blended with a base *huang jiu*. Similarly, animals, whole or in part, can be found soaking in wine to add medicinal properties and perceived value. Usually, such practices go hand-in-hand with Chinese medicine, and the choice of fruit, flowers, herbs and animal parts is intended to achieve particular health benefits, as either a cure for ailments or a preventative or restorative tonic. This opens up a host of options and, depending on the season, geography, time of day and personal traits – such as age, gender and health – different wines are prescribed for different occasions. Traditional wines are connected with Chinese festivals, for example osmanthus wine (*gui hua jiu*) for the Mid-Autumn Festival and *tusu* wine for Chinese New Year (yellow wine with Chinese rhubarb, Sichuan pepper, cassia bark, Chinese bellflower, aconite and rhizomes), each with its own repertoire of health-enhancing qualities, suited to the particular season. This has parallels with the modern beauty industry, in which there is seasonal emphasis on skincare regimes, for instance nourishment in winter, sun protection in summer and hydration throughout the year. Grape wine, lychee, chrysanthemum, osmanthus, lotus and even snake, scorpion, toad wine and others make up the kaleidoscopic pattern of Chinese winemaking to this day.

Can grain-based wines succeed outside China?

What is the potential for traditional Chinese wines in the international market? In recent years, the producer Kweichow Moutai (Maotai) has spearheaded efforts to raise the international profile of *bai jiu*. It is well positioned for the challenge: it is China's 'national spirit' and frequently graces state banquet tables, not least Richard Nixon's historical state visit to China in 1972, which paved the way for normalising the US–China relationship. It is also gifted by Chinese embassies across the world. Today, Maotai is positioning itself internationally as a sophisticated and luxury drink. Its marketing materials offer trendy Maotai cocktail recipes in an attempt to appeal to the younger international party set, vying for a slice of the lucrative metropolitan nightlife pie currently firmly occupied by large-format vodka bottles served with sparklers in clubs and bars. As mentioned, *bai jiu*'s profile can be an acquired taste – to the uninitiated palate it could simply be piercingly strong and throat-burningly spicy, and all its subtleties lost. Arguably, the best way to introduce it is as a cocktail base rather than to be drunk neat in the prevalent Chinese way. Due to its fame, Maotai is also a victim of domestic counterfeiting.

Huang jiu's position as an ingredient in Chinese cuisine is assured, although wines sold for cooking are the lower grade versions (for example, Shaoxing cooking wine). Premium *huang jiu* producers, in my view, should look to the domestic and international efforts of premium Japanese saké, which positions itself as an uncompromising product of traditional craftsmanship, sometimes aided by modern technical precision. The role of the restaurant trade in promoting home-grown wines is also crucial to attracting an international audience. The diversity of *huang jiu*'s characteristics and taste profiles could make it an exciting new contender for global food-and-wine matching. Its light and mellow mouthfeel and subtle yet complex aromas go well with many Asian and Mediterranean cuisines, and surely there will be many other surprising combinations.

A MIXED CASE: WINE IN MODERN CHINA

The 1980s: Reform and Opening Up

As the dust of a turbulent twentieth century settled, and the wounds inflicted by foreign aggression, civil wars and the Cultural Revolution began to heal, China embarked on a new kind of Long March back to glory with quiet determination. Since the 1980s, China has gone through decades of so-called 'Reform and Opening Up', embracing the market economy in a uniquely Chinese way. The New China rebuilt itself humbly and opened up to foreign ideas, economic models, technologies, products and lifestyles. This period also saw China loosening its controls over agriculture and enterprise, and made foreign investments attractive on both sides with policy incentives and preferences. The taste for imported wine was developing and the new prosperity was making wine more accessible to every part of society. From 1980 onwards, landmark joint ventures in the wine industry heralded a new age in which imported technology, oenologists, experience and vine cuttings joined hands with local knowledge, labour, connections and access.

Leading the pack of wineries was Dynasty, a Chinese-French joint venture founded in 1980 by Tianjin City Grape Garden and Rémy Martin. Dynasty is one of the most recognisable brands in China to this day. The Huadong winery, based in Qingdao, came under a Chinese-British joint venture in 1985 until 1990, with the vision of highlighting wine quality based on grape variety, vintage and appellation indicative of Qingdao. Pernod Ricard entered the fold in 1987 with the Beijing Friendship

Winery (Dragon Seal), until 1990. Today, Pernod Ricard's interest in China is best represented by its Helan Mountain Vineyard in Ningxia, established in 2012 and producing high-quality wines, mostly from Cabernet Sauvignon, Merlot, Pinot Noir and Chardonnay. Domaine Franco-Chinois (also known as the Sino-French Demonstration Vineyard) was established in Hebei province in 1998 as a cooperative project led by the Chinese and French governments, resulting from then-Premier Wen Jia Bao's state visit to France a year earlier. It produces high-quality, classic French-style wines.

Changyu, a true pioneer and the first commercial winery in China, is also prolific in its international collaborations. To name a few high-profile examples, in 2001 it joined forces with Groupe Castel, producing a signature Château Changyu-Castel Cabernet Gernischt blend from the Beiyujia vineyard in Shandong province. In 2006 it enlisted Canada's Aurora Icewine Co. to establish the Golden Icewine Valley in Liaoning province, setting its sights on half of the world's ice-wine output capacity. In 2013, the already mentioned Château Changyu Moser XV was unveiled in Ningxia, where the main varieties include Cabernet Sauvignon, Merlot and Syrah. The estate is named after its consultant Laurenz Maria Moser V of Austrian winery Laurenz V.

In recent years, the most luxurious of international brands have taken note of China's potential. Domaines Barons de Rothschild and China International Trust and Investment Corporation have been creating a vineyard on the Penglai peninsula in Shandong province, Penglai Estate DBR-CITIC, since 2008. Varietals planted include Cabernet Sauvignon, Syrah, Merlot, Cabernet Franc and Marselan. Moët Hennessy Louis Vuitton (LVMH), whose illustrious wine and spirits portfolio includes Moët & Chandon, Krug, Veuve Clicquot, Dom Pérignon, Château Cheval Blanc and Château d'Yquem, established Domaine Chandon China with local partner Ningxia Nongken Enterprise in 2013. The winery cultivates Chardonnay and Pinot Noir grapes to produce champagne-style sparkling wines. Even more alluring, perhaps, is LVMH's ambitious joint venture with Shangri-La Winery in Yunnan province, named after the legendary region near the foothills of the Himalayas. Vines are grown by 120 local families on over 300 parcels of land (sub-divided into 900 parcels) ranging from 2,200 to 2,600m above sea level, pushing the frontiers of winemaking into lofty clouds on one of the most mythical terroirs on earth.

The fanatical spenders: the noughties craze for Bordeaux

Since the 'Reform and Opening Up' programme, China's role on the world stage has shifted considerably. At first it served as the 'factory of the world', fuelling and feeding Western consumerism. While the wealthy West spent on a culture of debt, China was earning, learning and saving. After the turn of the new millennium, China's frugality began to emerge as a source of global economic strength. The dizzying growth rate, fuelled by Western demands for its low-cost manufacturing, created a huge appetite and ability for China to spend on foreign national debts as a means to manage its trade balance and currency, and on commodities and technologies to keep pace with industrial needs and infrastructure projects. If there had been any doubt about its strength, this became undeniable after the 2007–8 global economic crisis. At a critical juncture China came of age, offering financial lifelines to global markets and seizing opportunities for itself in the international arena. As the nation's wealth filtered down to private hands, the rapid emergence of Chinese billionaires and 'millionaires-next-door' created a formidable appetite for luxury foreign goods and lifestyles. The newly wealthy Chinese were not only flaunting their wealth with a passion, they were spending fanatically, as if, finally, to wipe clean several generations' blood and sweat.

The wine world could certainly testify to this astonishing rise of China, and for China, Bordeaux became its first and most passionate love. At the turn of the new millennium, mainland China (excluding Hong Kong) was importing 2,000 hectolitres of Bordeaux wine. Fast forward a decade and that figure has ballooned well over a hundredfold. China has now become one of the largest and most important markets for Bordeaux and the wine industry worldwide. How did it come about? And will it last?

In the 1980s, Hong Kong was a notable but minor destination for Bordeaux wines. Despite the small size of the market, some key networks were being established that turned out to be spectacular 'first mover advantages'. For example, Topsy Trading Company, the pioneer fine-wine importer in Asia, was founded in 1983 with the initial aim to supply wine to top hotels in Hong Kong. Among its early purchases were now legendary vintages such as Petrus and Lafite Rothschild 1982, and crucially, it established enviable access to large allocations of Bordeaux Grand Crus for years to come. In 1989, Château Lynch-Bages began a partnership with Hong Kong's Cathay Pacific Airways to provide first-class passengers flying between Hong Kong and London with the coveted claret – a boon for the airline among wine enthusiasts who dubbed the flight as the 'Lynch-Bages arbitrage', and in turn helped establish Lynch-Bages as one of the most recognised wine brands in Asia, even gaining an indigenised name in Hong Kong – 'Lang Chi Bak' – after a famous Cantonese opera artist.

During the 1990s, wine began to gain traction in mainland China, backed by a benevolent political stance that supported a shift towards grape-wine consumption. There were three main drivers behind this. First, in the face of rapid population growth, the government saw that grape wine could ease the pressure on the amount of grain consumed by traditional Chinese grain-based winemaking. Second, grape wine is better for health, as it is lower in alcohol than strong liquors such as *bai jiu*. Third, winegrowing can stimulate development and employment in less arable regions and reduce desertification of lands because grape vines can survive in infertile or rocky soils – in fact, stressed vines can make better wines. In 1997, the return of Hong Kong to China from British governance paved the way for mainland China to access the lifestyle of Hong Kong society, which, courtesy of its British colonial past, was already acquainted with the British partiality for claret. Bordeaux, with its long-established trading ties with the UK and, via the UK, Hong Kong, was uniquely positioned as first mover in the wine market to woo the Chinese. Hong Kong's advantageous hub position was further enhanced in 2008 when its 40 per cent wine import duty was waived.

Bordeaux's favourable positioning was by no means merely a stroke of good luck – it also owed a great deal to its unique trading system, known as the *place de Bordeaux*. This is a long-established and deeply entrenched web of local business relationships, in which the wine producer (the wine estate or *château*) sells wine via a broker (*courtier*) to a specialist wholesale merchant (*négociant*), who is then responsible for selling wines in the wider global market place. This division of labour is advantageous when well deployed. The merchants can use their web of contacts, resources and economies of scale to develop networks all over the world. They have strong sales channels and marketing arms that can sell wines quickly and widely and increase the global visibility of the wines under their representation. This leaves the wine producers to concentrate their resources on what they do best – producing wine – and to invest most of their money in the vineyard and winery. The broker gauges supply, demand, market sentiment and pricing, adding value with a fair view of the market, and brings together suitable deals between producer and merchant.

Such a set-up works particularly well for an elite group of wine producers, particularly the Classified Growths, which were based on an 1855 classification ordered by Napoleon III for the *Exposition Universelle de Paris*. These wines command premium prices and enjoy loyal followings. Merchants and brokers vie for the business of this group of Bordeaux royalty, and no effort is spared to represent their wines. The strength of the *place de Bordeaux* system spreads the prestige of top Bordeaux wines far and wide – and Bordeaux's image ignited something in the Chinese psyche.

The fire in the dragon's belly

Despite the passing decades, the soul-destroying Cultural Revolution continues to haunt China. In a bid to restore optimism, the government recognised that the first step to feeling good – both for the government and the people – would be taken through the nation's economy. Privatisation and entrepreneurship were supported, as well as foreign investments, which flooded in. A grand new slogan was born, 'To get rich is glorious!' and a generation of fortune's children responded.

Wealth, confidence and the feel-good factor rolled in for the winners of China's reforms. Flaunting wealth became a national sport to showcase success and happiness. For some, the cultural hollowness left behind by the traumas of yesteryear was plastered over with the pursuit of highbrow objects and activities. For others, the yearning to reconnect with culture had led them to rediscover what was once banned for being bourgeois. Luxury foreign lifestyles fitted the bill perfectly, having all the characteristics that the Chinese wanted: high price tags to show wealth, exoticism to impress, quality to indicate discernment, and all the romanticism of a far-away fairy-tale land without the emotional baggage of one's own backyard. By chance and by design, prestige Bordeaux wines ticked all the right boxes.

Western wine culture resonated naturally with the Chinese: the value of time in the diminishing and rarefying nature of wine; the concept of terroir, which finds parallels in *feng shui* (the study of natural elements and their effects on well-being) and *feng tu* (the regional characteristics of a place); the search for balance and compatibility in food and wine; and the purported health benefits. For a nation deeply interested in meanings, symbolism and gestures – in life, love, business and politics – fine wine and Chinese culture are no doubt 'heavenly born a double, earthly bound a couple', as the saying goes. Yet before even a fraction of the Chinese population had come to appreciate these cross-cultural compatibilities, something else about Bordeaux wine had ignited the fire in the dragon's belly. After all, many Chinese people got rich through number-crunching and fast-fingered opportunism.

In the first decade of the new millennium, top-notch Bordeaux wines were the thing to be seen with, the perfect gift to sweeten business deals and reinforce relationships. Thanks to Bordeaux's 1855 classification of top wine estates, it was easy enough for the Chinese to acquaint themselves with the best of the best. Wine knowledge, or the lack of it, is no problem in the gift-giving circus of classified Bordeaux wines – the giver and the receiver simply have to refer to a ranking chart to understand how much 'face' is being given and received. On the back of this phenomenon it did not take long for talk of financial returns from wines to catch on. It was one of those badly kept secrets that the rich bought fine wines as 'assets'. Fine wine could diversify an investment portfolio and increase in value over time, because a particular wine starts with a limited supply of a specific vintage, which diminishes over time as it is consumed, while demand increases as the population and markets expand. Even better, when the quality of a wine is affirmed by opening a bottle, it becomes simultaneously more desirable and rarer, thus enhancing its value. Because of this, your merchant would tell you, the usual trick is to buy two cases of a particular wine for the cellar: one case for drinking when the right time comes, and one case for reselling at a profit to fund your drinking pleasure.

The Chinese scrutinised classified Bordeaux prices with an unromantic numerical eye, yet smacked their lips at sensational but improbable fortunes such as the Jefferson's Lafite Rothschild going for £105,000 at auction in 1985. The sweet fragrance of wine money got the Chinese spinning into a virtuous cycle of their own enthusiasm, which peaked in 2010. As the Chinese saying goes, 'one spreads to ten, and ten to a hundred': hordes of punters bought wines for the right time to resell rather than the right time to drink. As far as they were concerned, this was a bandwagon not to be missed. Propelled by the Chinese passion, the revered 1982 vintage of Château Lafite Rothschild became the trade of the decade: a bottle bought around the year 2000 would have yielded the lucky owner about 1,000 per cent profit in ten years, with a steep

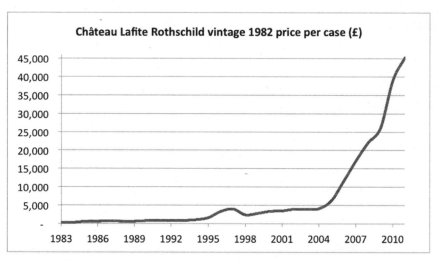

Château Lafite vintage 1982 price history: from under £300 to a peak of over £45,000

acceleration towards the end of the decade. Indeed, with a well-deliberated holding period (often helped with some chart-cropping, in hindsight), wine could massively outperform old favourites such as gold, real estate and equities, the traditional asset classes from which many Chinese have reaped lucrative rewards. The attraction of wine was simply irresistible to more and more people.

In the typical Chinese style of grand gestures, it was their turn to plot price charts that soared on a near vertical trajectory and to smash auction records. At the now-legendary Sotheby's auction held in Hong Kong on 30 October 2010, impeccable wines from the cellars of Domaines Barons de Rothschild estates were offered, among them coveted Lafite vintages including 2009, 2008, 1959 and 1869. The exclusive Chinese clientele, hand-picked by the auction house, showed just how thirsty they were for the Lafite name and the provenance guaranteed by a direct sale from the Rothschild cellars. This day set unforgettable wine auction records: three bottles of the Lafite vintage 1869 – the first Rothschild vintage following Baron James de Rothschild's acquisition of the estate in 1868, and one that predated the phylloxera epidemic and therefore, to some very particular drinkers, the loss of 'true' European vines – estimated at US $5,000 to US $8,000 each, sold for a record-breaking US $234,000 per bottle to one single, mysterious phone bidder. The day pulled in US $8.4 million of total sales compared to a pre-sale estimate of US $2.5 million. Then the record-breaking cohort went home, came back the next day and dropped another US $10 million with the gobsmacked auctioneer.

But there was still more to the attraction of classified Bordeaux wines: it was a bandwagon with a first-class compartment. The privileged circles were told with a wink and a whisper that Bordeaux wines were special for another reason: they could be bought *en primeur* – before the wine is bottled and released to the market – for extra potential profit.

En primeur and the time value of money

The most important calendar event for the *place de Bordeaux* system takes place in the first week of April every year, when the *place* organises barrel tastings across Bordeaux appellations of the most recently harvested vintage *en primeur* (that is, wines which are still in barrels and not yet bottled). The world of the wine trade and press descend upon Bordeaux during the *en primeur* week to taste, remark and exchange thoughts about the wines and the market at large. There is a great buzz of excitement and activity as wine professionals taste hundreds of barrel samples through purpled-tongue and teeth, forming impressions of the vintage in terms of quality, style and, not least, pricing expectations. The beautiful châteaux of Bordeaux really come to life during this time. As if hosting debutante balls, they put on lavish luncheons, dinners and soirées to showcase their wines in the best possible circumstances; journalists and critics sharpen their palates and their pencils; merchants gauge consumer sentiment while conducting negotiations behind closed doors. In the ensuing weeks the châteaux will take account of the proceedings and release the *en primeur* price at which the latest vintage will be sold.

Put simply, *en primeur* is a forward purchase agreement underwritten by wine merchants. The buyer pays upfront for a wine that is still barrel ageing and will be delivered 12–18 months later, when the wine is bottled. In this way, the producer secures cash flow and sales of the crop, and, for this benefit, *en primeur* wine tended to be sold at a lower price that would see future appreciation when the wine was released in the wider market.

In practice, *en primeur* pricing is far more than just economics. It is a complex matrix of mind games, politics and rivalry. Pricing too high means that the wine may not sell and the producer risks alienating consumers and business partners. Pricing too low means that the producer limits potential profits and may be perceived to have produced a lesser wine than its neighbours. The merchants, on the other hand, are anxious about the *en primeur* allocations they receive from producers, in particular from the high-profile châteaux. They tend to buy their entire allocation each year, regardless of the quality and price of the vintage, in order to protect their position in the allocation game. In any case, reputations and relationships are all at stake here. For many châteaux, getting the *en primeur* pricing right is the most crucial financial decision of the year, and, for many *négociants*, having enough money for their most coveted allocations every year is a key part of their financial planning.

One producer half-jokingly remarked about *en primeur*: 'We are all very friendly here at Bordeaux, except during the weeks of release [of *en primeur* prices]. During that time we study *The Art of War* behind closed doors.' Speaking of *The Art of War*, the Chinese would like to think that they possess a natural knack in the game. The motives behind *en primeur* make sense: buying wine this way, especially wine of the most desirable names and vintages, should offer attractive returns on investment over a 12 to 18-month horizon. Beyond that, in China in the first decade of the millennium, there was an incredible growth in wine demand fuelled by a populous nation with rapidly multiplying numbers of new young millionaires and a burgeoning middle-class. In many cities, people began to adopt the lifestyles of Beijing, Shanghai, Guangzhou and Shenzhen (the 'first tier' cities). All this gave enormous headroom for price growth in the secondary market (the buy-and-sell activity that takes place after the original release). Besides, the Chinese were already well versed in buying and reselling off-plan real estate and many had reaped lucrative rewards. The concept of *en primeur* has often been discussed among the Chinese in similar terms. The riskiness and speculative aspects seemed less significant and the whole notion appeared familiar. If any empirical evidence was necessary, the clincher must have been the 'lucky eight' vintage of 2008 Château Lafite Rothschild.

Against the gloomy backdrop of the Credit Crunch, the 2008 vintage *en primeur* started apprehensively, with prices on average 30 per cent lower than those of the 2007 campaign. The first tranche of Château Lafite Rothschild was released at around £2,000 a case. Within weeks the price doubled as a result of the highly influential wine critic Robert Parker awarding Lafite a higher than expected score of 98–100 (out of 100). By October 2010 the yet-to-be-bottled vintage had already appreciated to around £9,000 a case. On 26 October 2010 Château Lafite announced that the 2008 bottles would be etched with the Chinese character 八, the number 8, which symbolises prosperity in China. When the news broke, Lafite 2008 shot up in price overnight, with Asian buyers rushing for stocks. The price pushed above £11,000 for a case of 12 bottles in less than 24 hours.

The 'lucky eight' vintage was a watershed moment. In its aftermath, the 2009 and 2010 vintages were declared as 'vintages of the century' in Bordeaux, and the Chinese bought with insatiable fervour, overtaking long-established traditional markets in both trade volume and value. But instead of marking the beginning of a prosperous and long relationship between Bordeaux and its new best friend, as many had envisaged, the unthinkable happened. The upward trajectory of prices ground to a halt and then plummeted in 2011. This was not supposed to happen to a great vintage with a new-found fanbase of more than 1 billion people. So what went wrong?

Some blamed the sustained global economic woes since 2008, and gloomy economic headlines hardly bolster confidence or improve senti-ments. But despite this downbeat macro-economic backdrop, the Chi-nese millionaire class was still expanding healthily; luxury fashion houses continued to post robust earnings thanks to strong consumer spending from China; the art scene remained flamboyant; and rare coins, stamps, fast cars and designer clothes continued to bask in the warmth of China. But the Bordeaux wine market was heading for a major price correction. In contrast, other wine regions attracted more attention from China. Bordeaux was frequently outperformed by Burgundy at auctions and that region's Domaine de la Romanée-Conti became the new darling, robbing Lafite of its once-unassailable lustre. Soon rumours of cancelled orders from China began to circulate within the Bordeaux wine trade. Mer-chants went out of business, jeopardising their *en primeur* obligations, in turn afflicting more losses on their counterparts. It became evident that plenty of the 2009 and 2010 stocks had remained unsold. Bewilderment and fear gripped the Chinese, the Bordelaise and the wine trade at large, as defaults and bankruptcies suddenly became all too real. The dragons bearing ladders to riches suddenly felt more like snakes unravelling slip-pery fortunes. The Chinese were in turn seething with fire in their breath, feeling they were taken for a ride by opportunists who capitalised on their inexperience and enthusiasm.

To understand the undervalued risks that came to bite both the Chinese and the Bordelaise, let us digress for a lesson from the City trading floors of high finance. Money, traders would say, has a present value and a future value. One dollar today had a different value yesterday, and will have a different value tomorrow. As such, when we think of money, there should always be a parameter of time associated with its value. This is not an abstract notion: we are all familiar with the effects of interest rates and inflation on our spending power over time, and these are the drivers of the time value of money. Value is not the same as price, although they are related: value represents buying power, whereas price is driven by supply and demand. The concept of the time value of money is at the very heart of finance, and directly affects our lives and behaviour.

So, when a lucky man bought a case of Château Lafite '82 back in the 1980s and made a return of 15,000 per cent in 2011, what really happened to his money? Over the decades, the value of cash has diminished with inflation, but the price of the Lafite '82 had increased against a dwindling pool of unopened bottles. So the lucky man effectively swapped the reductive value of cash for an asset that turned out to enjoy enormous increase in value. To gain from investment in assets, you must believe that the chosen asset, which on day one has the same value as your money, will in the future maintain or increase in value over and above the value of your cash.

The vintage 2009 *en primeur* was much hyped and anticipated by the wine market. The vintage was sublime and the Chinese buyers were eager. Prices for the *en primeur* rocketed from the year before: Lafite Rothschild raised its release price by over 300 per cent compared to 2008. But what justified this increase? Surely it could not be perceivable differences in quality or any intrinsic change between the two vintages? And how did this pricing fit in with the logic of *en primeur* if a large premium had been slapped on it straight away? Such pricing was putting off the vast majority of traditional buyers who were more representative of normal market demand. It was a pricing mentality that grasped over-zealously towards an anticipated future value based on an unproven new market entrant. It is easy to pick on Lafite as a high-profile example in hindsight, but it was not the only bullish winery at the time. In fact, most classified Bordeaux wines were priced at a premium. By the time the 2009 vintages were bottled and ready for delivery some 18 months later, it became apparent that the 2009 *en primeur* pricing had overshot the mark and prices plummeted below *en primeur* levels in the secondary market, which invalidated the rationale for buyers to pay 18 months ahead of delivery, since they could have bought the same wine later as a finished product and paid less.

The 2010 vintage was again declared a triumph with strong pricing to match, but towards the end of the *en primeur* campaign the steam had finally run out. June 2011 marked a price peak that was followed by a sharp descent. Feeling duped, increasing numbers of Chinese buyers pulled out as prices dropped, but in fact most had barely understood the risks to start with. By the beginning of 2012, even the most optimistic merchants had to accept the price drop was not going to be a short-lived glitch. The Liv-ex index, which tracks the price movements of a basket of the most traded fine wine, had dropped over 20 per cent since the peak of 2011. The 'lucky eight' Lafite 2008 had lost over 40 per cent in value by this point and the devaluation did not look to be over.

There were prior warning signs, of course. Astute observers and traders had long been vocal about unsustainable prices that were not supported by solid demand growth based on drinking. By this time, Chinese wine imports had become extremely polarised, with logic-defying bids at the top end and price-crushing bulk trade at the bottom, neither of which suggests real interest in drinking: the top end is fuelled by speculation and ostentation, while the bottom end supplied mass-produced plonk, charged at a premium for its import status or even ending up in counterfeited wines. 'It was as if the Chinese market had no middle ground where normal middle-income families could enjoy a good-quality bottle of normally priced wine,' observed winemaker Edouard Miailhe at Château Siran, an estate next to Château Margaux that produces beautiful wines at more grounded prices.

By the summer of 2011 prices became unsustainable, which marked the start of a long way down. There were concerns about China's economy, fears about a Chinese property market bubble, and shadow banking defaults loomed large while Chinese banks tightened credit lines and lending. Suddenly the swaggering tycoons and state-owned enterprises felt a sharp pinch. Many buyers backed out of their orders and unloaded existing stock. In the absence of interested buyers in other parts of the world, the market became flooded with supply. The darkest days, however, were still ahead. In June 2013, sentiment soured further as China engaged in a trade spat with the EU: the EU accused China of selling solar panels too cheaply into Europe, and China retaliated by announcing a probe into European wines being 'dumped' in China. Although the situation was eventually diffused, it did no favours to an already fragile wine market. But more devastating was the Chinese president Xi Jinping's ongoing crackdown on government spending and corruption. As people came to realise that this president meant business with his austerity programme, a significant amount of Chinese wine money dried up as high-end hospitality and gift-giving suffered. It became clear to all that the downward price correction in investment-grade wines was not over yet.

A 'crowded trade', as they say on the City trading floor, is often a great idea gone awry. As more people pile in for a piece of the action for fear of missing out, they pay a premium to participate. The idea then ceases to be original or good value because the benefits are fully priced in. Bubbles happen when crowded and speculative trades blow up, then pop. While speculation usually stems from a genuinely good idea, the better the idea the greater the herd that gathers around it. At some point, a sensible trade becomes prey to hugely inflated expectations, wrapped in a false sense of safety and sanity driven by the consensus of a crowd.

In Bordeaux, the painful lesson was costly for many involved. It was particularly ruinous for those *négociants* without a luxurious cash cushion – on the one hand, they faced obligations to buy their allocated wines from the châteaux, and on the other were order cancellations and non-payments from buyers. The collapse of over-priced vintages also had a negative knock-on effect on older vintages. The vast majority of Bordeaux's modest vineyards, which had only benefited marginally from the halo effect of the classified growths, now faced hardship as a result of the general exodus from Bordeaux.

The subsequent vintages from 2011 to 2014 saw muted *en primeur* activities, not helped by the lacklustre reviews from critics and merchants. Many Bordeaux properties, however, could not bring down their *en primeur* prices to align with market expectations. It was difficult to come down from their high horse after having mounted it with elevated notions of brand value. But what could be more detrimental to brand value than a brutal secondary market price correction that not only invalidates the initial pricing but crushes confidence in the whole *en primeur* system itself, not to mention hurting goodwill? Chinese interests cooled significantly during this period and the fundamental rationale of buying *en primeur* was jeopardised. The system itself was thrown into extra uncertainty with the exit of Château Latour after the 2012 campaign. Further disenchantment ensued as some châteaux withheld stocks in a bid to prop up demand by limiting supply, fracturing their relationship with the trade community. Like buses, misfortunes seem to arrive not one by one, but all at once. The *en primeur* and the *place de Bordeaux* systems have not been the same since. In the face of uncertain market conditions, increased competition from other wine regions and technological disruption to distribution channels that demanded increasing price transparency and supressed margins, Bordeaux looked out of touch with market dynamics and consumer sentiment. Even another two back-to-back strong vintages such as 2015 and 2016 could not pacify the underlying need for reform.

Rebuilding resilience in Bordeaux *en primeur*

What sort of reforms could benefit the Bordeaux *en primeur* system and shore up confidence again? Its underlying concept as a forward market is sound, and the intended purpose of rewarding the roles and relationships between producers, merchants and consumers was a strength that carved out Bordeaux's unique position in the wine industry. But all this was built on pricing that benefited all participants in the system. The powerful outreach, marketing and distribution ecosystem of the *place de Bordeaux* is still much admired and envied by other wine regions, but *en primeur* needs to offer value, especially in a world where consumers have many more options. It is no longer the case that other wine regions cannot challenge top clarets for quality, production volume and ageing potential. Our data-rich and connected digital age is driving price transparency, and increasingly well-informed consumers are demanding pricing rationales that they can see, understand and accept. The powerful influence of wine critic scores on pricing should also be addressed, especially for *en primeur*, where such opinions are formed on barrel samples of unfinished wines. Do they offer sufficiently meaningful insights about the wine to justify the extent to which they dictate the market? In addition, since the 2011 price crash that wiped out many stakeholders, there should be more effort to reduce counter-party risks (i.e. the risks of non-payment or non-delivery).

The Chinese have a fine reputation for being sharp opportunists, and the messy love affair with Bordeaux left a deep impression of this. But they are also used to taking the long view over cycles of boom and bust. Like the Chinese civilisation itself, glory and doldrums are all fluid states, never the last word. What matters is the will and ability to adapt with the times and return to triumph. If we liken the years 2009–11 to a passionate first love affair between hot-blooded teenagers, then what will show real character is how the industry moves on from the experience.

The year 2015 marked an improvement in the general outlook, with wine imports returning to tentative growth. By this time, many wrong-footed merchants had been flushed out of the market or restructured. The industry had learned painful lessons and started to reposition with realistic long-term goals in China. Consumption growth for a mass market and cultivating interest and knowledge became the main focus. Despite the retreat from the 'liquid gold rush', the Chinese wine market remains a fantastic prospect. As the country with the largest population and the fastest-growing wine market in the world, the reality of demographics and wealth accumulation means that the market still enjoys enormous growth potential. Sustainable and adaptable strategies will determine who will prosper with China. Fancy packaging and a seductive sales pitch fall short in the long run, and instead we are seeing higher quality contextualised communication and tasting-led learning.

Growing numbers of Chinese wine drinkers are adept at appreciating nuanced notions of wine. Industry insiders who frequently travel there express admiration for the pace of learning that is taking place across China. The UK's biggest wine education body, the Wine & Spirit Education Trust (WSET), now counts China as its biggest market, and winemaker and sommelier are increasingly aspirational professions. The view that wine in China is overdone and yet little understood is both a crying shame and a great source of hope: it can only mean that the potential for the right sort of interest and awareness is vast. Everyone in the wine industry, from producers to distributors to educators, must look to strategies for the long haul over short-term gains, and continue to understand the Chinese more deeply. If we could turn China's public awareness of the scandals of fake Lafites into the awareness of terroir and the beauty of the ageing process of wine, the world may be in danger of running dry of wine!

The post-Bordeaux wine market in China

China presents unique opportunities and challenges to traders. In just over a decade, the wine trade has had to repeatedly reinvent itself, ruthlessly casting off players who could not keep up. Between 2005 and 2011, when Chinese buyers tended to be high rolling, brand-conscious customers, the fine-wine market dreamed of an ever-expanding population of wealthy Chinese continuously bidding up prices at the luxury end of the trade, because rapid urbanisation and wealth creation seemed to create young millionaires just like China's factory production lines. The importers, distributors and retailers added their margins along the sales chain, and many invested in luxury consumer experiences in first-tier cities, such as exclusive tasting clubs with fine dining. But modest actual consumption, sluggish economic growth and a government austerity programme to combat corruption dealt a severe blow to this rosy prospect. The years 2012–14 saw a period of market readjustment. The wine trade assessed the real demand in China and the importance of nurturing a mass market rather than just chasing the high net-worth consumers. The market learned the importance of buyers actually drinking the wines they buy, rather than stockpiling them like gold bars and trophies or passing them around as gifts, creating a bizarre overhang of excess supply that ultimately undermined demand.

Merchants also noticed a rather inconvenient social drinking habit: many Chinese drinkers would empty a glass of wine in the same way they would with *bai jiu*, where the tradition is to drink from small cups and empty the cup in one go, like a shot. While the more alcoholic *bai jiu* (typically 40 per cent or above abv) lends itself well to this drinking habit, and one bottle would usually suffice to send a table optimally tipsy, many more bottles of wine would be required to do the same job. This meant that merchants had to pay careful attention to wine pricing relative to *bai jiu* in order to challenge the incumbent preference for *bai jiu* at social gatherings. As a result, the average price of imported wines dropped, preparing for a normalised, price-conscious mass market that can realistically be expected to sustain long-term growth.

As wine consumption increased, so did the number of producers, importers, distributors and retailers vying for a piece of the growing pie. Downward pricing pressure became increasingly fierce, compressing margins. The main battle ground is the 100-yuan threshold price (around $15/£11), where the mass market consumers tend to divide themselves. Various countries having different trade tariffs as well as fluctuations in renminbi (the Chinese currency) exchange rates further complicate the competitive landscape. The market also became highly fragmented, with multiple players constantly emerging and submerging in an ocean of rapidly changing tides. Long gone are the days of counting the key players on two hands, or having sympathy for doomed opportunists who treated the Chinese market as one large single slate with the consumer profile of, in their view, ignorant suckers. Increasingly, local importers, distributors and retailers are catering to nuanced local trends and tastes. Regional wine preferences could be due to many factors, for instance local climate, food style, spending power, wine knowledge and social habits. Locally organised wine experiences are also gaining popularity across first- and second-tier cities, such as themed tastings or dining experiences with food and wine pairings. These serve to bolster buyer confidence and appetite. The battling forces of large distributors with economies of scale, and therefore pricing advantage, versus smaller merchants offering boutique experiences are the main ones at play in China's wine market today. Consolidation will likely take place through mergers and acquisitions, and we can also expect to see more collaboration between domestic and international producers as the quality and brand-value gaps narrow.

In a bid to encourage and recognise quality standards, the government is to grant 'Estate Wine' trademarks to qualifying domestic wine estates that satisfy a set of quality standards on their own vineyards. This is a move closer to the more rigorous EU classification laws. According to the trade committee of the China Alcoholic Drinks Association (CADA), the establishment of Estate Wine trademarking is to 'protect the reputation of Chinese estate wine producers in the domestic and overseas market', clearly indicating an ambition for Chinese wines to join the many other Chinese industries that have broken domestic borders and conquered the international market. A new era of 'made in China' is coming, with a new image of quality, value and innovation.

The qualifying conditions for Estate Wines include: that the producer has full control over their vineyards; the entire winemaking, storage and bottling process must be completed on site; the upper yield limit on grapes is 1000kg per mu (a Chinese unit of land measurement; in the context of winegrowing this translates to about 94–115 hectolitres per hectare, depending on whether white or red wines are produced; a lower yield indicates more concentrated, higher quality grapes); the annual production needs to be more than 75 hectolitres (around 10,000 bottles); the vines must be at least three years old before producing wine; the winemaker needs to hold approved professional qualifications in oenology; plus some additional technical and hygiene requirements for winemaking and storage. In 2017, the first cohort consisted of 16 estates: Château Bolongbao, Beijing; Tai Yi Hu, Shandong; Château Rongzi, Shanxi; Amethyst Manor, Hebei; Bodega Langes, Hebei; Château Martin, Hebei; Nobility Château, Hebei; Helan Mountain Specialty, Ningxia; Helan Qingxue Vineyard, Ningxia; Kanaan Winery, Ningxia; Ningxia Leirenshou Winery, Ningxia; Château Yuquan, Ningxia; He Shuo Guan Long, Xinjiang; Tiansai Vineyards, Xinjiang; Xinjiang Ruitai Qing Lin Wine, Xinjiang; and Château Zhongfei, Xinjiang.

A discussion about today's wine market would be incomplete without mentioning e-commerce. About 21 million Chinese people now buy wine online (according to a 2016 Wine Intelligence report). Buyers often search online for imported wines and seek value for money and price transparency. JD.com and Alibaba's Tmall are the leading online retail platforms for wine in China. Tmall (China's largest third-party online retailer) had sold 23 million bottles of wine during its first year of operating its Vineyard Direct programme in 2015, and noted the 18–22 age group as their biggest spenders, which is typical of a country largely built on the new wealth of the past 30 years since Reform and Opening Up, and the coming of age of the 'rich second generation' (*fu er dai*) millennials and Generation Z. JD.com, another gigantic Chinese e-commerce platform, is a market leader in online sales among Chinese imported wine drinkers, and logged over $200 million in imported wine sales under its own listings and via hosted merchant stores in 2016.

E-commerce is introducing new channels: producers and distributors can set up their own online stores and sell directly to consumers. This approach improves market transparency, give merchants more control over branding and pricing, and can guarantee authenticity of the wine. Despite the presence of established platforms, there are plenty of newcomers in this space, notably venture capital-backed online retailers who are able to buy in large quantities and sell at very competitive prices.

Online wine sales, however, are somewhat restricted by a lack of experience. General knowledge and confidence in wine buying are still in their infancy. Therefore the 'online to offline' (O2O) business model, which combines the convenience of online browsing, purchase and home delivery with offline experiences such as tastings, classes and themed events, offers a more complete consumer experience that bolsters consumers' confidence that they can make informed choices, and in turn increases willingness to spend. Social media platforms, most notably WeChat, are empowering social and content-driven marketing, promotion and sales, opening up unprecedented access to consumers, and work particularly well with the O2O model.

The war on counterfeits is ongoing. Although some high-profile media exposés and state-sponsored crackdowns have made stern examples of offenders, and would put off the faint-hearted, it is a challenge that demands effort from both suppliers and consumers. ASC Fine Wines, a leading wine distributor in China, has opted for a high-tech anti-counterfeit system that involves labelling every bottle of wine it sells with a hologram label printed outside China and a unique QR code that consumers can scan and verify with a purpose-built mobile app. Direct selling from wine estates to consumers via online platforms is also a growing trend that cuts out uncertainties in the distribution chain. There are also emerging blockchain solutions that strive for full traceability of the entire supply-chain lifecycle, for example the experimentation between Shanghai's Waigaoqiao Direct Imported Goods (DIG) based in the Pilot Free-Trade Zone (PFTZ), blockchain start-up BitSE and PricewaterhouseCoopers (PwC) to deploy the Ethereum-based VeChain platform for imported wine distribution in China. On the consumer side, improved wine knowledge will also help buyers to identify fakes. The bar for counterfeiting is rising to flush out the currently prolific, but mostly primitive, forgeries.

The future direction of the Chinese market will encompass experienced and knowledgeable wine drinkers who are confident in expressing their own tastes and embrace both domestic and imported wines that offer value, quality and character. China's native wine traditions are alive and well, albeit with a modern twist and an international flavour. While market dynamics are ever changing, and statistics can barely keep pace with reality, cultural values are much more constant and insightful about China's past, present and future directions.

International vineyard acquisitions

China's love affair with wine is also evident in the acquisition of foreign vineyards. Bordeaux is again the darling. Although there were a handful of Chinese buyers before 2011, that particular year marked a watershed, with 21 Bordeaux vineyards snapped up by wealthy Chinese individuals and conglomerates. By early 2015 the Chinese were already scoring their century in Bordeaux vineyard counts. Many buyers own distribution channels back in China, such as beverage companies and hotel groups. They have the money and the means to buy and sell entire harvests but could not do so via the traditional Bordeaux *négociant* system, let alone secure allocation or exclusivity with the producers directly. Owning a vineyard, on the other hand, means the entire production can flow directly to their own ready-made sales channels and waiting customers back in China, without the foreign middleman.

By and large, and despite some rather aggressive moves from certain Chinese buyers to undermine the *négociant* system, Bordeaux has been welcoming towards Chinese buyers, in stark contrast to many other French wine regions, such as Burgundy and Champagne. Bordeaux has historically been culturally diverse and used to foreign owners, winemakers and traders. Chinese owners also recognise their relative inexperience in running vineyards and tend to employ local expertise and retain original teams, while injecting much-needed cash into the upkeep and operations. The Chinese tend to buy in areas that are relatively cheaper than the star appellations, as most of the drinkers back home are less concerned about nuanced differences between Bordeaux appellations. Chinese investments in these lesser-known areas have turned around otherwise languishing vineyards strapped for cash and route to market. With the rise of wine tourism, many new owners are making more versatile use of their châteaux to promote holistic wine experiences, not only selling the wine production to the domestic Chinese market, but also offering luxury accommodation with culinary and wine tastings to an elite group of Chinese holidaymakers. (*See* page 228 for details of some high profile vineyard acquisitions.)

Drinking Château Lafite with Coke

Ask a Chinese person: would you drill through a Ming vase to make a lamp? Or add milk and sugar to highly prized Da Hong Pao tea? You are likely to receive a Chinese grimace of torture.

Now ask a French wine buff: how about adding some Coke to your Château Lafite Rothschild? You will probably get a similar reaction, plus cries of '*Sacré bleu!*' with associated 'up in arms' action. It is a widely circulated, and by now rather tired, anecdote that some super-rich Chinese would drink painfully expensive bottles of Château Lafite with a generous pouring of Coke in the mix. Inevitably, the story arouses a round of unanimous head-shaking and gasps of disbelief, side-glances of disapproval and a wave of low frequency sounds of heartbreak. The conclusion? That the Chinese lack wine culture and knowledge of wine. Well, yes, and no.

The practice of mixing Lafite with Coke may well be going on, out of ignorance, disregard or even dislike of the taste of foreign wine among some Chinese nouveau riche. To be fair, since over 50 per cent of Lafite sold in China is fake, it might be wise to add some Coke! (More bottles of the iconic Château Lafite 1982 were sold in China than were ever produced by the estate.) But all is not lost – this is by no means the prevalent way of drinking it in China. After all, a colourful anecdote is hardly a census. In reality, many winemakers and merchants who frequently visit China are greatly encouraged by the sustained interest from growing numbers of Chinese wine lovers in knowing more and tasting more.

Let us reconsider why someone might mix Lafite with Coca-Cola. The drinker may not have acquired the taste for foreign wine, let alone any nuanced notions of what the wine might represent, such as the nobility of a unique terroir, the story of the vintage, the art and skills of the winemaker in achieving balance between nature and nurture, between sweetness, acidity and tannins. Out of ignorance or indifference, it may seem perfectly reasonable to carry out some DIY to alter the taste, as though mixing a cocktail. This does not imply, however, that the drinker is unfamiliar with *all* wines, in the Chinese sense of the word. The same drinker probably wouldn't dream of doctoring a bottle of reserve Maotai, one of the most revered brands of Chinese *bai jiu*. It is, after all, a matter of taste and values based on understanding and customs. How many casual Western tea drinkers pause to remember that fine teas might have been picked at the break of dawn by young girls with nimble wrists, hand-cooked repeatedly by experienced, calloused fingers in hot pans, painstakingly rolled manually to retain the flavour of the tea terroir, before they add their milk and sugar? As I have described, China has had a long tradition of drinking blended wines, such as liquors infused with herbs, spices, flowers and even animal parts. For a culture unfazed by drinking snake wine and bitter gall wine, adding Coke to Lafite looks pretty tame then.

Of course, it is a great pity to waste a fine wine on someone who doesn't appreciate it, when it could have brought joy to a discerning drinker or someone eager to learn. If a wine is made with a great deal of skill and love, and is intended to be enjoyed in its glorious unadulterated form, it deserves to be treated so. This respect and understanding will only come with greater awareness and genuine interest in the wine. The taste of a wine may be altered by the choice of food, rather than by adding Coke – this knowledge will also come with learning and experience.

Wine and calligraphy: making wine communication relatable

One of the key challenges in promoting Western wines to a Chinese audience is that of communication. Often there is a feeling of things being lost in translation on both sides, not just due to language or cultural differences, but relevance: why should we care about a wine's birthplace thousands of miles away, and why does it matter that the vines grow on gravel soil with clay subsoil? Delving straight into a deep discussion about the uptake of nutrients and water in the vines based on soil types that eventually manifests in certain flavour and tannin characteristics is likely to meet blank faces. Only when we make the connection of relevance can we ignite genuine interest. For example, likening an understanding of wine terroir to that of the styles of Chinese calligraphy, so that the appreciation of the final work can be contextualised, might be a helpful way in to explain soil types and vines.

Discerning taste in calligraphy is not the birthright of the Chinese, nor is understanding wine the prerogative of the French, but imagine the challenge of teaching the French about Chinese calligraphy. The trick is to make foreign concepts native and relatable.

When explaining the basics of wine tasting, we might say that a good wine is first and foremost balanced: it does not have too much or too little of any characteristic that typifies a wine of its kind, and the integration of sugars, acidity, tannins and alcohol result in a harmonious whole, without any one element dominating. This kind of evaluation can feel rather abstract to a novice. What is more relatable is the tactile sensation of a wine in the mouth. This is usually a good starting point to appreciate it: the 'mouthfeel' (the weight and texture of a wine) is easily perceivable, even for novices. Most of us can relate to varied sensations in the mouth through eating and drinking. For example, we frequently borrow terms like heavy, soft, velvety, tingling, fresh and chewy to describe the effects of alcohol, sugars, acidity and tannins. Even without understanding their causes and effects, everyone can observe sensations and assess whether the overall impression of the wine is pleasing, intriguing, unremarkable or unpleasant, and that would be a good first step in discerning wine.

With Chinese calligraphy, you could describe the aesthetic impression of a work without necessarily knowing the meaning of the writing. How does the writing occupy the space? Does it look balanced? Does it appear well considered or impromptu in style? Is there any particular part of the work that draws your attention or demands specific focus? Do the brush strokes convey energy, emotion or confidence? Do you imagine a supple, soft wrist at work, or a strong arm that had applied particular force and pressure? Just like a wine, we can talk about the 'body' of calligraphy, its bone structure, flesh and joints. Is it broad, lean, athletic, elegant, voluptuous, sinuous, muscular? You might be surprised by how much knowledge of wine can help you to discern elements of Chinese calligraphy. And the reverse is also true.

Of course, to take the step from basic appreciation to connoisseurship requires much more time dedicated to learning and experience. To be able to derive the story of a wine from its mouthfeel – its age, grape variety, terroir, winemaking techniques and ageing potential – requires a lot more knowledge of wine, but also makes the experience of drinking it infinitely more interesting and rewarding. In calligraphy, knowing Chinese characters, schools of style, brushstroke techniques, the manipulation of the human body, the meaning and mood that suits the work and so on, would further enhance our appreciation of calligraphy and the master's greatness.

Yet even with an understanding of an art, there would still remain the million-dollar question: what are the qualities that really set a masterpiece apart, above and beyond great balance, impression and techniques? Complexity and intrigue, perhaps. A great wine has the ability to reveal a range of pleasing aromas and tastes. It has spatial and temporal dimensions, depths and lengths to savour. It engages the senses and concentration for a long while. As with a great work of calligraphy, there are details and nuances to discover and contemplate. And with every level of enhanced knowledge, yet another layer of intrigue is revealed.

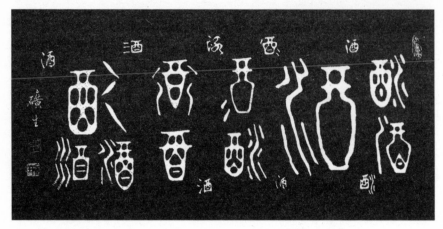

Calligraphy of one Chinese character in various playful renditions. Can you guess the meaning of the character? (Answer on page 120)

Expanding the international vocabulary of wine

'Oh! Marvellous! That unmistakable aroma of cassis!'
'Oh! Not again! What on earth is cassis?'

However it may be rendered in various tongues, cassis, blackcurrant, *heijialun*, is a common word used to describe the aroma of Cabernet Sauvignon, but it is not a familiar smell to many people, even less so to Chinese people; likewise gooseberries, to which Sauvignon Blanc is often compared.

A large part of learning about wine is to acquaint yourself with new aromas and flavours, and sharpen your sensory awareness. But what if the blackcurrants or the *crème de cassis* from Dijon that we are supposed to train our faculties with are not easily obtainable in a country such as China?

It is time to take a step further, beyond the cassis and gooseberries, and look for alternative vocabularies. The way truly to speak to a different audience, to convey the aromatics, flavours and everything that is alluring about wine, is to find terms that are relatable to local experience.

I have marvelled at wines with subtle scents of *longyan* (long'an) and lychee, or that reminded me of *shanzha* (hawthorn fruit), *sang guo* (mulberries) or *pipa gao* (a throat drop made of loquat fruit), or wines that conveyed the fleshy richness of *dong po rou* (slow-cooked melt-in-the-mouth pork belly) or a nose reminiscent of Chinese herbal medicine. Sometimes, I know in my heart that what I perceive with my own world of familiar fruits, foods and childhood memories from China are the best way I can describe a wine, but the challenge is how to share the same language with someone else in a tasting room in London or a château in Bordeaux. To enrich the language of wine, and the understanding among an increasingly global fanbase, it is no longer enough simply to increase the awareness of cassis, but also of *shanzha, longyan, pipa*, even slow-cooked pork belly.

Furthermore, where the Chinese might lack in distinguishing between blackcurrants and blueberries, they more than make up for in discerning between variations in tea flavours that might pop up in the wine glass. So perhaps the generic 'tea leaf on the palate' of one wine critic could be made more specific to another Chinese taster as 'aged *pu'er*' (a type of semi-fermented Oolong black tea, especially susceptible to the effects of terroir) or 'first flush *bi luo chun*' (a famous Chinese green tea). As the appreciation of wine expands into new cultural territories, the addition of new languages to talk about wine will only enrich wine culture as a whole, and promote cross-cultural learning and fun.

Tea culture and wine culture

Many wine lovers lament how the Chinese drink wine. As I have mentioned, the widespread habit of throwing back whole cups of *bai jiu* at once has made a direct transfer to grape wine in social settings, where keeping up is essential for saving face. Many Chinese people would fill large glasses of wine and toast *ganbei!* (bottoms up!). This seems rather wasteful of a good bottle, as no effort is made to savour the wine. Luckily, a happier cultural fit is readily available, and it can be gleaned from Chinese tea culture.

In tea terms, it is intuitive for the Chinese to understand notions of revered terroirs, single estates, hand harvests and vintage labelling.

Similarly, when it comes to tea, the Chinese are familiar with assessing the colour, aroma and taste, intriguing palate, complex mouthfeel, balanced tannins, enduring lengths, effects of oxidisation and much more. Comparing a fine bottle of wine to prized Chinese teas, such as premium Da Hong Pao ('Big Red Gown') or Pu'er, would immediately summon a respectful attitude in the Chinese drinker, and sips, rather than gulps, are likely to be taken with conscious effort to appreciate the sensation. Da Hong Pao may be likened to Bordeaux's classified growths in terms of tiered prestige, quality and price tags, and vintage Pu'er may be compared to the most cellar-worthy wines because certain varieties improve and gain character with ageing, just like fine wine. Some of the finest Pu'er teas are aged for over 60 years.

In a tea ceremony, great care is taken in the setting, the skills and preparation of the service and the tea-ware. Similarly, careful storage, suitable serving temperature and appropriate decanting and glassware are also important to serving wine. Furthermore, a tea ceremony demands a contemplative state of heightened sensory awareness and harmony that is the essence of *chan* (more commonly known in the West by its Japanese rendition as Zen). This resonates with discerned wine tasting, where the experience is not just the act of drinking, but a holistic experience that assesses the look, aroma and taste of the wine. In both tea and wine culture, sensory acuity and awareness bring out the best experience, and much pleasure is in store for those who care to learn and bank memories.

Health–wealth–happiness: why red wine is lucky in China

Around 90 per cent of grape wine drunk in China is red. Red is the most auspicious colour in China: it's the colour of joy, happiness and good tidings. Red lanterns, red firecrackers and red envelopes heighten the spirit of Chinese New Year. Red carpets, red ribbons and red banners herald the opening of a new establishment. Traditionally, a bride and groom dress from head to toe in red on their wedding day. Even the stock exchanges display gains in red – the opposite to international market convention. When it comes to the imported wine market in China, it is the red wines that bask in the limelight. It all makes sense, of course: red is the natural choice to express, and aspire to, happiness. So it seems that the favouritism towards red wines is unchallenged in China because it is a matter of cultural partiality.

But wait. Long before the arrival of this infatuation with red wines, the Chinese had been celebrating with grain wines for millennia, and continue to do so. Grain wines come in a multitude of colours, including clear, white, yellow and orange. The Chinese certainly have no hang-ups about drinking wines that are not red. And let's be honest, most red wines are more purple or brown than auspiciously red. Of course, the lucky colour associations of red wine is a stroke of marketing genius, but why is it that, say, the golden-hued sweet wine from Sauternes – which has a more accessible taste profile and is the ultimate colour symbol of wealth and power – did not crack the Chinese market with nearly the same impact as its red neighbours from the Médoc? We have to look a bit deeper to understand the popularity of reds.

Over 2,000 years ago, at the peak of trading activities along the Silk Road, Emperor Han Wudi (156–87 BC) of the Han dynasty learned about grape wine beyond the western borders of China and took a personal interest in cultivating grape vines. During the prosperous Tang dynasty (618–907) many more famous personalities were noted lovers of grape wines. Li Bai (701–62), the 'poetry saint', and Lady Yang (1719–56), one of the 'Four Great Beauties' of China, were ardent red wine lovers. Then, at the zenith of the Qing dynasty's imperial might, the longest-reigning emperor of China, Emperor Kangxi (1654–1722), was advised by a French missionary from Bordeaux to drink red wine every day with meals to maintain good health. A most esteemed emperor's longevity was now linked with the daily consumption of red wine.

Although red wine has long featured in China's history and culture, it has never been as widespread as it is today. Production levels and transport logistics have never been as advanced as they are now. Cultivated wine grapes were not native to China, technology was limited, lack of knowhow restricted domestic production and imported foreign wines were scarce. For a long time, red wines were the preserve of royalty and nobilities, and few outside the privileged classes had access to it. Nevertheless, with a historical fanbase of 'sons of Heaven' (emperors), scholars and beauties, red wine had always enjoyed prestige in the collective consciousness of the Chinese.

Fast-forward to the 1980s and 1990s, and as an increasing Chinese population progressed from *xiao kang* (modest comfort) living standards towards becoming middle class, wine consumption began to flourish once more. *Bai jiu* and beer were popular incumbents, and the wealthy flaunted a little Rémy Martin for a splash of class (the marketing department at Rémy Martin spotted the Chinese fascination with the centaur that is its logo, and really exploited it). *Bai jiu* was too alcoholic, however, and, with its associated habit of *ganbei* it was hardly healthy. Beers are lower in alcohol, but many loyal fans fell victim to the 'beer belly' physique. Rémy Martin gave a touch of luxury, but secretly many considered it merely a more exotic alternative to *bai jiu*, except that one would 'frugally' drink *bai jiu* while displaying the Rémy Martin bottle in the living room where guests could see it.

In 1996 the then-premier Li Peng remarked to the National People's Congress that people should drink more red wine instead of hard liquor, on health grounds. Spurred on by such exalted endorsement, the talk about red wine being a healthier and sophisticated alternative began to gather speed and took hold among the well-to-do Chinese population, a group who had a better education, higher-paid jobs, travelling opportunities and interactions with foreigners, foreign goods and foreign lifestyles. Traders and entrepreneurs also took note of new opportunities that seemed to come with the government's blessing. When the twenty-first century dawned, China's interest in red wine took off on a near-vertical trajectory, fuelled by the emergence of newer social classes who wielded enormous spending power.

It was as if people had suddenly connected up the dots, and the distant historical prestige of red wine became the new trend of the age. Emperors of bygone dynasties were now reincarnated as the children of fortune under socialist capitalism, and red wine, which was revered then, was once more revered. Underpinning all of this was the same quest for good health and longevity through a rich culture of food and drink. Somehow red wine seemed to fulfil the role of elixir.

In the West, wines are generally not marketed on health grounds. There are stricter regulations for making health claims, and consumers tend not to make wine choices in this way. In China the market landscape is rather different. Many consumer surveys suggest that health benefits are an important aspect in wine choice, and red wines are widely considered to be the most, if not the only, health-providing alcoholic beverage. Against this backdrop, plenty of enterprising wine merchants are taking advantage of the health angle to sell wines in China. I was bemused to find an example of a cassis wine marketed as the ultimate health wine, with a label covered in dense writing extolling the health benefits of cassis. The canny wine producer recognised 'cassis' as a term frequently used to describe red wine and, therefore their logic went that a cassis wine would deliver an even greater concentration of health benefits than red grape wine. Although Western wine producers do not usually intend to market their wines in China as health drinks, sales strategies may get out of their hands somewhere along the distribution chain. In any case, the voices of consumers, who clearly value the health aspects of wine, cannot be overlooked. Many wine websites in Chinese inevitably include a section on 'wine and health', with the latest scientific research and beauty tips, including using leftover wine for anti-ageing facials.

In more recent decades, many scientific findings provide supportive evidence that moderate and regular wine drinking offers anti-thrombotic protection against heart diseases and strokes, and possible benefits in relation to diabetes, mental illness and some cancers have been noted. It is also suggested that resveratrol, a phenolic compound found in red wine, has antioxidant properties and may even act as an antibiotic. It is found in grape skins and gets into red wines because of the sustained skin contact with the pressed juice. Little is found in white wine, as the juice is run off from the skins. In China, many people have heard of red wine's health benefits, perhaps in a simpler narrative, and as a result they buy red wines for elderly parents as a gesture of filial piety, an important lifelong virtue in Chinese society.

As well as its lucky colour and health benefits, there is another aspect to red wine's popularity. Anecdotally, red wine is for the serious wine drinker. While women are more likely to be seen drinking white, rosé, sparkling or ice wines, the man of the world should be seen with a glass of red. According to this attitude, a true connoisseur must prefer red wine because it is the least accessible in taste profile, often with drying and bitter tannic characteristics and complex structures that take some getting used to. Therefore, the appreciation of red wine demonstrates the taste that has come with training and discernment. Drinking red wine is thus associated with class and taste, which in turn implies wealth, expertise and power.

Red wine's prominent status is well deserved, but there is plenty to be celebrated in wines of other hues. As for taste preferences, there is much to discern in the nuances of white, pink and golden-coloured wines. As people become more experienced drinkers, wines of all colours will have their deserving place in China. The appreciation of other wines might take a while longer, and develop at a steadier pace than the heady trajectory enjoyed by the reds, but it will come, and we should take heart from China's own kaleidoscopic traditions of producing wines of varying colours, ingredients and characters.

Heaven–earth–people: the terroir for success

The Chinese believe in three elements that hold the key to success – the natural conditions sent from heaven, such as climate and weather; geography, in other words the lie of the land and the advantages of a location; and the motivation, wisdom and collaboration of the people – encapsulated by the concept of 'heaven–earth–people'. This ancient Chinese wisdom, endorsed by the celebrated Confucian philosopher Meng Zi (Mencius, 372–289 BC) and the pre-eminent war strategist Sun Zi (Sun Tsu, 544–469 BC), has stood the test of time. To this day, it is ingrained in the Chinese psyche and imparts guidance in all aspects of life. It is perpetually relevant in agriculture, business, politics, project planning and some say even love! Sun Zi, in *The Art of War*, sees the three elements of 'heaven—earth—people' as equally important, like the legs of a tripod. If the three elements are incomplete, you may find favour for a short while, but adversity is pending.

Winemakers worldwide have long held a strong belief in terroir: the notion of, and respect for, a place's natural conditions that impart unique characters to its produce. Terroir, from the word *terre*, meaning 'land', often refers to terrain, soil and topology, but many winemakers insist that it is more than just what the earth embodies. Terroir, in its wider sense, could encapsulate 'heaven—earth—people', though the role of humans is contentious. Do natural elements ultimately dictate human behaviour, or do human endeavours transcend nature? This ancient debate is very topical to viticulture today, thanks to expanding winegrowing frontiers as a result of globalisation and climate change that threatens the very existence of traditional wine regions.

Broadly speaking, soil attributes are key determinants of an area's suitability for winegrowing. Well-drained soil that supplies steady, but not excessive, water and the nutrients nitrogen, phosphorus and potassium to the vines is preferable. Soil also affects the temperature and heat transfer above and below the surface, which will affect vine growth. Winegrowing benefits from just the right amount of stress to the vines so that the vigour and yield are balanced and the vine's energy is prioritised for producing good berries rather than too much foliage. Therefore, less fertile land is actually preferred. In particular, gravelly and rocky soils can store and transmit heat efficiently and hold great potential for fine winemaking, as can be found in some classified Bordeaux estates.

Sunshine is essential for vine growth and ripening of the berries, and is generously afforded to regions with a Mediterranean climate. Temperature range and variability, from season to season, day to day, and between day and night, all have a strong influence on vine health, berry quality and wine style. For example, a big diurnal temperature contrast between warm days and cool nights tends to create a good balance between sugar and acidity in the berries. The timing and amount of rainfall throughout the year is crucial, as excessive water during ripening would dilute the flavour in the berries and may induce infections. Wind is also important: while a gentle breeze will moderate exposure to heat and moisture, and ventilation reduces the risk of fungal diseases, strong winds may cause damage to vines and the yield. Furthermore, humidity has implications for the rate of water loss in the soil and vines (low relative humidity leads to faster evaporation from the soil and transpiration through the vines), risks of infection (high humidity increases the spread of diseases) and flavour characteristics (high humidity benefits wine quality, particularly the freshness of the flavour and aroma).

Areas with a Mediterranean climate, characterised by long, warm, dry summers and mild, wet winters, are generally favourable for wine-growing: sunshine is ample and reliable for a long growing season. Low rainfall during the growing season also reduces the risk of fungal diseases. Hot, dry summers, however, increase the risk of drought and water stress, and irrigation is often necessary. Examples of wine regions that enjoy such a climate include the Mediterranean basin, the west coast of the United States, southern and western Australia, the west coast of South Africa and central Chile. Some wine regions have a continental climate where seasonal temperature variations are large. In such areas, hot summers with large diurnal temperature variations are conducive to growth, ripening and balance of flavour in the berries, but the onset of a rapid temperature drop and unpredictable rainfall in autumn heighten uncertainties around harvest, so in these areas vintage quality can differ considerably from year to year, but can also produce more varied and characterful wines. Wine regions with a continental climate include Central and Eastern Europe, Canada, Burgundy, the northern Rhone, most of the Loire Valley, Rioja, Douro, northern Italy and Mendoza.

The opposite of a continental climate is a maritime climate, where the annual temperature ranges are not wide, typically places near large bodies of water or the coast. Such areas tend to enjoy a long, temperate growing season with warm rather than hot summers and mild rather than cold winters. Risks of excessive rainfall and humidity, however, may bring hazards such as a ruined harvest or diseases. Maritime-climate wine regions include Bordeaux, Champagne, England and New Zealand.

China, on the other hand, straddles vast territories with a tropical and sub-tropical south and a frigid north. Most of the vine-growing regions have a maritime and/or monsoon climate in the north-eastern coastal area, where the Asian monsoon systems bring about hot, humid and wet summers but winter is mild; or a semi-arid/continental climate in the central-north and north-western areas, where summer is hot but winter can be very cold and dry. Neither of these are ideal winegrowing conditions for the reasons set out above. In short, it is a toss-up between a wash-out summer and a fatal winter – winemakers must choose their battle in China.

Thus, the suitability of a location for winegrowing involves many considerations, subject to nature's endowments and challenges. Inevitably, winemakers from different regions have rather different attitudes towards how much human intervention is required in their art: winemakers from areas with naturally favourable conditions tend to promote a light touch approach so the terroir speaks for itself, while areas with challenging conditions may play up human ingenuity in overcoming natural obstacles.

I have been privileged to discuss the fascinating topic of terroir with several Bordeaux winemakers, who are at the helms of some of the world's most envied terroirs. Their interpretations of 'heaven–earth–people' are particularly telling.

Jean-Hubert Delon, proprietor of Château Léoville-Las Cases and Domaines Delon in Saint Julien, described terroir as 'the primary influence that gives a wine its character, which encompasses the climate, microclimate, soil, subsoil, lie of the land, environment and much more, that influence and interact with the vine, which ultimately expresses itself in the wine produced. All these factors are revealed in the wine, to showcase the essence of a specific place, and to celebrate the character, nobility and soul of the earth.'

Unlike Sun Zi's view of the equal importance of 'heaven–earth–people', some winemakers believe that the notion of terroir, in its purest form, is really about the natural elements. The human touch is to process the gift of nature with a faithful interpretation of the area's character, and not to embellish it with the winemaker's personality. Thomas Duroux, chief executive of Château Palmer, Margaux, explained: 'When a wine is made by someone who has a very strong personality, and when you feel the personality in the wine, then this wine is no longer speaking of its birthplace, but of the winemaker. Such a wine is no longer unique to a place, but can be reproduced elsewhere with the travail of humans.'

Understandably, this belief is especially strong among those vineyards blessed with the most celebrated terroirs in the world. 'A wine is characterised through soil, vines, climate and man. But a Great Wine, with capital letters, is characterised by all these elements, plus the nobleness of the terroir,' said Jean-Paul Gardère, the late veteran director of Château Latour, Paulliac.

Jean-Philippe Delmas, managing director of Château Haut-Brion, emphasised to me that, although the precise blends vary each year, 'through each vintage, you can taste Haut-Brion – there is something that tells you it is Haut-Brion, and I believe that is the notion of terroir'. This echoes Samuel Pepys's 1663 diary entry, in which he wrote of 'a wine called Ho Brion that has a good and most particular taste I never met with'. In what was perhaps the first tasting note about Haut-Brion, Pepys recorded that 'particular' taste of a unique terroir.

The Confucian philosopher Meng Zi took a different view of 'heaven–earth–people'. While acknowledging the importance of all three, he considered people to be the most important factor: one can argue that heaven and earth are the premises that we start with, but the actions of people deliver the end results. Véronique Sanders, director general of Château Haut-Bailly, Graves, observed: 'The people – the human efforts of many who bring the elements of heaven and earth and present their life and soul in the form of a wine – is a blending of passion, care, know-how, experience, intuition ... and an expression of philosophy.' In winemaking, people who enjoy favourable initial conditions, such as the winemakers with the superior terroir, are grateful, respectful and nurturing towards their natural assets. For most of them, less is more when it comes to human intervention, allowing nature's own exquisite expressions to be the unique qualities celebrated in their wines. Yet winemakers with initially challenging conditions need to be more creative, improving potential through human craft.

Professor Li Demei, a leading Chinese wine educator and consultant, believes that the Chinese terroir is a case in point of the heaven–earth–people mantra, in which human endeavours are necessary to conquer environmental challenges as described above – in particular the ingenuity of developing and irrigating previously desolate lands and painstaking efforts of burying vines to overcome harsh winter conditions.

Laurenz 'Lenz' Moser, winemaker at Changyu Moser XV in Ningxia, even took the bold decision to make a white wine from the 'king of red wine grape' – Cabernet Sauvignon. 'We needed a white wine for the export market, but our current plantings of white varieties are not yet ready to produce good-quality white wine,' Lenz explains. 'I have previously made a white wine using Cabernet Sauvignon in Austria, out of desperation due to a bad harvest, but it turned out to be very pleasant and aged well too. So I decided if I don't have other good white grapes to work with right now, then I will make white wine from Cabernet Sauvignon in China! It is a wine born out of necessity, being solution oriented. The Chinese language reminds us that every crisis, *wei ji*, has two elements – a danger (*wei*) and an opportunity (*ji*) – we have problems but we have solutions as well.'

There are, therefore, different approaches and philosophies at work. Sometimes, significant human effort must be employed to compensate for natural inadequacies. At other times, when nature endows greatness, a light touch is the most desirable.

A Chinese proverb says that endeavour is the pursuit of man, but outcome is the will of heaven. 'That's why you always have to stay humble in front of nature. It will always have the last word, it will always deal the last hand', says Alexander Van Beek, general manager of Château Giscours and Château du Tertre in Margaux. This rings true for the uncertainty of weather conditions every year. Furthermore, climate change is likely to reshape the landscape of wine regions worldwide and pose serious challenges. Higher average temperatures, and more frequent and extreme cases of heat waves, droughts, flooding and hailstorms, will render some traditional winegrowing regions unsuitable, possibly within half a century. Inadvertently, China's north-west could improve its prospects as a wine region, where a warmer winter would be beneficial for viticulture. Then, perhaps, Chinese terroir will really sing for itself. It is no coincidence that large multinationals are diversifying their vineyard portfolios into cooler climates, including parts of China, just as champagne houses are hedging their bets with English sparkling wines.

To combat climate change, shore up resilience in the world's habitats and reduce further damage to our planet, we all have collective responsibilities. The belief in patrimony and responsibility is strong among winemakers. 'The most important thing in wine is the notion of heritage,' says John Kolasa, managing director of Château Rauzan-Ségla in Margaux and Château Canon in Saint-Emilion. 'You are just passing by, but a bottle of wine stays. You pick up something that somebody left in the cellar fifty years ago, and you have to be sure of putting something in its place that somebody will drink fifty years later. And that notion of heritage is the key factor in everything we do in our work.' This mindfulness of continuity and of future generations will hopefully spur on our collective efforts to do more for the environment.

The most vocal and active winemaker to address climate change is Miguel Torres Senior of Bodegas Torres, one of Spain's leading wineries, which has vineyards in Spain, Chile and California. The Torres & Earth programme is already in motion to reduce its carbon footprint throughout its winemaking and distribution process, with practices such as recycling water, using lighter bottles, reducing packaging and installing solar panels for electricity generation. It is also testing CO_2-capture technologies with the goal of preventing harmful emissions into the atmosphere and converting CO_2 into useful resources such as fertiliser.

It can certainly be argued that the human element in 'heaven–earth–people' is crucial to the future potential and resilience of terroir. Moreover, we cannot assume favourable conditions to be everlasting. We need to stay alert, take a longer view and be prepared to adapt. But even with the best intentions and the greatest efforts, we also have to allow for factors that we can neither control nor foresee. Life's uncertainties are the flavours of challenge, beguilement and gratification. 'It's a very good thing that we don't know everything and all that happens. The terroir will always retain some mystique and mystery,' says John Kolasa.

'The keys to making a great wine? Weather, terroir, people … and a bit of luck,' concluded Didier Cuvelier, proprietor of Château Léoville Poyferré in Saint-Julien, with a wink.

Chinese philosophy and *in vino veritas*

Chi in wine

Chi (or *qi*) is the essence of the universe, the source of life, the spirit of a soul. *Chi* requires balance to achieve harmony, from the microscope of particles to the macroscope of the universe. The yin and yang of *chi* are mutually supportive and interactive to attain balance.

For many wine lovers, the most alluring aspect of a fine wine is its ability to improve with age. It seems to have a mysterious life force that follows a unique path of development through time. A wine that ages gracefully is celebrated and revered, like a life well lived. But what gives a wine life, evolution and character?

Calligraphy depicting *chi*: *chi* is an important quality in calligraphy itself that brings a life force to the writing, which communicates between the artist and the viewer

It is thanks to a balanced complex of compounds, tannins, acids and sugars that, under the orchestration of oxygen, interact and resolve into harmony over time.

The lifespan of a wine can be described in the same way as the cycle of *chi*: when *chi* amalgamates, life; when *chi* gathers strength, vigour; when *chi* weakens, frailty; when *chi* relinquishes itself, death.

A wine is given life and attains *chi* through the cultivation of vines and the nourishment of soil, rain and sun, followed by harvest, fermentation, barrel ageing and bottling that sees it through conception to birth. The balancing of *chi* continues inside the bottle, as the wine resolves among its constituents and develops complexity and harmony over time. How well the wine ages, and for how long it retains liveliness and *chi*, are partly determined by the terroir, the condition of the vintage, the winemaker's skills and the level of balance in the components of the wine – the sugars, acidity and tannins – and the supply of life-affirming oxygen inside the bottle. Yet *chi* is also a force of mystery, and the exact way in which a wine will age always has an unknowable aspect that is fascinating.

Underpinning the concept of *chi*, and also of fine wine, is the notion of balance. When *chi* is at its most harmonious, wellness, beauty and peace are found. The central aim of Chinese medicine is to attain balanced and well-channelled *chi* in the body, which will manifest as health and strength. Similarly, a wine with balanced *chi* flourishes with its best qualities. When *chi* is disturbed a discord arises between yin and

yang, the flow of *chi* is blocked, and this brings about an ailment. Analogously, heavy-handedness in aspects of winemaking will lead to a flawed wine, which even if not immediately obvious will manifest in the long term. *Chi* also has natural cycles of vitality and decline that apply to all living things. And so, as it is with wine, the *chi* in a wine will experience youthfulness, exuberance, maturity and decline.

The wisdom of *ren*

Calligraphy depicting *ren*: the practice of calligraphy is linked with the contemplation of virtues

Ren: control, discipline, patience, tenacity, endurance, tolerance and forbearance. Countless scrolls of

Chinese calligraphy are dedicated to this single Chinese character, which is hung on walls in both private homes and public halls. *Ren*, in its most concise and monosyllabic motto form, encapsulates a whole world of Chinese philosophy.

Ren means to think before using actions and words, to curb knee-jerk reactions, to show forbearance in the face of adversity, injustice or ignorance, to be patient and wait for the right time and place for action. Outwardly *ren* may appear timid, but the true way to *ren* requires steely inner resolve and perseverance. *Ren* is an attitude, a technique, a principle, an approach to life's situations or a path to self-discovery. The virtues and best practices in winemaking can be succinctly summarised by this single Chinese word.

The art and science of viticulture and oenology require discipline, control and patience. Knowing how to balance the natural elements with technical knowhow is a skill that has no shortcuts, and requires tenacity, fortitude, curiosity and passion, all invested over time. A young vine takes 15-plus years before it bears fruit that may yield wine with good potential. It takes further decades for the vine to fully mature and reveal its distinctive character. For a well-made wine, one may wait for several decades before it comes of age to be drunk. From vine to glass, a fine wine could be in the making for generations.

Yet in our modern age of instant gratification, a wine is often judged prematurely. In Bordeaux, a region famed for the most age-worthy wines in the world, one of the most important occasions is the annual *en primeur* tasting from barrel samples, when wines are tasted and evaluated. The pricing of these wines is often heavily influenced by first impressions and the critics' scores. Age-worthy wines can be disadvantaged by such an exercise, since complex wines made for ageing tend to be difficult to drink when very young, and may score badly compared to wines made for easier and earlier drinking. Yet many consumers look to high scores as a simple benchmark of quality.

What can the winemaker do when facing such a dilemma? After all, a wine estate needs to sell wines and maintain cash flow for what is a hugely capital-intensive operation. Under such pressure, some winemakers have adopted techniques that produce high-scoring wines at the expense of age-worthiness, thereby following the fashion and taste dictated by influential critics and wealthy regional markets. At the same time there are others who practise the principles of *ren* by staying true to the style of the terroir in their winemaking, believing that even if their wine may be out of favour with current fashion, in the long haul its true beauty will shine through with time and patience. In the meantime, they must possess the inner self-belief to endure and tolerate any unjust dismissal from the mass market.

Ren is that quiet confidence and deep-rooted faith to know that ultimately the truth will reveal itself and triumph.

Kung fu wine and *kung fu* masters

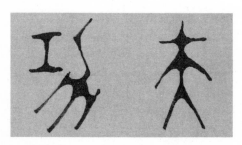

Calligraphy of *kung fu*: a calligraphy master is as much a *kung fu* master as a martial arts maverick

Kung fu (or *gong fu*): the unceasing learning, application and improvement of technique and art in human endeavour; the spirit of relentless pursuit for knowledge, ability, advancement and truth in a chosen discipline.

When the subject of *kung fu* comes up, we often think of awe-inspiring martial arts epitomised by brave heroes who dedicate their lives to arduous training and endless pursuits for betterment, and then apply their skills to fight injustice. They represent the best of the human spirit and command the utmost respect. Yet *kung fu* in its broadest sense could apply to almost every aspect of our lives. In classical Chinese teachings, anything worth doing is worthy of dedication and enquiry. There is *kung fu* in tea, in soup, in music, in calligraphy. When you attain *zhen gong fu* (real *kung fu*) your art becomes genuinely worthy and you become a master. Chinese parents frequently yell at their children to '*xia gong fu!*' – apply real effort to your studies!

Adong, the highest Ao Yun vineyard at 2,600 metres above sea level, Yunnan province

A drone-shot landscape of villages and plateaux, Meili mountains, Yunnan province

Wine Regions in China

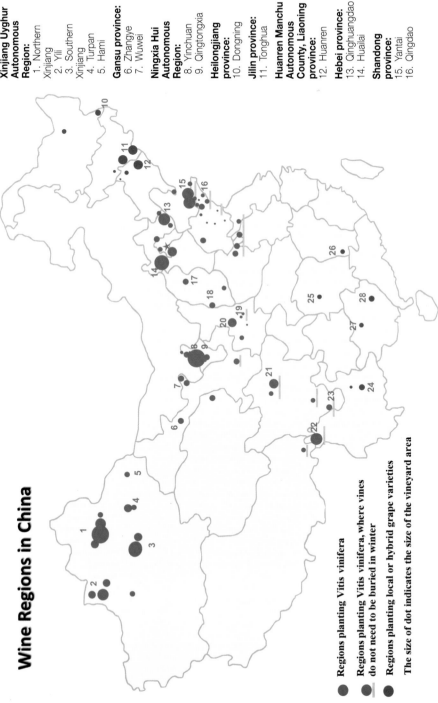

★ Beijing

Xinjiang Uyghur Autonomous Region:
1. Northern Xinjiang
2. Yili
3. Southern Xinjiang
4. Turpan
5. Hami

Gansu province:
6. Zhangye
7. Wuwei

Ningxia Hui Autonomous Region:
8. Yinchuan
9. Qingtongxia

Heilongjiang province:
10. Dongning

Jilin province:
11. Tonghua

Huanren Manchu Autonomous County, Liaoning province:
12. Huanren

Hebei province:
13. Qinghuangdao
14. Huailai

Shandong province:
15. Yantai
16. Qingdao

Shanxi province:
17. Taigu
18. Xiangning

Shaanxi province:
19. Xi'an
20. Xianyang

Ngawa Tibetan and Qiang Autonomous Prefecture, Sichuan province:
21. Aba (Ngawa)

Diqing Tibetan Autonomous Prefecture, Yunnan province:
22. Diqing

Sichuan province:
23. Panzhihua

Honghe Hani and Yi Autonomous Prefecture, Yunnan province:
24. Mile

Hunan province:
25. Huaihua

Jiangxi province:
26. Chongyi

Luocheng Mulao Autonomous County, Guangxi province:
27. Luocheng

Du'an Yao Autonomous County, Guangxi province:
28. Du'an

● Regions planting Vitis vinifera

●| Regions planting Vitis vinifera, where vines do not need to be buried in winter

● Regions planting local or hybrid grape varieties

The size of dot indicates the size of the vineyard area

Skyline of Gobi vineyard, Xinjiang province

Helan Qingxue Vineyard in summer, Ningxia province

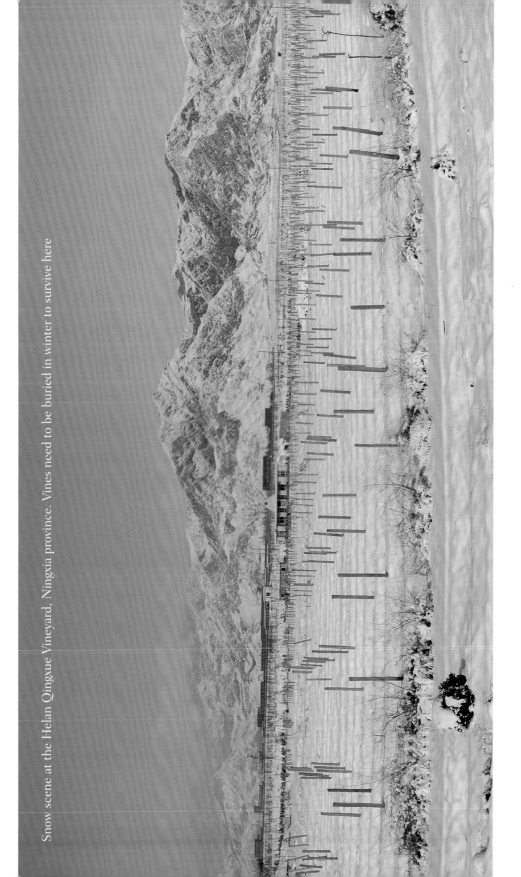
Snow scene at the Helan Qingxue Vineyard, Ningxia province. Vines need to be buried in winter to survive here

Burying vines for winter at Château Changyu Moser XV,
Ningxia province

A Merlot vineyard just after unearthing in spring,
Ningxia province

COFCO-Great Wall seedling incubator, Penglai,
Shandong province

Young vines at a local seedling company in
Xinjiang province

Cabernet Sauvignon planting at the foot of the
Flaming Mountains – red sandstone hills in the
Tianshan Mountain ranges, Turpan, Xinjiang
province

Sorghum is a major grain ingredient in traditional
Chinese winemaking

Traditional grain wine cellar at Youyuan winery,
Sichuan province

Wine is synonymous with many traditional Chinese
festivals. Raising the wine cup to toast the full moon
is an archetypal image of the Mid-Autumn festival,
immortalised in lyrics by Su Shi (1037–1101)

Tao Yuanming (*c*.352–427) – *garagiste*
winemaker and disillusioned scholar. His love
for wine and chrysanthemum is celebrated to
this day

A *Dream of Red Mansions* is among the greatest classical novels and portrays many wine scenes that give us a glimpse into luxury living in eighteenth-century China. Was it all but a dream?

The art of inebriation, according to Taoism,
is to free the mind and return to one's most
natural state

In winemaking, *zhen gong fu* is evident in the greatest wines. A wine from even the most noble estate with the most favourable terroir will not fulfil its potential without applying *zhen gong fu* to understanding the nuances of the land, cultivating the most suitable vines, conditioning the soil and vines to give the best possible fruit, harvesting at the most appropriate moment, selecting the best quality grapes, controlling temperature and fermentation, ensuring the most suitable barrels and cellaring conditions, careful tasting, blending, bottling, corking, transporting and storing. Passionate winemakers are tireless in their pursuit of quality and improvement. They learn from other masters, they respect tradition, heritage and experience from previous generations, and they have a sense of honour to carry a sacred baton forward. They embrace new technology and strive for progress and excellence, but only after careful testing and evaluation. They draw from learning, experience, memory, advice, discovery, intuition, humility and confidence, and for all this, time rewards them with wisdom, mastery and respect that no fast-track route could possibly replace.

Real *kung fu* is true mettle. It is a spirit that never stops and never ceases to be curious. In the temples of martial arts and the vineyards of celebrated wines, *kung fu* masters exude increasing authority and command more respect with age, awarded by the hard grit of time. Through the pursuit of *kung fu*, the Chinese have a deeply ingrained heritage of respecting elders, most strongly embodied in the notion of filial piety. As Confucius highlighted in his teachings, respect for the master is a key virtue of civilisation and the act of drinking wine should be an act of paying respects. On this note, let us toast the *kung fu* masters of past and present, and reflect on our own endeavours. Will we attain the way of *kung fu* in our chosen fields?

> *In winemaking, you need one quality: the drive of ceaseless craving, wanting. To want – in the past, the present and the future – I wanted, I want and I will want.*
>
> Jean-Paul Gardère, the late veteran director of
> Château Latour, Pauillac

The growth of wine tourism

The Chinese now spend hundreds of billions of US dollars each year on holidays – the highest of any nationality – and this trend is still rising. Traditionally, package holidays have had mass appeal, with ambitious itineraries of the must-sees and must-shops all taken care of. A caricature of a Chinese tourist would see him donning a cap advertising his travel agent with a camera strapped across the chest and one too many duty-free shopping bags in hand, hollering to his fellow travellers about the famous landmark in front of their eyes, or beckoning the pack to keep up with the raised umbrella ahead of them somewhere in the crowd. For many Chinese tourists, the ultimate objective remains the coverage of multiple destinations and the fulfilling of an extensive shopping list. The journey can be something of an irrelevance, if not a nuisance, full of cramped long-haul flights and pot noodles. The destination itself is allocated the minimum amount of time necessary to get a glimpse and the gist before being ticked off the list, then onwards to the next item on the agenda.

The global boom in Chinese tourism has certainly affected the picture-perfect wine regions, and mass tour groups do not fit well with the essence of wine holidays. A wine tour is better undertaken holistically. The sight, smell and sound of the journey through the wine region, and the food, ambience and company that complement the wine, make up the experience as much as the customary trips to must-see wineries and the purchase of must-buy bottles (or cases, for that matter).

In fact, the more holistic approach to travelling is being embraced by the younger generation of Chinese tourists, and they are setting the trend for wine holidays. As exposure to and interest in fine wines are largely the preserve of the Chinese elite, these tourists tend to be already well travelled, well heeled and well educated, with international connections or upbringing. Some command prominent positions in society, some are self-made high-flyers or *fu er dai* (rich second generation), younger than the average profile of wine tourists. They go to wine regions not like Grand Tour first-timers, but as an emergent breed of Chinese who favour a tailormade itinerary and treat the journey, not just the destination, as an integral part to the whole travel experience. They appreciate culture in a slower, more immersive way. It is an approach aligned to the essence of wine regions. Conversely, wine holidays, as holistic presentations of wine culture, are the perfect ambassadors for this new philosophy of travel.

Wine tourism is a fledgling industry within China, drawing in domestic visitors, and is starting to attract international interest. Many high-end Chinese wine producers consider tourism an essential part of their operation, incorporating brand marketing with sales. Wine tourism ranges from grand statement projects to boutique experiences. There's a Chinese saying that 'even great wines are afraid of obscure alleys', so Chinese producers appreciate what wine tourism could bring to brand recognition and communication. Immersive experiences and face-to-face communication are the most personal ways to attract new followers and sell wine. (For some suggested places to visit in China, *see* page 226.)

Matching wine with Chinese food

There is a natural parallel to the multisensory pleasures in wine and in food, where colour, aroma and flavour are the essential aspects of the quality of cuisine. 'Having good colour, aroma and taste' is a phrase frequently used to describe Chinese food or to praise a delicious and well-rounded dish. In food as well as wine, taste means far more than simply flavour: the mouthfeel, texture and balance between complementary or contrasting ingredients are important considerations.

Matching wine and food is not a new concept in China. Historically, taverns often offered food to complement their wines in order to be competitive, so wine has inspired and elevated food culture in many ways. Restaurants are commonly referred to as 'wine houses' (*jiu jia*) and banquets are known as 'wine feasts' (*jiu yan*). These everyday words remind us of the closeness of food and wine. As China becomes increasingly interested in Western-style wines, pairing Chinese dishes with a global repertoire of wines is becoming more popular. As general guidelines, light dishes should be matched with delicate wines. Rich, weighty foods and

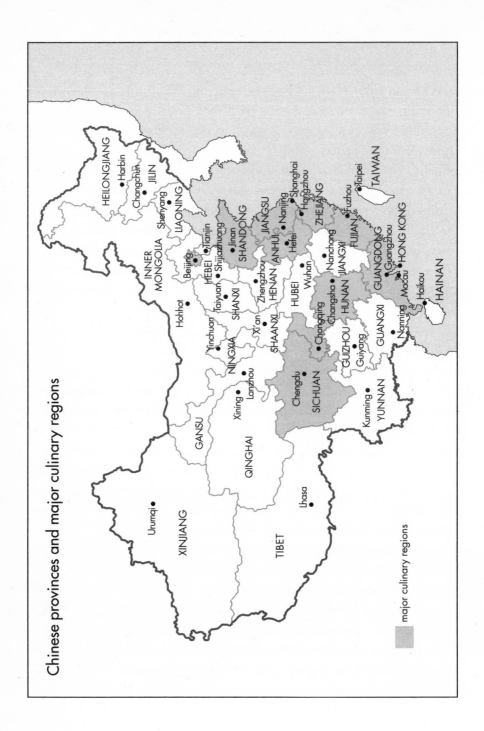

Chinese provinces and major culinary regions

major culinary regions

sauces go well with bigger, bolder wines. More textured food warrants higher tannins in the wine. Saltier dishes would find balance in fruitier wines, while spicy food would benefit from sweeter wines. Acidity in wines complements fatty and oily foods.

Unlike in Western cuisine where food is served in courses so that a particular wine may be paired with a particular dish, in China a large variety of food may be served at the same time, thus making it very difficult to do 'pairings'. It may be possible to pair one wine with a beef steak or another with a delicate fish, but what do you do when faced with chicken, lamb, beef, fish and vegetables, served all at once? When matching wine to Chinese food we also need to consider how the Chinese eat.

To tackle this puzzle, we could first simplify the challenge a little. Chinese cuisine has a natural affinity with grain-based beverages such as rice wine, *bai jiu* and beer. This seems reasonable, as Chinese cooking often uses soy sauce as a base condiment, which is made with fermented wheat, soybean and brine. Thus grain-based wine and grain-based sauce is a natural match. So the first step in matching Chinese food with other types of wine is to examine the base seasoning and style of the food. China is a vast country with many diverse cuisines (*see* map of the major culinary regions on page 92). Very broadly, there are eight main established regional cuisines, which are characterised by geography, climate, local produce and tradition. One approach to selecting wines is to choose styles that suit the cuisine.

Yue – Cantonese (Guangdong) cuisine

This is a comparatively young cuisine style, but one that has been successfully popularised in the West thanks to early Chinese migration from the Canton region. Cantonese cuisine is generally mild and sometimes with pronounced sweet flavours. Dishes tend to be served with ample sauce of a weighty but silky consistency. Texture, colour and freshness of ingredients are especially important, with quality benchmarks such as 'delicate yet flavourful' and 'rich but not greasy'. Dim sum (small plates steamed in bamboo containers or shallow fried, often delicate flour parcels with meat fillings) is a brunch culture traditionally accompanied with tea, and now much loved across China and all over the world. Cantonese cuisine is also famous for *Kung fu* soup, which uses seasonal ingredients to complement seasonal nutritional requirements, and is cooked very slowly for hours.

Wine style suggestions: dry, fresh whites with good acidity; dry sparkling whites and rosés; medium-bodied fruity reds with low tannins.

Signature dish pairing suggestions: sweet and sour pork (*gu lu rou*) with a Chinese vidal ice wine; steamed dim sum (*dian xing* or *zheng dian*) with champagne or Chinese sparkling wine; braised seafood (*hai xian bao*) with dry Riesling; sizzling hot-plate beef (*tie ban niu liu*) with mature Pinot Noir; BBQ *char siu* pork (*cha shao*) with a fruity Merlot; roast goose (*shao'e*) with a mature Sangiovese.

Chuan – Sichuan cuisine

Fiercely spicy, *Chuan* cuisine is often characterised by numbing and hot sensations known as *ma la*. Generous use of dried chillies, chilli oils and hot peppercorns are the hallmark of Sichuan dishes. Hot pot is also a much-loved eating tradition, in which assorted raw food items are thrown into a fragrant boiling broth before being eaten – a sociable way to eat and cook at the same time.

Wine style suggestions: off-dry or sweet, aromatic whites; off-dry rosés; ice wines.

Signature dish pairing suggestions: Ma Po tofu (*ma po dou fu*) with Torrontés; Kung Pao chicken (*gong bao ji ding*) with Gewürztraminer; boiled fish in chillies (*shui zhu yu*) with Riesling Spätlese.

Xiang – Hunan cuisine

This is a cuisine characterised by dry spice and bold flavours with a twang of acidity. Foods with complementary flavours and textures are often mixed in the same dish. Thick and nutritious seasonal soups are also famed in this region.

Wine style suggestions: aromatic, unoaked whites; medium-bodied fruity reds.

Signature dish pairing suggestions: 'dry wok' chicken (*gan guo ji*) with Viognier; braised pork ribs (*hong shao pai gu*) with New World Shiraz.

Su – Jiangsu cuisine

This region promotes the natural flavours of the ingredients, without heavy seasoning. 'Delicate but not bland' is the nuanced benchmark in flavours. Good presentation and attractive colours are also important. This region is famous for intricate knife-work and artistic presentation, and cold dishes are also popular.

Wine style suggestions: zesty, unoaked whites; off-dry sparkling whites and rosés.

Signature dish pairing suggestions: brine-boiled duck (*yan shui ya*) with off-dry to sweet Riesling; sweet and sour Mandarin fish (*tang cu gui yu/song shu yu*) with off-dry Chenin Blanc; steamed shredded crab and pork meatballs (*xie fen shi zi tou*) with Sauvignon Blanc.

Zhe – Zhejiang cuisine

The cuisine of this area is similar to that of Jiangsu, a neighbouring province. Particular attention is paid to seasonality and freshness of produce. Seafood features prominently among signature dishes.

Wine style suggestions: fresh, zesty whites; sweet wines; sparkling whites and rosés; mature reds with rounded tannins.

Signature dish pairing suggestions: braised pork belly (*dong po rou*) with Sauternes; tea infused stir-fry shrimps (*long jing xia ren*) with dry white Longyan (Chinese grape variety); drunken chicken (*zui ji/diao hua ji*) with Fino sherry.

Min – Fujian (Hokkien) cuisine

This region favours sweet and sour flavours and rarely uses chillies. Fujian cuisine pays particular attention to seasoning, the fragrance of the sauce, and the control of timing and fire temperature in cooking.

Wine style suggestions: fuller bodied and more complex whites; fruity reds.

Signature dish pairing suggestions: drunken pork ribs (*zui pai gu*) with a Chinese unoaked Chardonnay; sautéed scallops and white radish (*ban zhi gan bei*) with Pouilly-Fumé.

Hui – Anhui cuisine

This style originated from one of the most scenic mountain regions – the Yellow Mountain – and is particular about the 'fire power' of cooking techniques: the skilled control of and interaction between fire, oil and sauce (usually soy sauce) come across in the colour, flavour and texture of food. Boldness in colour and flavour are favoured.

Wine style suggestions: oaky Chardonnay; full-bodied jammy reds with mature tannins.

Signature dish pairing suggestions: 'stinky' fermented soya-braised Mandarin fish (*chou gui yu*) with Chardonnay; braised short ribs (*hong shao xiao pai*) with Californian Zinfandel or Chinese Marselan.

Lu – Shandong cuisine

The oldest and the most influential style, *Lu* is representative of northern Chinese cuisine. Soy sauce, garlic and spring onions form the basis of seasoning. Savoury tastes are prominent.

Wine style suggestions: local examples of fuller bodied whites with good acidity; fuller bodied reds with soft tannins.

Signature dish pairing suggestions: steamed sea bream (*qing zheng jia ji yu*) with Shandong province dry Italian Riesling; braised sea cucumber and spring onions (*cong shao hai shen*) with Shandong province Cabernet Gernischt (Carménère) or Liaoning province ice wine; vegetables in a creamy broth (*nai tang pu cai*) with Shandong province Chardonnay.

Jing – Beijing cuisine

This cuisine takes on many influences, particularly from the northern and eastern parts of China. As the undisputed imperial capital of China for three consecutive dynasties, Beijing cuisine is also influenced by palace cookery, giving meticulous attention to the quality and seasonality of ingredients, nutrition, balance of flavour and presentation.

Wine style suggestions: dry or sweet Rieslings; fruity, riper examples of Pinot Noir, Marselan, Merlot or Shiraz.

Signature dish pairing suggestions: Beijing roast duck or Peking duck (*bei jing kao ya*). The proper way to serve it is in two waves: first the crispy skin is carved and rolled up in pancakes with plum sauce, cucumber strips and spring onions. Then the meat is served as a dish or wok-fried with dry noodles. This dish could pair well with many wines but opt for bright acidity that can cut through the richness. For whites, consider Chinese examples of unoaked Chardonnay, Sauvignon Blanc or Riesling. For reds, consider Chinese examples of Cabernet Sauvignon, Marselan, Merlot and Cabernet Gernischt (Carménère) blends.

Generally speaking, Chinese food tends to work well with off-dry to sweet and more acidic wines. Also, heavily oaked or tannic wines can cause tartness, and high-alcohol wines would add fire to spicy food. In addition to the cuisine style, bear in mind the local climate – sometimes a chilled bottle on a hot day will trump any other considerations! Also consider local specialities and preferences. Coastal regions are more likely to excel in seafood, while areas close to river basins prefer the more delicate texture of river fish over sea fish. People from mountainous regions may eat more game and prefer bold, rich, earthy flavours, so matching the weight of the food and wine is a good general guideline.

It is worth noting that the Chinese are particularly sensitive towards the texture of food. Silkiness, chewiness, crunchiness: the texture of food reflects the quality and freshness of the ingredients and the '*wok kung fu*' of the chef. Countless combinations of complementary or clashing textures, classical or experimental, feature in Chinese cuisine. This offers a further dimension in working out wine choices because mouthfeel and the body of the wine could add or detract from the texture of the food, just as flavours may harmonise or clash.

Although the basic challenge – that multiple dishes tend to be served at the same time – remains, which makes it difficult to juggle wine choices among the different food items, matters in this regard are not entirely arbitrary. Every cuisine has cold and hot dishes, vegetable and meat dishes, light and heavy dishes. Certain similar or complementary dishes can be served in 'waves'. Some statement dishes, often called the 'head dish', for example the world-renowned Peking duck, are served on their own before waves of other dishes arrive together. In other regions, cold dishes, and sometimes 'dishes to down wine', are served before hot dishes. Sweets and fruits are served at the end of a meal. Professor Li Demei, the wine educator and consultant, advocates a considered approach to serving Chinese dishes if food and wine matching is to be a meaningful endeavour. Items with similar styles should be served in waves, with lighter dishes first, and choose wines that suit a particular wave of dishes or a main dish served on its own. Chinese restaurants would benefit from a more holistic approach to their menu, wine list and service, otherwise diners tend to opt for the simpler option of not having wine with Chinese food at all.

Food and wine matching can be challenging and even intellectual, but ultimately it is a social and pleasurable aspect of wine and culinary culture. The incredible diversity in Chinese cuisine is a boon, and we await more Chinese wines to join the kaleidoscopic global repertoire, and no doubt making the subject ever more intriguing, confusing, contentious and amusing! So let us experiment with open minds and a sense of adventure.

Wine etiquette and customs

In China, wine is steeped in legends of divine origins. Its sacred and noble status is reflected in its function as tribute to heaven, gods and ancestors. Over time, the uses and types of wine broadened, but the central place of honour and rites within wine culture remained. To this day, wine still conveys notions of honour, respect, thanksgiving and tribute in Chinese customs, and is used to mark births, marriages, business ventures,

A pair of wine cups with flowers and mandarin ducks motifs (auspicious symbols), gilt silver, Tang dynasty. Height 3.2cm, weight 0.146kg. Currently housed in Shaanxi History Museum

achievements, gift-giving and remembrance. Classical Chinese texts have given us oft-quoted phrases such as 'without wine there is no propriety' and 'without wine there is no banquet', which reveal wine's social cachet. Traditions, some of which are discussed in more detail later, have led to terms such as 'daughter red' (cellared wine to mark the first full month of a daughter's birth), 'scholar red' (cellared wine to mark the first full month of a son's birth), 'happy wine' (wedding banquet wine), 'hundredth-day wine' (served at a banquet to celebrate a new-born's hundredth day), 'red-bonus wine' (served at company year-end parties) and so on, which emphasise wine's irreplaceable position in Chinese customs. The word *jiu* not only refers to all types of alcoholic beverage in China, it is often also synonymous with hospitality. For example, *he xi jiu*, 'to drink happy wine', is to celebrate a wedding; *bai jiu xi*, 'to put on a spread of wine', is to host a party or banquet.

The etiquette and symbolism embedded in the act of serving and drinking wine are also important. Throughout history, wine etiquette has been accompanied by social rituals from rigid and highly complex ceremonial formalities to unbridled drinking games and till-you-drop frolics. Wine provides a kaleidoscopic view of an age, its people and its cultural and moral values. To this day, certain aspects of ceremonial wine etiquette are still observed. Beginnings, milestones and endings are often accompanied with offerings of wine, first and foremost to heaven and the ancestors for their blessings, then between the living to bolster relationships and express shared aspirations for a new career, a new home, a new agricultural year, a harvest or a college degree, or for the remembrance of a loved one. In ceremonial contexts, the first cup, or sometimes up to three cups, of wine are poured on the ground or onto the object to which the wine is offered. In social gatherings, toasts of wine are proposed from the most senior to the most junior, in order of social hierarchy or age, echoing the notion of honouring the leader, the wiser and the elder first. Since toasting is a gesture of respect, a toast must be accepted with thanks and is often reciprocated. Among a group it is an expression of solidarity and common aspirations, and a rallying call for everyone. When commemorating or expressing a wish, a ceremonial 'three cupfuls' are often toasted and drunk in succession to seek blessings from heaven, earth and people. Usually the host initiates the pouring and toasting and ensures that the wine does not run dry throughout the feast. At a wedding, the new couple may link arms and drink wine simultaneously from each half of a split gourd or wine cups known as paired mandarin duck cups, to symbolise everlasting unity, prosperity and fertility. Since the twelfth century, the ethnic Jurchins and Mongols, with their reputation for 'boundless' and 'ocean-like' drinking capacities, wielded great influence over the Central Plain of ethnic Han China and, to this day, the Chinese still try desperately to keep up with each other in the custom of *ganbei*, in which cup after cup of wine is emptied in a succession of proffered toasts.

Because wine is rich in symbolism, its service is taken seriously in China. The history of Chinese wine ware that accompanies archaeological discoveries is a near-continuous account of Chinese civilisation and technology. From Neolithic potteries to Bronze-Age vessels ranging from the colossal to the dainty, and through lacquerware, glass, coloured-glaze porcelain, jade, crystal, agate, gold and silver wares galore, Chinese wine ware takes on innumerable shapes and showcases some of the finest human achievements in craftsmanship, creativity, technology and ingenuity. Sometimes a gigantic cauldron for ceremonial offerings, sometimes an auspicious animal shape as a banquet centrepiece, sometimes an exquisitely carved miniature worthy of the hands and lips of a celebrated beauty. Besides its elegant forms, wine ware also serves many different functions designed for the optimal expression of the wine it serves, from winemaking to storage, to warming, to table service, to drinking. This rich wine heritage can be found scattered all over the world in museums with shapes so varied, exquisite or concealing that one may not immediately recognise their wine-related function. With such a history, modern Chinese wine drinkers are likely to appreciate the contemporary parallel in Riedel wine glasses and decanters, which are designed specifically for different types of wines or even grape varieties.

In many parts of the world it is customary to commemorate a child's birth by cellaring wine, and in China this tradition also exists with varying regional characteristics. Perhaps the most evocative is *nüer hong*, 'daughter wine' or 'daughter red'. In parts of China the birth of a daughter is marked by cellaring rice wine, usually Shaoxing wine, to be brought out for her wedding day. Traditionally, rice wine is prepared and sealed in plain ceramic wine pots and is ready for cellaring when the baby girl reaches one month old. When she marries, elaborate hand carvings are added to the wine pots, usually of auspicious motifs such as flowers, mandarin ducks, phoenixes and dragons. Because of this tradition, 'daughter wine' is also called *huadiao jiu*, 'flower-engraved wine'. On the wedding day the pots of wine are carried along with the bride on a palanquin and served at the wedding banquet. Similarly, *xi jiu*, 'happy wine', is matrimonial wine. Traditionally, the wines served at weddings were grain wines, but in modern China *bai jiu* and red grape wines are usually served.

A similar tradition exists for the birth of sons, too. Cellared Shaoxing rice wine, called *zhuang yuan hong* ('scholar wine' or 'scholar red') expresses the hope for sons to become learned and wise, with the prospects of high office in adulthood. Other widespread customs to celebrate early landmarks for newborns include *man yue jiu*, 'full month wine'; *bai ri jiu*, 'hundredth day wine'; and *zhou sui jiu*, 'full year wine'. Adults will enjoy the wine on the baby's behalf with banquets and parties and generous spreads of wine and food. Again, grape wines are increasingly replacing traditional rice wines on such occasions, especially in the first- and second-tier cities.

Chinese hospitality extends with pride towards friends and guests. The colourfully named drinking traditions of *jie feng*, 'wind-bracing', and *xi cheng*, 'dust-cleansing', welcome a guest from afar and revive the traveller after their arduous journey. Likewise, *jian xing jiu*, 'send-off wine', bids a good journey and good fortune to someone embarking on a trip or making a new start in life. In the diplomatic or business world, a wine-and-dine culture plays an important part in strengthening bonds and smoothing differences. Wine is brought out to mark the establishment of new ventures, the building of new premises and the start of new partnerships. *Fen hong jiu* – year-end 'bonus wine' – is poured to mark achievements, give thanks for hard work, motivate the workforce, reinforce team spirit and, last but not least, allow workers to let their hair down.

Throughout Chinese history, state-sponsored public drinking gatherings have been notable occasions during prosperous times, designed to showcase the wealth of the nation or the benevolence of the government, and to promote long-held Chinese virtues such as paying respects to elders with wine. District symposiums – where people gathered at officially sponsored banquets to perform wine rituals and feast – have existed since the Zhou dynasty in the first millennium BC. This tradition had a long-lasting legacy and has been revived time and again down the ages. In 1713, Emperor Kangxi celebrated his 60th birthday by inviting all elders above the age of 65 to several days of feasting inside the royal palace. All the young princes served wine to the elders, setting aside their royal rank. It is estimated that no fewer than 7,000 elders participated in the celebrations. Another such banquet was held in 1722, for Kangxi's 70th birthday, for which the emperor composed a poem entitled 'The Thousand Elders Banquet', and the name caught on. Kangxi's grandson, Emperor Qianlong (1711–99), followed his grandfather's example and held two more such banquets during his reign. As the Qing dynasty began its decline after the reign of Emperor Qianlong, however, no more such large-scale banquets were held. In recent years, Elders' Banquets are re-emerging in modern-day China, usually organised by district officials with the approval of the central government. They are a show of peace and prosperity, and the continuation of age-old Chinese values.

Wine and festivals

The origins of Chinese festivals are closely linked with nature and the agricultural year. Traditionally, festivals are occasions for worship and giving thanks to gods and ancestors, to mark important agricultural activities and to commemorate heroes and legendary figures. They are also occasions to appreciate human relationships, to admire scenery and to enjoy food, wine, tea, arts, poetry and games. (*See also* the list of festivals with Gregorian calendar dates on page 253.)

Chun Jie (Spring Festival – Chinese New Year)

The Spring Festival has existed in various forms since the time of Emperor Shun of the mythical Five Emperors period more than 4,000 years ago. Subsequent eras have used different calendars to mark the occasion. The Chinese Lunar New Year, as we know it today, originated from the revision of the calendar in 104 BC, during Emperor Han Wudi's reign. The Spring Festival marks the beginning of the year and is celebrated with worship, feasting, wine, fireworks, decoration of icons, art and auspicious poems. Traditionally, *tusu jiu* (yellow wine infused with Chinese rhubarb,

Sichuan pepper, cassia bark, Chinese bellflower, aconite and various medicinal rhizomes) and *jiaohua jiu* (yellow wine with capsicum flowers) are drunk to defend against winter ailments. Contrary to the usual etiquette, where elders are offered wine first as a mark of respect, at New Year wine is offered first to the youngest and last to the eldest. As a saying goes: 'The young gain a year; the old lose a year'. Thus, the occasion of New Year celebrates the young, who grow in physique and gain in worldliness.

As a result of rapid urbanisation, the Chinese New Year now creates the largest annual human migration in the world. Dubbed the 'Spring Rush', this is a phenomenal time when hundreds of millions of people are on the move simultaneously, homeward bound from all corners of the land to be reunited with family. More than 3 billion trips are made around the festival period, taking up 99 per cent of China's transport network capacity. Yet, no matter how arduous the journey, few would question making it, because the New Year's Eve dinner – epitomised by the scene of parents, husband and wife, siblings and children sitting together around the table with steamy dumplings and New Year delicacies, accompanied by the sound of laughter and the clinking of wine cups and chopsticks – is the most important family occasion of the year, charged with emotions and the symbolism of love, safety, comfort and filial piety. Richer or poorer, the sentiments are common to all Chinese people. Among the *nian huo* ('New Year goods') that are brought home, red grape wine is increasingly prominent. This is the most important period for wine sales in China. Many Chinese wineries launch auspiciously named and labelled wines at New Year, vying to outdo each other in artistic flair. Several vineyards also release red sparkling wines and 'nouveau' wines (wines fermented for a short period after the latest harvest) which are crowd pleasing and festive, made with the New Year's Eve family dinner in mind.

> *Sounds of fireworks herald the passing of a year;*
> *Spring breeze accompanies warmth into the wine of tusu.*
> *A new sunrise casts light over thousands of households;*
> *Each had changed the old board of Icons for new ones on peach wood.*

'New Year' by Wang Anshi (1021–86)

Yuan Xiao Jie (Lanterns Festival)

The Lanterns Festival marks the first full moon of the New Year, on the fifteenth day of the first lunar month. It was promoted by Emperor Han Wudi as a day of worship. On this day, lanterns and bonfires are lit from dusk to dawn and people celebrate with dragon and lion dances, displaying beautifully handcrafted lanterns, feasting and eating *yuan xiao* (also known as *tang yuan*), a hot dessert of glutinous rice balls with sweet fillings. Often the *yuan xiao* are served in a warm soup of sweet, unfiltered rice wine called *jiu zao* or *jiu niang*. *Jiu zao* may well resemble an ancient form of basic rice wine, or might have come from the gruel left over from filtering wine. Its production method is simple, and many people today still make *jiu zao* at home with glutinous rice. Warm *jiu zao* is a hearty drink or dessert for winter and is known to be nutritious and good for circulation. A drink of warm rice wine or *jiu zao* followed by outings with lanterns, accompanied by guessing lantern riddles (riddles written on paper lanterns) is a particular highlight for this festival, and a sure way to end the night on a jolly high!

SIMPLE HOMEMADE *JIU ZAO* (酒糟) RECIPE

> 500g glutinous rice
> filtered water for soaking (as needed)
> 250g filtered water for winemaking
> fermentation inducer (酒曲; it can be found in larger Chinese supermarkets)
> red fermentation inducer ('red yeast rice' 红曲米; optional): in addition to the main inducer, a red inducer makes a red-coloured *jiu zao* that has extra health benefits and gives an auspicious red colour
>
> Equipment: large cotton muslin (or a thin white cotton T-shirt); steamer; deep casserole dish; clingfilm

1. Wash the rice thoroughly then place it in a large container. Cover with plenty of fresh filtered water and leave to soak for around 12 hours, or until the rice breaks easily when lightly crushed between the fingers.

2. After soaking, throw away the soaking water. Prepare the steamer with about 6cm of water in the lower tier. Line the upper tier of the steamer with cotton muslin and lay out the rice evenly on top. Use the cotton muslin to wrap up and cover the rice completely. Place the steamer lid on firmly to minimise steam escaping.

3. Bring the water in the lower tier of the steamer to the boil, then turn the heat down to medium for 30–45 minutes to steam the rice. While the rice is steaming, check the casserole dish is completely clean and free from any oil or grease, then put it into a hot oven to be sterilised.

4. Remove the steamed rice and transfer to the casserole dish. Let the rice cool down to about 37°C (about body temperature to the touch).

5. While the rice is cooling, crush the fermentation inducer into fine crumbs or powder. Refer to manufacturer's instruction for exact quantity to use. Dissolve the inducer in around 250g of filtered water. If using, do the same for the red inducer.

6. Once the rice has cooled to around 37°C (it must be below 40°C for the inducer to work), start to pour a little of the inducer into the rice and mix well. Slowly add all the inducer solution into the rice and keep stirring and mixing to ensure an even spread of the inducer solution in the rice. If using, add the red inducer in the same way.

7. Spread the rice evenly in the casserole dish and gently press down to flatten and smooth out the rice. Make a round hole in the centre of the rice, so you can see wine welling up in this hole as fermentation progresses.

8. Cover the dish with clingfilm and a lid. Keep it at around 30°C for around 24–36 hours (you can wrap it in an electric blanket or duvet). If the ambient temperature is lower, allow for several more days. You should be able to observe progress over the clingfilm as the round hole left in the centre of the rice will gradually fill up with wine (don't open it in order to prevent unwanted bacteria from entering).

9. Store in a sealable container and refrigerate.

The rice and wine mixture is not usually drained – the two are consumed together. Serve warm with any combinations of *yuan xiao* (glutinous rice balls), poached egg, goji berries and jujube dates (red dates). If you prefer to drain the wine from the rice, you will have a basic filtered rice wine.

The variation with 'red yeast rice' that makes a red *jiu zao* (*hong jiu zao*) is often given to post-natal women as part of a rigorous month-long confinement programme to restore health and strength.

Qing Ming (Clear Bright Festival or Ancestor Day)

This festival has its origin in ancient times, when rulers paid tribute to their ancestors in spring. Over time, this celebration has filtered into folk tradition. *Qing Ming* falls on the 15th day after the spring equinox, usually around 5 April in the Gregorian calendar. Wine is offered to the ancestral tomb as tribute, along with food, incense and provisions for the afterlife, such as paper money. Wine is also drunk by the living to soothe their heavy hearts. There is a tradition of eating only cold or raw foods for several days around the time of *Qing Ming*, although it is no longer widely practised today. Wine was an important drink during these few days of 'eating cold', as a way to warm the body and supplement nutrition. *Qing Ming* is also a time to enjoy the beauty of springtime, when 'the air is clear and the scenery is bright' and the 'mind and faculties are clear and bright' – and in keeping with these popular old sayings, the festival is known as 'Clear Bright'. It is a time to plant trees and go on excursions to see nature, along with picnic food and wine.

> *The rain of Qing Ming drizzles,*
> *On the road, the traveller's heart is heavy.*
> *Pray where is a wine tavern to be found?*
> *The cowherd boy points to the distance –*
> *The Apricot Flower Village.*
>
> 'Qing Ming' by Du Mu (803–c.852)

Duan Wu (Double Fifth or the Dragon Boat Festival)

The *Duan Wu* festival falls on 5 May of the Chinese lunar calendar. It commemorates the death of the patriotic hero and romantic poet Qu Yuan of the third century BC, in the Warring States period. Qu Yuan's poems were some of the earliest written records of Chinese drinking culture – his writing mentioned winemaking techniques, ingredients and drinking customs, such as medicinal wines with capsicum or osmanthus flowers for worship and drinking.

> *All in the world is muddied and I alone clear; everyone is drunk and I alone sober.*
>
> Qu Yuan (c.340–278 BC)

You may be familiar with dragon-boat racing, but did you know it is a tradition steeped in wine culture and commemorates a patriotic hero from over 2,000 years ago?

He would not have known, however, that his own life would be celebrated in a wine-related tradition that endures to this day. When the enemy state, Qin, was destroying his home state of Chu, Qu Yuan was heartbroken and threw himself into the river. The locals who loved him raced out in boats to rescue him, but when their search proved in vain they threw rice parcels into the river to lure away the fish from harming his body. Legend tells that an old doctor poured a barrel of realgar wine (*xiong huang jiu*) into the river, which was said to anaesthetise water creatures that might feed on Qu Yuan (realgar is a red arsenic ore mineral). Sure enough, a benumbed dragon soon emerged from the river. Thus, the traditions of eating rice parcels, called *zong zi*, racing dragon boats and pouring realgar wine as protection on the 'double fifth' day came to form the *Duan Wu* festival. Realgar, although it possesses medicinal properties, is also toxic. It is now more commonly poured on the ground, to drive away pests and 'bad spirits'. For drinking to mark *Duan Wu*, other types of herbal wines are more suitable, for example *chang pu jiu* (calamus-infused yellow wine), *wu jia jiu* (a medicinal herb in the ivy family with blue berries), *yehe huan hua jiu* (silk tree wine) and (harder to swallow for some, perhaps) *chan chu jiu* (toad wine).

Qi Xi (Lovers' Day, Young Girls' Day, Chinese 'Valentine's Day')

Qi Xi falls on the seventh day of the seventh lunar month when the stars Altair and Vega are high in the sky. It celebrates the love story of a young cowherd (Niu Lang), who fell in love with a visiting goddess, Weaver Girl (Zhi Nü). The lovers were torn apart when Weaver Girl was summoned to return to heaven. The cowherd's old buffalo happened to be the Star of Taurus incarnate and helped the cowherd to give heavenward chase to his beloved. His impertinent persistence angered the Heavenly Empress, who turned the lovers into the stars Altair and Vega, forever divided by the Milky Way. Eventually, the Heavenly Empress relented and allowed the couple to meet once a year on the seventh day of the seventh lunar month. On this day, all the magpies in the world would fly over the Milky Way, forming a bridge for Niu Lang and Zhi Nü to cross the heavenly river that is the Milky Way for their brief reunion.

During the *Qi Xi* festival, girls traditionally display their home-making skills, such as needlework. Young women make offerings of wine, tea, flowers and fruits to Zhi Nü, wishing for a good husband and a happy family life. People admire the night sky and look for the stars of the Cowherd and the Weaver Girl. It is said that if you stand beneath grape vines you will be able to hear the celestial lovers' tender words to each other.

Zhong Qiu (Mid-Autumn Festival or Moon Festival)

The Mid-Autumn Festival, first mentioned in the classical text *Rites of Zhou*, originated as a time to celebrate the harvest and give thanks to gods. The choice of the fifteenth day of the eighth lunar month coincides with the moon at its fullest – thus, Mid-Autumn is also a day to admire the moon and to contemplate the full moon's symbolism for unity among family, friends and beloved. On this day, the tale of 'Chang'er ascending to the moon', in which a superhero's wife drinks too much of an elixir of immortality – meant for two – all by herself, is commemorated. The overdose makes her lighter than air and she floats up to the moon. Instead of enjoying eternity with her husband, she has to endure immortality alone. (Although Chang'er is usually pitied for her loneliness, a variation on the story suggests that it was no bad thing, and in fact there was a hunk on the moon and a jade rabbit to keep her company.)

Traditionally, tributes of wine, flowers and fruits are made to the moon and to Chang'er. The beauty of the full moon is admired by gatherings of family and friends, with the accompaniment of mooncakes (a round, filled pastry to represent the full moon), tea, fruits, nuts and fragrant wines such as *gui hua jiu* (osmanthus wine – a plant celebrated for its fragrant autumn flowers and medicinal properties). Artists and poets would take inspiration from the moon and the effects of wine, and produce paintings and verses, usually on the theme of unity or the longing for it. Many timeless pieces of poetry dedicated to wine drinking and moon watching were composed at Mid-Autumn.

This festival, with its enthralling legend of the Moon Goddess and the universal human desire for fulfilment and unity symbolised by the full moon, is one of the most important and captivating Chinese festivals. It is also one of the most significant gift-giving seasons of the year, second only to the Chinese New Year. There are many regional customs associated with gift giving at Mid-Autumn and, in our modern times, smart marketing executives have fully commercialised this social fixture to channel consumer habits and to mould gift-giving etiquettes. The traditional art of pairing food and drink at Mid-Autumn has naturally played into the hands of mooncake, tea and wine producers. Mooncakes are available in an increasing repertoire of ingredients and flavours, offering many pairing options for different types of wine and tea.

How often does a bright moon grace the sky?
Raising my wine cup to the heavens, I asked...
We know of sorrow and joy, parting and meeting;
the moon knows shade and shine, waxing and waning.
Such is the imperfect ways of the world, and have always been so.
I only wish we may be blessed with health and longevity,
even though thousands of miles apart, we could share the beauty of the same moon.

Excerpt from 'Prelude to the Water Melody',
Su Shi (1037–1101)

WINE PAIRINGS WITH MOONCAKES

Cantonese-style mooncakes have a thin pastry skin and a rich filling such as sweet lotus paste, sweet red bean paste or dried fruits and nuts, sometimes with salted whole egg yolk (symbolic of the full moon) embedded in the fillings. Lotus paste pairs well with a delicate sweet wine with fresh

Mooncake and wine pairings are increasingly popular for the
Mid-Autumn festivities

fruits and bright citrus notes, such as a young Sauternes or Barsac. The
fruity and nutty characters of sweet red beans could be complemented by
Tokaji Aszú, Muscat or tawny port. The heavy and mixed texture of dried
fruits and nuts needs good acidity to cut through the richness. Cognac is an
'out of the box' pairing that works well for this. The opulent, dense fillings
mellow the cognac and make it feel rounder and smoother. With salted egg
yolks, off-dry Riesling, Gewürztraminer or Pedro Ximénez sherry could be
thrilling choices.

'Su' style mooncakes have layered flaky pastry with sweet or savoury
fillings that strive to be indulgent but not greasy. With savoury or meat
fillings, Burgundy Pinot Noir brings the right amount of fruitiness and
fine, delicate tannins. With sweetmeat/sweet paste/dried fruits and nuts,
Chinese ice wine or lightly sparkling rosé would add a refreshing lift to
the delicate sweetness and delectable pastry.

'Snow skin' mooncakes are sweet modern creations, often served cold or frozen. There are countless combinations of skin and fillings, such as green tea, chocolate, coffee, sesame, even ice-cream. Just pop the champagne (demi-sec) and get giddy with it!

Chong Yang (Climbing Day or Elders' Day)

The origin of this festival, an occasion for thanksgiving after harvest, can be traced back to the first millennium BC. On the ninth day of the ninth lunar month, people admire chrysanthemum blossoms and drink chrysanthemum wine (*jü hua jiu*), which is said to promote long life. Active outdoor types wear a branch of cornel flowers and go climbing to enjoy autumn scenery. Since the word for 'nine' (九 *jiu*) and the word for 'persistency' or 'longevity' (久 *jiu*) in Chinese are homophones, it is also a festival for respecting elders and remembering family ties.

Xiao Nian (Little New Year or God of the Stove Day)

The celebrations of Chinese New Year start about a week before New Year's Eve, a time known as the 'Little New Year'. The house will be thoroughly cleaned in preparation, and the kitchen becomes the main focal point, for it is of paramount importance that the kitchen god is well pampered on this occasion.

This domestic god watches over every household in some elusive corner of the kitchen, offering protection and observing good deeds and bad. Each year, he makes a journey to the heavenly realm on the Little New Year (the 23rd day of the last lunar month) and reports to the Heavenly Emperor all that he has observed. He then returns to hand out the appropriate karma to each household. 'Go up with good words, and come down to bring peace' is the common prayer to the god of the stove. In order to sweeten the mouth of this messenger god, sweets and cakes are offered to him on this day. As a more drastic measure, many households lay out a generous spread of wine in the hope of rendering him drunk and incoherent when he reports to the Heavenly Emperor.

The drinking cultures of Chinese ethnic minorities

Although the Han ethnic group accounts for over 91 per cent of the Chinese population, China boasts another 55 ethnic minority groups within its borders. The drinking cultures among these peoples are varied and colourful, but several common themes bind them all: hospitality, respect, the act of sharing, the passion for music and dance, the joy of celebration, the expression of love and the marking of important life events.

Sipping wine with long reed straws from a common pot is much more sociable!

The Zhuang ethnic group from southern China is the second largest ethnic group in China after the Han, yet accounts for only just over 1 per cent of the total population. Their culture maintains a delightful drinking tradition after a young couple's betrothal. The groom-to-be will pick an auspicious day and visit his fiancée with gifts of wine and meat. Before receiving him, the girl will visit the ancestral chamber, light candles and incense and line up several bowls of tribute wine in front of the ancestral shrine. Under one of the bowls she will place her horoscope. The groom-to-be will then be admitted to pay his respects to the ancestors and to locate his future bride's horoscope. If he picks up a bowl of wine without the horoscope he must first empty it before picking up another, and keep going until the horoscope is found. Afterwards, a great party is held at the girl's house, with wine and a feast for friends and the matchmaker. The matchmaker can never escape a heavy bombardment of toasts from all sides!

The Yi people, from south-west China, usually celebrate the New Year over three days. On the first day every household brings out wine, makes tributes to gods and ancestors and drinks over a family feast. On the second day all the men in the village gather together and 'house crawl', going from door to door with greetings of song and dance, receiving some wine in return from each house. As the day wears on the group gets smaller as the 'lightweights' gradually fall by the wayside. On the third day everyone takes some wine and goes on an outing. Whenever the group meets an acquaintance, a drink of wine is offered as the 'starting mouthful', to wish good tidings for the New Year.

The Miao of southern China have a saying: 'without wine there will be no music of Miao'. For them, singing and dancing are the necessary accompaniments to wine. Songs tend to take the form of a contest, like a drinking game, with one side posing a lyrical question and the other coming up with an impromptu song in reply. Several 'wine adjudicators' decide which side wins. The winner pours the wine and the loser drinks the forfeit. The Miaos are known, too, for their hospitality: if a household has a visitor from afar, all the neighbours come round with food and wine, and the guest must drink with them all. When a family elder passes away, the news is broken not with words, but with wine. A family member visits each relative in turn. Upon entering a house nothing is said, but the messenger first kowtows and then pours a bowl of wine. The gesture is instantly understood.

Among the Tujia ethnic group of central-southern China, when a child is born, the first guest to visit is received with great honour. The parents will offer warm sweet wine, often with a poached egg. An auspicious date is then set for a banquet to thank the visitor for their blessings. The Tujia people treat building projects as solemn occasions, creating, as they do, the 'foundation for a hundred-year legacy', and thus worth marking with wine. Before choosing the timber, the woodworkers are given rice wine. Before the tree is felled, wine is offered on site to honour the tree. When the timber is ready for the building work to commence it is wrapped in red ribbons and all the workers are thanked with three cups of wine before the timbers are carried off, accompanied by the sound of firecrackers. Once the main beams are erected, two songsters will be invited to drink wine and sing alternating verses in praise of the *feng shui* of the location.

The Korean ethnic group from north-east China celebrates elders' birthdays with a folk dance called 'the wine dance'. The performers, usually daughters, daughters-in-law and grand-daughters, dance gracefully while sporting small wine bottles on their heads. After the performance, the ladies bring down the wine and pour it for the 'longevity star'.

To propose marriage among the Ewenki of northern China, a matchmaker will represent the prospective groom and visit the girl's family. The matchmaker must present a bottle of wine to the girl's elders, and pour out the wine for them. Some detailed enquiries are made by the girl's family and, if the answers are to their satisfaction, the elders will empty their cups to indicate consent. Otherwise the wine is undrunk. During the wedding a bonfire is made, into which the new couple pour wine. All the guests drink, sing and dance by the fire late into the night.

Some traditions are more widespread and are observed across many ethnic groups, with slight variations among them for added distinctiveness. For example, 'flicking wine' is a sign of respect or a gesture for toasting: the surface of the wine is gently flicked with a finger to splash a few drops of wine in the direction of the tribute. Another common ethnic custom is to gather around a large pot of wine and share it together over conversation, singing, dancing and games. This practice is simply known as 'sipping wine'. Each person has a pipe, usually several feet long, made of bamboo or reed, which is used like a straw to sip wine from the common pot. The wine is usually a basic, unfiltered rice wine and, as the wine depletes, it becomes more viscous owing to the sediment. The pot is periodically topped up, often simply with water. The party ends when people finally realise that the wine is so diluted they are actually drinking water.

There are many more ethnic wine cultures around China, far too many to detail here. With the rise of wine tourism, which ventures from the Central Plain to far-flung corners of China, this is yet another fascinating aspect of Chinese wine culture awaiting the wanderlust of the explorer.

A VERTICAL
TASTING OF
HISTORY

Wine has evolved side by side with Chinese civilisation itself, sometimes as witness, sometimes as character in legends and stories. A great variety of wines (*jiu*), made with grains, fruits, herbs and even animal products, has existed since antiquity. Winemaking developed through trial and error down the ages, ranging from natural fermentation through the use of fermentation inducers (a mixture of cultured moulds, yeasts and grains to induce and control the fermentation process) to distillation and blending.

Throughout China's history, wine's symbolism has been even more influential than the drink itself. The most long-lived wine stories endure because of their historical context, or because they are related to the remarkable deeds of colourful figures, or because of the lessons and philosophies in life that they present down the generations. The moral of the tale always outlives the wine-drinking experience. Wine has been important in the notion of rites since ancient times: from the elixir of divine origins, fitting as a tribute to gods and ancestors, to the gesture of respect and honour paid through toasting seniors and elders. For those who left their names in the history books, wine was an important chess piece in political intrigues and power plays between banquet table and battlefield. Wine revealed the human condition, from heightened emotions and deepened human bonding to the loss of form and control, even to the downfall of kingdoms. It compelled philosophers, scholars and rulers to examine the duality of its virtues and vices. Indeed, wine culture proved to be a potent barometer of the rise and fall of political, social and economic fortunes of China. Wine-induced states of release, pleasure and freedom unleashed creativity for poets, musicians, artists and calligraphers. Wine is food, drink, medicine, tonic; wine is ritual, politics, status, philosophy; wine is poetry, art, music, calligraphy; wine is brotherly bond, political plot, family fun, society salon. Wine is part of life and soul, and of the cultural bloodline of the proud Chinese people, who call themselves the Dragon's Descendants.

The origins of *jiu*

A vessel ![glyph] containing wine ![glyph], with a topper or filter ![glyph] to make ![glyph], forms the earliest Chinese pictographic representation of 'wine'. Variations such as ![glyph], ![glyph], ![glyph] and ![glyph] eventually led to the Chinese character 酉. A stream ![glyph], flowing and splattering ![glyph] down a mountain cliff ![glyph], depicts 'water'. Variations such as ![glyph], ![glyph], ![glyph] and ![glyph] evolved to form the character 水. The 'water radical' 氵 was derived in the same way, and is often used as part of a character to suggest a semantic association with water or liquid. The modern Chinese character for wine, 酒 (*jiu*), is made up of the water radical 氵 and the archaic character for wine 酉.

As is the case with many Chinese characters, which began life as pictograms, fascinating stories arise from the etymology of these characters. Let us begin with a folktale about Du Kang the winemaker, who is widely hailed as the father of wine in China. The origin of Du Kang himself is shrouded in mystery: some say he was a prince, a god incarnate, or a court winemaker, yet others claim he was simply a conscientious ordinary winemaker. Regardless of which version is true, this folklore offers a colourful alternative interpretation of the pictographic origin of *jiu* 酒 = 氵 + 酉.

Du Kang finds out how to improve his wine

Legend has it that the tireless endeavours of Du Kang to improve his wine impressed a saint, who came to Du Kang in a dream and revealed the secret of winemaking. The saint said to him: 'Go to the village cross-road on the ninth [九 *jiu*] day of the month, at the time of *"you"* [酉, or

5–7pm; this is the same character that means 'wine' in old Chinese], take a drop of blood each from three volunteers, and add them to your wine.' Upon waking, Du Kang eagerly made preparations according to the divine instructions. On the ninth day, at the appointed time, Du Kang stood at the crossroads of the village with his wine and waited for passersby. Presently, a scholar strolled by. Du Kang greeted him and explained his purpose. The scholar returned some pleasantries, politely obliged and donated his blood. After a while, a warrior crossed his path. Again, Du Kang went up to him and explained his intentions. The warrior generously slashed his arm without hesitation to make the second donation. Now dusk was deepening, the village falling quiet and the time slot was fast approaching its end. Du Kang began to feel anxious, as he had yet to meet a third person. Just then, the village fool trotted by, carefree and happily talking nonsense to himself. Feeling more the beggar than the chooser, Du Kang approached the fool with his story. The village fool laughed in great amusement and also obliged him. In the nick of time Du Kang completed his mission, and hurried back home to make his most incredible wine yet. The result, true to the saint's word, was stunning. Du Kang, delighted, named his wine *jiu* in honour of the divine inspiration. For his great achievement in winemaking, Du Kang was promoted to saint status, and was appointed by the Heavenly Emperor as the wine saint in heaven.

According to this tale, the Chinese character for wine, *jiu* (酒), is thus made of two parts: on the left, the three drops of blood that went into the wine and which make up the water radical (氵), and, on the right, the time of day, '*you*' (酉). *Jiu* is a homophone of both the word 'nine' (九 *jiu*), to mark the date of the month in this story, and the word for 'a long time' (久 *jiu*), a nod to the virtue of patience in making and appreciating wine.

But the story does not end there. Have you spotted the three volunteers' contributions to wine? In China, it is symbolic to drink three cupfuls of wine. The first cup, we drink as the scholar does: a polite toast with pleasant words of praise, good wishes, even poetry. The second cup, we drink like the warrior: bold, spirited and candid. The third cup, alas, makes us akin to the fool: uninhibited, giddy, perhaps even nonsensical. Although some may argue, of course, that this is actually 'divine madness', the ultimate state of being induced by wine.

Wine's ancient beginnings: a tribute to gods and ancestors

China is a contender for the title of the world's earliest archaeological finding of fermented beverages. Radiocarbon dating and sediment analyses of ancient Neolithic pottery from Jiahu village, in present-day Henan province, suggest that, some 9,000 years ago, the Chinese may have produced wines from rice, honey and fruits. Researchers even conjectured that the fruits may have been native wild grapes or hawthorns, owing to the prominent presence in the pots of tartaric acid, the principal organic acid in such fruits, which were known to have grown in the area.

The earliest dedicated tools and wares for making, storing and drinking wine found in China come from Juxian, Shandong province, and date to the Neolithic Dawenkou culture that flourished in this region some 5,000–6,000 years ago. These include earthenware utensils for heating the ingredients to encourage fermentation, for filtering, straining and storage, as well as an assortment of drinking cups. We can therefore conclude that Chinese winemaking took shape no later than this period.

By the time that written records appeared, c.1500 BC, a variety of wines and winemaking techniques, along with wine's religious, political and social functions, were apparent. The use of wine in healing, ancestor worship, state ritual and upper-class indulgence during the prehistory eras of the Three Sovereigns, Five Emperors and Xia dynasty (over 5,000 years ago) has been well documented by latter-day scholars. Scripts found on animal bones from the Shang dynasty (c.1600–c.1046 BC) made references to a type of tribute wine made from millet and infused with turmeric. Fermented grains, fruit (probably including native wild grapes) and milk products were the most common ingredients in these primitive wines, and they tended to be weak, sweet and viscous. In ancient China, grain-based winemaking was more widespread and sophisticated than fruit-based winemaking, including grape wine. Despite the fact that over half of the world's grape species are found in China, they have remained largely wild. This is in contrast to China's early domestication of grain crops such as millet around the Yellow River valley, widely considered the cradle of Chinese civilisation. China's main climatic characteristics are the cold and dry north versus the warm and moist south, conducive to the agricultural output of grain and rice crops. The Middle Eastern and Mediterranean regions, however, where the climate is hot and dry, were quick to domesticate grapes.

The development of *jiu qu* (fermentation inducers), possibly around the second millennium BC, illustrates the level of sophistication in the use of grains. The application of *jiu qu* has remained the predominant way to kick-start fermentation in Chinese grain-based winemaking because it enables greater control over the fermentation process, alcoholic strength and wine style.

By the time of the Western Zhou dynasty (c. 1046–771 BC), winemaking and wine etiquette had become remarkably precise and refined, while the thriving Bronze Age culture produced vast quantities and types of exquisite wine vessels. Wine-related affairs, from every aspect of production to consumption, were supervised by state-appointed authorities and stipulated in official documents, which have provided a lasting legacy of an age of rites.

The creation of wine

There are numerous origin tales for wine, which are fascinating. Many attribute wine's beginnings to divinity: that it was a gift from heaven via the hands of demi-gods or their descendants, or that it was taught by gods through the medium of dreams or by gods visiting earth in human form. The true identities of the earliest winemakers are impossible to know, but the association made between wine and divinity is telling: like the emergence of the world and of human life, the discovery of fire and of agriculture, wine is something wondrous, mythical and miraculous. Besides regional folklore passed down through oral traditions, the texts dedicated to wine by scholars and historians through the ages are testaments to wine's importance in China's history.

It is most likely that, back in the age of hunter-gatherer communities, the natural process of fermentation of gathered ripe fruits would have produced the earliest 'wines', by virtue of the yeasts naturally found in fruits converting sugars into alcohol over time. To our early ancestors, this primitive wine would have been intriguing for its mere occurrence, as well as its effects on the body and mind. Without the benefits of scientific knowledge, it would be natural to attribute a divine origin to the serendipitous appearance and remarkable effects of wine, and, with that, to confer upon wine the highest status. Wine's importance is also indicated by its medicinal use since ancient times. The origin of medicinal wine is credited to demi-god sovereigns such as Shen Nong, the 'divine farmer', also known as Yan Di (Emperor Yan) and Huang Di (the 'Yellow Emperor').

The Chinese often refer to themselves as the 'descendants of Yan and Huang' (*Yan Huang zi sun*) to pay respect to the embodiments of the collective wisdom of ancestors: Yan Di of the Three Sovereigns and Huang Di of the Five Emperors. They are the legendary forebears of the late Neolithic and early Bronze Age Huaxia civilisation that gave life to the Han ethnicity, which makes up most of the Chinese population today.

Neolithic clay pot for warming wine. Height 19cm, diameter at mouth 8cm, diameter at widest 42cm. Currently housed in Anhui Museum

Grains were found to have a similar natural ability to ferment and produce wine, so it appears that the development of wine and agriculture were correlative and complementary. The earliest known written source to suggest that natural fermentation of grain-based wines was an accidental discovery was *Jiu Gao* (The Edict of Wine) by Jiang Tong, c.AD 300: 'Wine existed since the time of the Three Sovereigns and Five Emperors ... Leftover rice piled in the hollows of mulberry trees would ferment and produce wine, and retain its fragrance over time. It is a natural process, no particular effort is required.' Indeed, one school of anthropology and archaeology believes that the domestication of grains may have stemmed from the desire to make alcohol in a more organised way. These early beverages would have been a gruel-like beer: tasty, mood enhancing, nutritious, made hygienic by virtue of the fermentation process, and offering certain medicinal benefits. One type of rice-wine gruel, *jiu zao* (*see* page 104), is still popular in China today. Some people consider it a beverage, others a food, but all value its health-giving properties.

Over time, people gained experience, honed their knowledge and started to refine the process of winemaking. In China, grains became a dietary staple, first and foremost as food. Only if surpluses were available would it have been possible to make wine, and the existence of excess food crops indicates a community abundant in land and produce, and likely to be wealthy and orderly. As a result, wine quickly took on political and social symbolism, signifying prosperity and power. It is not hard to imagine, therefore, thanks also to its divine associations, that wine was immensely appealing and useful to early rulers in their efforts to appease the gods and show strength. In ancient societies, wine was less of a recreational beverage and more of a utilitarian product for worship and politics.

Early masters of wine

Yi Di was a legendary winemaker said to have made wine of 'five flavours' – possibly with five grains. Yi Di's identity, and even gender, is widely contested. Earliest records suggest that Yi Di was the daughter of the Emperor Shun, the last of the Five Emperors. It is believed that matriarchal societies were prevalent in China 6,000 to 9,000 years ago. The demigoddess Nüwa was said to have created humans and social structure, and tales of women creating wine from fruit and milk have also been attributed to this period. Since the first century AD, however, history books began to record Yi Di as a man, reflecting the patriarchal society that China had become. Yi Di's reputation in history has had a similarly mixed fate: on the one hand, he/she is glorified as the pioneer winemaker and, on the other, he/she is demonised and exiled by Yu the Great – Emperor Shun's chosen successor – for popularising 'the liquid that could end kingdoms'.

A popular legend recounts that after Emperor Shun passed away, Yi Di made wine to honour her father's memory. Two batches of wine were produced. She presented one cauldron to her father's tomb, and the other to her father's chosen successor, Yu the Great, as a gift. The wine was much appreciated by Yu, and for a while he indulged in its pleasurable effects. Upon sobering up one day, however, Yu exclaimed: 'Someone will lose a kingdom due to this liquid!' Instead of thanking Yi Di for the wine, Yu banished her from his kingdom and swore never to touch wine again.

Yu the Great, a semi-mythical, Herculean hero, is honoured for his legendary efforts to use dredging to control the flooding of the Yellow River, which destroyed settlements and farmlands and threatened lives. He is an embodiment of collective wisdom and courage, and he personified the unrelenting spirit of the Chinese, the triumph of human endeavour over nature. It is easy to imagine that Yu, a ruler keenly concerned with agriculture and social welfare, would have been alarmed by Yi Di's seductive wine, especially if it was extravagantly made with 'five grains'. This is the earliest story that reveals something of wine's effects on morality and social order.

The development of winemaking is also widely attributed to Du Kang, our chapter-opening protagonist. His ancestry is shrouded in myth. Some say he lived in the time of Huang Di, the first and most famous of the Five Emperors. Others say he was Prince Shao Kang, a descendent of Yu the Great. Du Kang was said to have created wine from sorghum and paid special attention to the spring water used to enhance the fragrance of wine, giving rise to the Chinese notion of a 'wine spring' (*jiu quan*) – a mythical water fount in the case of Du Kang, or more generally a superior water source that gives wine a sense of place and identity.

The wine stars

The Chinese were among the first to study celestial phenomena and produce fairly accurate records. A system called the 28 Mansions was established to categorise the stars observed in the night sky, as well as their relative positions and their influences on nature and human activities. The earliest evidence of this system dates back to the Shang dynasty (1600–1046 BC). The wine stars are a group of three stars within the Mansion of Huang Di. In the Western astrological system, they are found in the constellation of Leo.

The wine stars inspire a school of philosophy dedicated to wine-making based on the principles of yin, yang and change, which explore forces of nature that are opposite, complementary, interdependent and mutable. 'The School of Wine Stars' argues that the properties of nature – sun, moon, water, fire, wind, rain, thunder, lightning and the celestial mansions representing heaven, earth and people – are responsible for the quality of wine. The winemaking process must consider the season, date and time according to astrology and divination. The choice of place, water, grains, medicinal ingredients and barrel age also merit deliberation. These practices were said to be the guiding principles for Yi Di and Du Kang, and still influence modern Chinese winemaking. Those familiar with the concept of terroir – the notion that a place's special characteristics are imparted to its produce – would undoubtedly find resonance in these ancient Chinese philosophies.

Early wine traditions

Our ancestors developed crucial skills out of necessity, for survival. Among these, the ability to make wine was regarded as essential. Why so? Because wine not only provided sustenance that was nutritious, hygienic and healing, it was also considered sacred and a symbol of honour – a worthy offering to the gods and ancestors. To the ancient Chinese, respect for the masters of heaven and earth who determine the fate of living beings was of paramount importance. They studied astronomy, devised calendars, improved winemaking and created art, music and rituals in order to live in harmony with their world and their gods.

The ancient Chinese regarded wine first and foremost as a tribute to gods and ancestors. Within the earthly realm, wine was also used for political means, laid out for state functions, and for figureheads and dignitaries. In ancient societies, wine was valuable as a drink for grand and noble occasions. Elaborate ceremonial rituals and drinking etiquettes thus grew up around the making, presenting and serving of wines. Arts and sciences flourished alongside wine culture, most notably relating to wine vessels and ceremonial music. The contemplation of wine in moral and philosophical contexts also emerged, forming part of the system of 'rites' – a central pillar of Chinese culture. Winemaking thus developed from its serendipitous beginnings, evolved into a form of skill through observation and experimentation, and became a culture that encouraged human expression and creativity.

Ancient rites are extremely complex and elaborate, quite unfathomable to most modern observers. It will suffice here to give a taste of what was once prolific. Ceremonies with wine and food tributes were frequently performed to seek blessings, give thanks or commemorate agricultural events such as planting and harvest, military campaigns and life events such as betrothal, wedding, conception, birth, illness and death. The highest quality wine was always used as tribute and took pride of place (sometimes in the north corner of an inner ceremonial chamber), and lesser quality wines, such as unfiltered, weaker or unaged wines, were ranked and positioned in various corners and orientations of inner and outer chambers. These wines were sometimes presented ahead of the ceremonial day. On the day itself, large cauldrons and wine ware of varying sizes, containing tribute wines and foods including large sacrificial animals that would be cooked during the ceremony, were carefully arranged. Sometimes a main cauldron was placed on the north side of a ceremonial gate. Specifically composed music accompanied the ceremony, played on instruments such as bells, cymbals, drums and woodwind instruments, and the diviner or priest may have chanted, sung and danced as well as overseeing the proceedings.

Outside of sacred settings, social drinking or banqueting also required intricate etiquette. First, the host welcomed the guest at the entrance, and the guest then entered from the west side of the entrance. Host and guest bowed to each other three times, then the host, followed by the guest, bowed towards the north. Once inside, the host sat on the east or south-east side of the room, the guest faced south with their back to the north, while the attendant sat in the west and faced east. Host and guest first paid respect to each other. When wine was served, a small portion was poured on the ground as tribute, then the wine was tasted and appropriate praise and comment was made. Only after this could the wine be drunk. Three cups was the limit of civilised drinking. Note that rites varied a great deal in their details and procedures.

The obsession with orientation is still common in China, most notably in the practice of *feng shui*. Its ancient origins are closely linked to people's desire to understand macro- and microclimatic traits in the various directions and the relationship between time, space and human activities, and then assign symbolism to them, which may seem abstract to us today. In modern winemaking too, the study of microclimate and mesoclimate (site climate) are important for choosing vineyard locations and effective vineyard management. These have parallels in Chinese studies of *feng shui* (literally 'wind and water') and *feng tu* (literally 'wind and soil'), which at their heart are ancient forms of environmental study.

Myths morph into facts

Until the Five Emperors period, rulers followed a system of abdication and nomination of leadership. Yu the Great was said to be the last of such leaders. Around 2070 BC, Yu founded the first dynasty of China: Xia. He was succeeded by his son, Qi, who subsequently overthrew the republican mode of abdication and nomination in favour of the hereditary state system that was to stay in place for the next 3,900 years. Due to Yu's own mythical status and the absence of contemporary written evidence, however, the Xia dynasty's existence is still contested. What is certain is that Chinese civilisation continued its forward march during the period covered by the Xia dynasty (c.2070–c.1600 BC), which encompassed the early Bronze Age and left us a wealth of bronze wine vessels.

Wine in the Bronze Age: wine ware and wine rules

The Bronze Age marked a new phase in Chinese wine culture. Multiple ancient urban sites along the Yellow River and its tributaries have yielded vast quantities and types of bronze wine vessels, mostly from the tombs of nobles. Specialised wares for preparing, storing, presenting, serving and drinking wine

Late Shang dynasty ceremonial wine warmer and container, *jia*, with phoenix columns. Height 41cm, diameter at mouth 19.5 cm, depth 5.7cm, weight 2.86kg. Excavated in Shaanxi province, 1973. Currently housed in Shaanxi History Museum

were evident, suggesting that winemaking was taken seriously then, and was important for ceremonies and rituals.

Of particular interest is Erlitou, an early Bronze Age site discovered in Yanshi, Henan province, in the Yellow River valley. It reached prominence around 1900–1500 BC and was a major hub for bronze production, specialising in ceremonial bronze wine vessels. Chinese historians generally consider the Erlitou culture as archaeological evidence of the Xia dynasty.

Over time, wine began to depart from its sacred ceremonial role and move towards pleasure-seeking among the ruling class. After 471 years and 17 kings, the Xia lineage came to an end with Jie (*c*.1651–1600 BC), a cruel ruler, infamous for drinking and frolicking, who was overthrown. He would not be alone in history, however, in losing his realm to pleasure and wine.

The Shang dynasty (*c*.1600–*c*.1046 BC) was founded following the fall of Xia. It was a dynasty that bequeathed several landmark archaeological findings to the story of China, most notably a script ancestral to Chinese writing, and occurred at the height of the Bronze Age.

The art of bronze working flourished during Shang. Of the bronze ware unearthed from this period, almost half of the known varieties are designed for the purposes of making, preparing, storing and serving wine. They range from large ceremonial vessels for religious and ancestral worship through winemaking and processing equipment to drinking vessels that demonstrated the status of the nobles as they enjoyed their wine. The art of bronze working and wine culture appear to have progressed hand in hand, evidencing prosperity and technological advancement. Of the different kinds of wines available at the time, rice-based sweet wines and millet-based fragrant wines were especially popular.

Serving and drinking vessels, for this life and the next

Over the generations, Shang rulers became increasingly indulgent. Lavish night-long carousing gradually filtered down the social strata and pleasure-

Numerous exquisite wine vessels were excavated from the warrior queen Fu Hao's tomb in Henan province; collected by the Institute of Archaeology, Chinese Academy of Social Sciences

seeking came to the fore. Many considered wine the ultimate earthly joy, and prepared for the journey to the afterlife with suites of drinking vessels. At Yinxu, the site of an ancient Shang capital, wine vessels were frequently found in excavated tombs. The grand tomb belonging to a warrior queen, Fu Hao, was particularly noteworthy for the quantity, variety and quality of the wine ware it contained: wine vessels for daily use, occasional use and for ceremonies, inscribed with her various names prior to her marriage, as queen consort and posthumous. They revealed wine's practical and ritualistic significance throughout her life. Among 900 other Shang tombs belonging to lesser occupants, around 500 contained wine vessels large and small, mostly ceramic.

Remarkably, several tomb sites dating back 3,000 years to the Shang and early Zhou dynasties yielded tightly lidded bronze wine vessels still filled with wine. For example, at the Zhang Zi Kou tomb in Henan province more than 90 bronze vessels were unearthed, among which 52 lidded vessels were still a quarter- to half-full of liquid. This is incredible: thanks to the advanced bronze working by this time, which produced extremely well-fitted lids, and the gradual corrosion over joints and gaps that made the containers airtight, the liquids escaped the fate of evaporation. Analyses of sampled contents suggest some of the liquids are likely to be rice or millet wine (corresponding to *jiu* in written records). Additional compounds found in some samples hint at the presence of fermentation inducers and aromatic ingredients such as herbs, flowers or tree resins (which would correspond to the aromatic tribute wine, *chang*). Also of note was one particular vessel containing osmanthus, validating popular references to osmanthus wine in written records.

Oracle bones tell wine stories

Although earlier forms of basic writing, in the form of simple shapes and pictograms, were found in cave markings and on pottery, inscriptions dating back to the Shang dynasty reveal a fairly developed writing system. The so-called 'oracle bone script' has been found mostly on tortoise shells and ox bones used for divination and record-keeping, and is an important ancestral script to the Chinese writing system. Of the characters deciphered, several represent wine or ingredients, characteristics, objects or activities related to wine. There are even narratives relating to the process of winemaking, types of wine and wine's function in the performance of divination and worship, which give us a glimpse into Shang dynasty life and underlines wine's importance in rituals. The Shang rulers were extremely interested in divination, the topics of which were all-encompassing, ranging from the outcome of war through the timing of rain, the yield of a harvest, the suitability of tributes for worship, the appropriate date for con-

Shang dynasty 'oracle bone' inscriptions; collected by the Institute of Archaeology, Chinese Academy of Social Sciences

ceiving and the root cause of a toothache, to whether an old flame has married someone else. During divination, the date, place, attendees and question were inscribed onto the 'oracle' bone, which was usually the scapula of an animal, and heat was then applied to the bone to produce cracks. The cracks were then interpreted by the diviner and the verdict noted on the bone. One question was deciphered as follows: 'Would our ancestors be happy to receive wine as tributes?' The answer was interpreted as 'yes', and a large tribute of wine was subsequently made.

Fermentation inducers

Using a fermentation inducer is a long-established tradition in grain-based winemaking in China. The earliest attribution of its use appears to be in the Shang dynasty, in the Confucian classic *Shang Shu* (*Book of Records*), although the practice may have been conceived earlier. We have already discussed the use of *jiu qu*, which incorporated mould, yeast and grain, to make wine (*see* page 36), but another type of fermentation inducer, *nie*, used malted (germinated) grains to produce *li*, the beer-like beverage which was sweet in taste and rather weak. Most historical records on the subject of early fermentation inducers tend to mention *nie* and *qu* together, but some were conscientious in differentiating their properties and their end products. This suggests that *qu* and *nie* coexisted as alternative fermentation techniques. *Qu* was more versatile, however, as the mixture and proportions of the ingredients can be varied to control the degree of fermentation. *Nie*, by contrast, was a weak fermenter and would always produce a low-alcohol sweet drink. *Li* had fallen out of favour by the third century AD, as drinkers developed a taste for stronger and more complex wines, and, with it, *nie* also became a lost art. *Jiu qu* making, on the other hand, would become firmly established as a discipline in its own right, as a great deal of skill is required to prepare the various combinations and proportions of moulds, malts and yeasts. Its development greatly enhanced the technical repertoire of Chinese winemaking.

Grain over grape

As winemaking became more disciplined and integrated into agriculture during these formative eras, grain-based wine became better established than fruit-based wine. This is telling, as basic fruit wines are technically simpler to make than grain wines as fruit ferments more easily without fermentation inducers, because its high sugar content readily converts to ethanol in the presence of naturally occurring wild yeast. Before fermentation of grain starch can take place, by contrast, it first needs to be broken down into sugars by starch-digesting enzymes, which are abundant in the cultured moulds or malts that are made into *qu*. The rise of grain-based wines, most notably those made with rice and millet, points to the successful domestication of grain crops by the communities living in the early Yellow River and Yangtze River settlements. Fruit, on the other hand, was less readily available for winemaking at this time, and natural fermentation relying on wild yeast can be unpredictable, to the extent that some early Chinese literature on winemaking did not realise that natural fermentation was possible without inducers. By the time of the Shang dynasty (*c*.1600–*c*.1046 BC), three types of wine were well established: the beer-like *li* made with rice or millet and malted grains; *chang*, frequently mentioned on oracle bones, was an aromatic tribute wine used in religious rituals and divination, made with black millet and turmeric; and *jiu* was a fully fermented, filtered rice or millet wine, stronger than *li*.

Mandate of Heaven and *Admonition of Wine*

Alas, an all-consuming love affair with wine and an over-indulgent life-style were to spell the demise of the last Shang ruler, Zhou (1105–1046 BC). He ordered meat to be hung around the palace so that he could eat as and when he pleased. He filled a large pool with wine and ordered groups of men and women to chase each other in it naked. He would drink and feast in such surroundings all through the night. The still-used phrase 'wine pool and meat forest' was coined to describe such excess. In 1046 BC the Shang dynasty fell at the Battle of Muye, where the people of Shang revolted and joined the campaign of Lord Wu, the leader of an expansionary Zhou tribe (not to be confused with the name of their antagonist Shang ruler – the characters and intonations are different in Chinese). After vanquishing Shang, Lord Wu set up his capital in Hao on the western outskirts of present-day Xi'an, and established the Zhou dynasty (also known as the Western Zhou, *c*.1046–771 BC).

Zhou rulers were keen to learn from the lessons of their predecessors. They wanted to warn their heirs and subjects of the treachery of excess. Yet aspiration to fine things was not disapproved of: moderation and deliberation were the keys to striking the balance between virtue and vice. A famous bronze ritual vessel of the period – the Great Yu vessel – was inscribed with a substantial admonition that warned against a demise similar to that of the Xia and Shang rulers due to an overindulgence in wine, while also praising loyal and competent service to the state, to be rewarded with fine wine, fine clothes and other material wealth.

The Duke of Zhou, the brother of the dynastic founder, King Wu of Zhou, and regent for King Wu's 13-year-old son, was the most revered figure of the Zhou dynasty, and stands as a giant and a saint among the greats of history. He promoted the belief that the king's power to rule came from the will of the Lord on High, and the deeds and behaviour of the ruler must meet with approval from Heaven, or the privilege may be withdrawn and reassigned. Virtuous rule would therefore increase the likelihood of the ruler retaining the so-called Mandate of Heaven.

Philosophical thought began to flourish around this time, along with an emphasis on standards relating to ethics and morals. Laws and codes were established to educate at every social level. The Duke of Zhou was himself a leading philosopher and legislator, and was among the first to evaluate the pros and cons of the effects of wine. He commended the ceremonial role of wine and further refined wine etiquette and rites. The duke was keen to promote wine's noble role as an accompaniment to ceremonial occasions, as a religious and ancestral offering and as a means of paying respects to parents and elders. The indulgent and disruptive aspects of wine were discouraged.

The duke's *Jiu Gao* (*Admonition of Wine*) was the earliest written code of conduct regarding wine drinking in China. In the document, he urges all to heed the examples from the demise of Shang and other tribes whose rulers have abused the power of wine, and to adhere to wine's ceremonial role at every level of society lest the moral fibre of the nation becomes corrupt and Heaven hands out punishment. Nobles and officials should only drink at ceremonial occasions and must not get drunk. They must also educate people to save grain and propagate virtue in society. As for the ruled people, they must dedicate themselves to working the land and engaging in productive enterprises. They must also be filial children, so when returning home to pay respect to their parents, wine could be enjoyed at a family feast. Zhou laws further set out prohibitions on people congregating for non-ceremonial wine drinking, with penalties including death, in order to stamp out plotting and unrest. Through his legislation and counsel, the Duke of Zhou demonstrated a deep concern for the conflicting nature of wine and the related political, social and moral implications. His legacy affected all political thinking that followed in China.

The Rites of Zhou

Winemaking techniques advanced in leaps and bounds during the time of the Duke of Zhou, thanks to better record-keeping that instilled enquiry and precision. *Zhou Li* (*The Rites of Zhou*) is an important classical text, the authorship of which is popularly attributed to the Duke of Zhou, although its origin is shrouded in mystery and it could have been a latter-day compilation after the fifth century BC. *Zhou Li, Li Ji* (*The Book of Rites*) and *Yi Li* (*Etiquettes and Rites*) form the Three Rites of canonical Confucian classics and lie at the core of Chinese notions of civilisation and humanity. *The Book of Rites* coined a phrase that sums up the essence of Chinese wine culture: 'wine maketh propriety'.

Late Western Zhou dynasty drinking cup with two handles. Bronze, height 14.8cm, diameter at mouth 8.5cm, weight 0.89kg. Excavated in Shaanxi province, 1961. Currently housed in Shaanxi History Museum

The Rites of Zhou covered the topic of wine in a section named 'Offices of the Heavens'. It categorised 'five conditions of wine' (*wu qi*), 'three wines' (*san jiu*) of court and 'four drinks' (*si yin*). It also described the various official positions in governance, and recorded the first Chinese public servant post for wine-related affairs:

> *The wine administrator is in charge of all affairs related to wine at court ... The administrator is in charge of monitoring the viscosity and texture of the drinks in order to provide for the king's requirements for the Four Drinks, and the presentation of the Three Wines, and, similarly, the drinking requirements of the queen and princes.*

Drinking and banqueting rituals were recorded in great detail and strictly observed. Elaborate proceedings for paying respect with wine depended upon the occasion, and the rank and relationship of the hosts and guests. Rites involved specific wine ware and complementary food and music. An excerpt from *The Rites of Zhou* gives an example of the details:

> *For sacrifices and rituals, provide the Five Conditions (Wu Qi) and Three Wines (San Jiu) according to formality, which will require the filling up of eight ceremonial containers (zun). The Three Wines must be refilled three times during a large ceremony, twice during a medium ceremony and once during a small ceremony. Each refill will have their corresponding ladle count.*

Apart from ceremonies and banquets hosted by the ruler for his dukes and ministers, there were also officially organised symposiums hosted at district levels for citizens to forge bonds, dispel disputes and demonstrate respect for seniors and elders. This tradition has been revived by many subsequent governments, even to this day.

Despite the Zhou dynasty's austere insistence on ritual and ceremony, drinking games evolved from hunting competitions and archery contests accompanied by wine and feasting. The Chinese saying 'drink the toast or drink the forfeit' originated from drinking games where wine is either the prize or the punishment (or just an excuse to drink!). Zhou dynasty protocol, however, insisted that all wine-drinking activities be adjudicated by at least one toastmaster, to prevent disorderly behaviour. After all, propriety must be observed under all circumstances. At least that was the official line.

Replicating the archaic complexity of Zhou drinking etiquette as a reflection of decorum and morality would be utterly impractical today, but wine's association with civility, as a way to show honour and respect, is very much alive in Chinese culture. As we have seen, toasting with wine and making gifts of wine are still widely practised. *The Book of Rites* describes etiquettes that are observed in many parts of Asia to this day, for example the rule that before the senior person raises his cup, the junior person may not drink. If the senior grants wine to the junior, the junior may not refuse it.

Zhou dynasty rites often refer to three cups as the appropriate amount to drink, and when it comes to drinking etiquette in China, three is still the magic number. For ceremonies, worship, remembrance or gestures of respect, three cups are often dedicated to the recipient of the honour, or as tributes to heaven, earth and people. Other sayings stipulate strict protocols for the first three rounds of drinking, such as that people should drink in order of seniority. After three rounds or three cups, one can loosen up and enjoy wine freely. A similar saying states that after three cups all are equal: distinctions are no longer made between host or guest, senior or junior. *The Book of Rites* also describes a marriage ceremony rite that is still popular today: a bottle gourd, a symbol of fertility, prosperity, health and longevity, is split in half, and wine is poured into each half. The new couple would each take one half of the gourd and simultaneously drink the wine.

The Five Conditions, Three Wines and Six Essentials

The Rites of Zhou recorded *Wu Qi* (Five Conditions) that summarised the process of fermentation and corresponded to the five stages of grain-based winemaking. Some scholars also believe that they referred to five types of wine, all fairly weak and sweet in profile.

1. *Fan qi*: the start of fermentation. Alternatively, a basic, unfiltered, viscous wine.
2. *Li qi*: the activation of sugars. Alternatively, a gruel-like wine. This is the early form of a sweet, low-alcohol rice wine now known as *jiu zao* or *jiu niang* (*see* page 104).
3. *Ang qi*: the peak of fermentation, the liquid becomes cloudy. Alternatively, an opaque wine.
4. *Ti qi*: the increase in alcohol content gives a red tinge to the liquid. Alternatively, a wine with a red tinge (it is unclear how this colouring was achieved at that time).

5. *Chen qi*: the end of fermentation, the sediments fall and the liquid becomes clearer. Alternatively, a clear wine, achieved perhaps through multiple rounds of fermentation and a higher proportion of added water, or through filtering. Achieving clarity in grain-based winemaking was a technical breakthrough.

The *San Jiu* (Three Wines) are the types of wine reserved for different purposes.

1. *Shi*: wine for religious ceremonies. This is typically made for a specific occasion, without ageing.
2. *Xi*: wine for hosting esteemed guests. This is aged for several months ('made in winter, ripe in spring').
3. *Qing*: wine of the highest quality, filtered, usually royal reserve; wine that has undergone a longer ageing process ('made in winter, ripe in summer').

In the same vein, *Li Ji* (*The Book of Rites*), which covers the Zhou dynasty administration and ceremonies, delves into the topic of winemaking with the *Liu Bi* (Six Essentials). These set out quality imperatives in the wine-making process:

1. The grain must be carefully selected and prepared.
2. The fermentation inducer must be made in favourable conditions.
3. The raw material must be cleaned before soaking and boiling.
4. The spring water used in winemaking must be of good quality and taste.
5. The winemaking tools and wares must be well crafted.
6. The temperature for winemaking must be well controlled.

The Book of Rites also mentions multiple fermentation (*zhou*) as a means to create wine of a weightier and purer quality (*chun*). The word *chun* is usually associated with distillation or to describe the quality of distilled liquor. This has prompted conjecture that multiple fermentation could actually be distillation. The Chinese character for *zhou* (酎) is no longer in popular usage in China, but is still common in Japanese, where it is rendered as '*chu*'. Japanese distilled liquors are called *shochu* (their Chinese counterparts are *shao jiu* or *shao zhou*).

Wine as tonic and medicine

The ancient wisdom of Chinese medicine is steeped in wine. Wine is believed to promote circulation and mediate the pulse. Several medical texts claim that the mythological Shen Nong and Huang Di of the Three Sovereigns and Five Emperors era should be credited with the invention of wine, which they put to medicinal use. Although these claims are founded on legends, it is certain that wine has long been an intrinsic part of Chinese remedies and healthcare. Indeed, many Chinese medicines and tonics were wine. Traditionally, medicinal ingredients were either fermented to make wine or infused in a grain-based wine for a specific duration to attain the desired strength and effect. The wine wares used to make, prepare and serve medicinal wine were also carefully selected for material, shape and quality so as to enhance the health-giving ingredients. The wine would also be served at an optimal temperature depending on the weather, the ingredients and the drinker's constitution.

Gathering and studying plants was an important part of traditional Chinese medicine. Watercolour of Shen Nong, Chinese deity of medicine

The traditional Chinese character for medicine (醫) contains the wine radical (酉),

and is a composition of pictograms meaning 'wine to cure ailment'. The earliest written records describing methods of making medicinal wine date to the Zhou dynasty, but these innovations are likely to have evolved since earlier times. Known ingredients for tonic wines in use during this period include Sichuan pepper and osmanthus. These wines can still be found in China today, and continue to be revered for their health-giving properties.

Wine in the *Book of Odes*

Shi Jing, variously translated as the *Book of Odes*, *Classic of Poetry* or *Book of Songs*, is the first anthology of Chinese poetry, comprising 305 works spanning over 500 years from the early Western Zhou dynasty (1046–771 BC) to the sixth century BC. It is revered for its richness in literary style, expression and subject matter. It brings to life the people of the Zhou dynasty across all social spectra and brims with memorable verses that the Chinese still quote in everyday conversation. The works are divided into three types: the *feng* (airs of the states) are compilations of folk songs that cover 15 culturally diverse regions of China and archive the voices and lives of the common working people; the *ya* (odes of greater and minor courts) are stylised poems written mostly by nobles and sung at ceremonies and banquets to accompany feasting and wine drinking; and the *song* (hymns) are praises and prayers to gods and ancestors, often accompanying a sacrificial ritual.

Wine has been associated with the 'longevity star' since ancient times

Wine is a common subject across all categories of the *Shi Jing*, in particular in the odes of greater and minor courts. There are descriptions of the methods and processes of winemaking, including mention of the raw materials, tools, methods and seasons. Good wishes for health and longevity are expressed through the offering of wine. Sincere prayers are made with the presentation of wine. Philosophical and moral lessons are given on the virtues and ills of wine. Meticulous accounts of wine-drinking etiquette and the formalities of various types of banquets are recited. The book even contains political satires depicting the drunken and disorderly behaviour of nobles at supposedly formal occasions.

Grape makes its documented debut in the *Shi Jing*, for example in the *Odes of Bin*, which recount the customs of an agricultural area in present-day Shaanxi province. In the poem *Qi Yue* (which means seventh month but refers to September in the Gregorian calendar), grapes were eaten in the 'sixth month' (August). It seems that the grapes were eaten fresh, however, rather than used in winemaking, as the verse goes on to show:

> *In the tenth month, harvest the rice;*
> *In with the harvest, wine will be made for Spring;*
> *To wish the bushy-eyebrow longevity ...*
> *In the tenth month, sweep the stack-site;*
> *Fill to the brim paired bottles of wine,*
> *Say, Let us kill our lamb,*
> *And go forth to our lord's great hall,*
> *There raise our horn shaped wine cups,*
> *And toast to him, long life with no bound!*

This poem depicts the agricultural and social year of the peasant class, and it indicates that although grapes were harvested and eaten, a good rice harvest was the prerequisite for winemaking. Wine is also an important tribute to honour the elderly 'bushy-eyebrow' landlord. After the harvest is in and the stack-site cleaned, the landlord would host a feast for his workers. Wine is generously poured and enjoyed by all at the feast, and toasts are made to the landlord's longevity. Wine's health-giving qualities are evident in its association with longevity and its role in honouring the elder or 'longevity star'.

Wine, wisdom, wiles: age of *The Art of War*

Even the Duke of Zhou's *Admonition of Wine* (*see* page 135) could not prevent pleasure-seeking in wine to seep back in. Towards the latter part of the Western Zhou dynasty, wine was openly enjoyed by all social classes, and although its role in ceremonies and rituals was undiminished, the people performing the rites had lapsed in their fidelity. Because of this, the Mandate of Heaven – the sacred baton for rulers envisaged by Duke of Zhou – began to slip away from the Zhou rulers by the eighth century BC as regional powers broke away from central control. In the 500 years that followed, China entered a highly volatile and unsettled period in which vassal states vied for more land and power.

In 770 BC, King Ping of Zhou moved his capital eastwards to Luoyi (present-day Luoyang) in order to escape an attacking enemy force, the Quan Rong tribe. Thus began the period known as Eastern Zhou dynasty (770–256 BC). By this time, the central power of the Zhou court had become largely irrelevant as regional fiefdoms were increasingly powerful. The Spring–Autumn period (c.770–476 BC) saw hundreds of vassals whittled down to a handful. By around 475 BC the merely symbolic Zhou dynasty entered the Warring States period (c.475–221 BC), so-called for its increasingly turbulent political climate as power consolidation intensified among the few remaining hegemons. Eventually there were just seven standing, fighting to the death to be the next overlord of all China: Qi, Chu, Yan, Han, Zhao, Wei and Qin.

During this time, a mass of people fled from upheaval and sought new opportunities. Scholars, warriors and merchants alike travelled far and wide in search of the best bidder for what they had to offer, whether that was intellect, skill or merchandise. Social discourse took centre stage while power changed hands ceaselessly and, naturally, wine took on an increasingly prominent role as a social lubricant. The complex political climate produced countless tales and lessons in diplomacy, warfare, wiles and wisdom for all posterity. Wine's decorous credentials preserved modesty and disguised treachery.

As wine was increasingly drunk rather than displayed or sipped, winemakers became more experimental and innovative. New wine varieties appeared as people exchanged ideas and tastes. Grain wines enhanced with spices and herbs to add flavour dimensions and health benefits began to emerge in contemporary writing. The 'body' of a wine became a benchmark for quality. Fuller, weightier wine was considered superior, as it generally required more ingredients and expertise to make.

The sparring warlords demanded talented advisors, while political instability also brought on an age of intellectual collisions. Symposiums, at which philosophical discourse was accompanied by wine that served both as beverage and subject matter, became a social phenomenon around this time. Many fables from this period involve wine, but the emphasis is rarely on the profile of the wine but, rather, its effect on the mind and the body and its potency as a diplomatic and political tool.

Heroes arise out of troubled times, and this period produced more than its fair share of strategists, diplomats, thinkers and warriors, among them Confucius (Kong Fu Zi) and Sun Zi (Sun Tsu, author of *The Art of War*).

The power play of wine

Numerous stories from this time show wine playing a role in political and diplomatic contests, in war and truce, between the most eminent of power players. Many of them remain well-loved household tales that have been passed down through the generations. One incident praised by Confucius as a diplomatic triumph, which prevented a war between the Spring–Autumn states of Jin and Qi, came about as a test of wine etiquette.

The tale relates to the powerful state of Jin, which was harbouring plans to invade the state of Qi. Before making the decision, the Duke of Jin sent his envoy, Fan Zhao, to visit Qi and gauge the strength of the state. The Duke of Qi received Fan with a sumptuous feast at his court. Halfway through the banquet, Fan Zhao, seeing that most of the courtiers were drunk and relaxed, feigned inebriation and said to the Duke of Qi: 'Sir, please honour me with a cup of *your* wine!' The Duke of Qi started: court etiquette dictated that a duke did not share his wine cup with his subjects. Fan Zhao, however, was not his subject, but a guest of a stronger state. To oblige would be to swallow an insult from a foreign envoy. Not to oblige might offend Jin with disastrous consequences. The Duke of Qi decided to play safe, and said to his servant, 'Fill my cup and give it to our guest.' Fan Zhao emptied the cup triumphantly. Just as the servant was about to return the empty cup to his lord, the Duke of Qi's prime minister, Yan Ying, rose to scold the servant: 'Don't you know to throw it away and bring a new cup for our lord?'

After the feast, the Duke of Qi thanked Yan Ying for helping him to save face, but he was also worried: 'I know you were trying to make me look good, but maybe you should not have done so – what if we have offended them?' Yan Ying answered confidently: 'Don't you worry, my lord, Fan Zhao was not drunk – he was deliberately stepping beyond bounds to test us. He wanted to see if you have subjects who would stand up for you.'

As Yan Ying predicted, Fan Zhao returned to Jin and reported: 'Right now is not a good time to invade Qi. I tried to test the Duke of Qi's men, but Yan Ying saw through my trick. With such loyal and courageous talent around the Duke of Qi, we cannot guarantee victory.'

The following story is particularly rich in anecdotes. It also suggests that wines at the time must have been very weak indeed, even after making allowances for gross exaggeration on the protagonist's part about his capacity for drink!

A CAUTION FOR KING OF QI

King Wei of Qi (*c*.378–320 BC) was an indulgent wine lover. During his early reign, he frequently drank through the night and could not rise in the morning to attend to state affairs. One night, he summoned his close adviser, Chunyu Kun, to drink with him. After a few rounds, the king was in a teasing mood and he turned to Chunyu Kun to ask, 'So how much can you drink before you are done in?' Kun replied, 'I can drink two litres, or twenty litres.'

'How so?' The king was fascinated by this answer. 'If you are drunk after two litres, how can you drink twenty?'

Chunyu Kun replied: 'When you are graciously granting me this wine, my lord, there are your guards and attendants standing in front and behind you, lest I do something out of line. I am wary, and I drink kneeling with my body on the floor. As such I would not pass beyond two litres.

'Yet if I am serving wine to an honoured guest on my parents' behalf, I would roll up my sleeves, serve the wine with bended knees and waist, ever so courteously. I will drink now and again when the guest grants me the honour of any remaining wine. Like this, I can handle four litres.

'If old friends come to visit, and it's been a long while since we last met, we would talk eagerly about the good old times and open our hearts in each other's confidence. I would be in high spirits, and gladly put away ten to twelve litres.

'But when I drink among casual company, where men and women are mixed in friendly company, taking rounds, with board games and pot-pitching, no distinction of rank or seniority, where touching hands and openly staring are not frowned upon; and there are plenty of missing earrings, lost hairpins – I would be secretly delighted, and even sixteen litres would only make me two or three parts drunk!

'Now, if by nightfall, people begin to combine their drinks together and squeeze very closely to share the leftovers, men and women on the same mat, with their shoes all mixed up, the bowls and plates a mess, and the candles burning out – if, just then, the fair hostess bid all guests farewell, but tells me that I alone should stay, and her thin robes are loosened, exuding fragrance … now I am in heaven, and shall drink up to twenty litres!

'So you see, my lord, wine enjoyed to the extreme may lead to chaos. Chaos will bring calamity!'

The king realised that this was intended to warn him of the consequences of his excessive drinking. He admired both Chunyu Kun's reply and his good intentions, changed his uncontrolled ways and became an esteemed ruler.

Wine often played a potent role in military campaign and strategies. Before a campaign, wine was offered to gods and ancestors as prayer, and to the army to unite and ignite spirits. Upon a victorious return, wine was poured to thank the heavens and reward the heroes. And ceremonies aside, wine could do even more in the wiles of war.

KING GOUJIAN UNITES HIS ARMY WITH THE WINE OF YUE

King Goujian of Yue reigned in 496–465 BC and was famed for his sheer grit. He exploited the duality of wine to its full extent in his long and arduous campaign to defeat the state of Wu. Having at one stage been captured and enslaved by King Fuchai of Wu, he began sending his enemy lavish tributes such as gifts of fine wine, precious objects and beautiful women. Fuchai became so infatuated with one particular beauty, Xishi, that he built a large 'wine fort' at great expense in present-day Suzhou, and gathered the best winemakers to produce vast amounts of wine to satisfy his insatiable appetite for wine and beauty.

By 473 BC, Goujian was finally ready for his revenge. As his army marched towards Wu for his long-awaited campaign, the Yue people rushed out onto the streets to give their king a send-off with pots of wine they had been saving over the years, pining for the day of liberation. Goujian was deeply touched by these patriotic scenes. He dismounted and knelt before his people to receive the gifts of wine. He then encouraged everyone to pour the wine into the river, and beckoned one and all to drink from the fragrant water of Yue. This gesture of unity was a great boost to the army and civilians alike, and the soldiers marched on their way in high spirits. Yue's campaign was a resounding success and Fuchai killed himself in shame. After enduring decades of humiliation and hardship, Goujian finally ended the lineage of one of the mightiest states of his time and restored the state of Yue as a strong force to be reckoned with.

Taoism endorses wine as a source of elation from the common realm into the spiritual realm, in harmony with nature and the universe

Wine in the Hundred Schools of Thought

Among the greatest legacies of the Spring–Autumn and Warring States periods were the rich and diverse schools of philosophy and studies known as the Hundred Schools of Thought, which flourished around that time. The political requirements of the day, with vassal lords vying for talented thinkers and strategists to aid their conquests, nurtured a golden age of intellectuals and merit-based social opportunities. Scholars roamed among states to seek patronage and employment. Public debates, the compilation of books and royal audiences were the order of the day. It was common for wealthy patrons to keep talents as house guests and to host symposiums where intellectual discussions, music and poetry making, board games and martial art contests were accompanied by wine and banqueting. Taverns, teahouses and restaurants also served as hotspots for public speaking and debates. It was a period of enlightenment, and the profound influence of various schools of thought from this era – including Confucianism, Taoism and Mohism – were not only significant to their contemporaries but have also helped to landscape the social, cultural and political consciousness of China and beyond.

The various schools of thought differed or borrowed from each other in formulating their philosophies. The phrase 'the contention of the Hundred Schools' was coined for this golden period of debate and exchange of ideas, and wine was certainly a contested topic. The Mohists, followers of a school of ethics, logic and rational thought, had little interest in wine, due to their distaste for ceremonies and belief in frugality and minimalistic living, whereas the Agriculturalists emphasised land use for food as the basis for stability and growth of a nation, and made little room for wine in the days when food mountains did not exist. The Legalists took the view that laws must be clearly set out to discourage riotous behaviour that might threaten social accord, and legislated bans on public gatherings of drinkers. On the other hand, the Medics studied the functions of wine as a tonic and medicine, while the Naturalists inspired winemakers to apply the principles of yin and yang and the Five Elements to the development and balance of wine. The two most influential schools in the wine culture of China, however, were Taoism and Confucianism. Taoism speaks to the free-spirited, artistic aspects of wine, while Confucianism deals with the practicality of drinking etiquette, social symbolism, the virtue of moderation, and the need to understand and control all the aspects of wine, good and bad.

Taoists believe in freeing the mind and returning to its most natural state, which can be achieved through inebriation. The famous Taoist master Zhuang Zi was renowned for advocating wine as a way to find joy and naturalness. He believed that wine drinking should be a casual affair, without ceremony, for the real value of wine is in enabling people to loosen the bindings of social expectations and realign with their true selves. Thus, 'the purpose of drinking wine is finding joy, not finding the right cup'. In such a state of mind, one is safe from one's own conscious perception of fear and harm, and the self is in harmony with the universe.

As such, it is a protected state. The sense of unbinding from social order and expectations, the relief from physical sensations and pain, the creative energy and enlightenment attained through intoxication – these are the gifts of wine. Wine offers a way to escape the so-called 'dusty realm' of worldly concerns and reach a purer plane in harmony with the universe. According to this way of thinking, the state of inebriation is virtuous, pure, liberating and desirable. The Taoist view played particularly well to the temperaments of artists and disillusioned scholars, endorsing wine as a source of elation that delivers one from the common realm into the spiritual realm. As a Chinese saying goes, wine is the beautiful connection between heaven and earth.

Confucianism, on the other hand, promoted the notion of 'wine virtue': wine is precious, as its production competes with food and labour resources. Therefore, wine drinking must not be wasteful. It follows that wine should be used as a means to contemplate and express virtuous deeds, such as honouring gods, ancestors, guests and elders. A virtuous person will drink with moderation and will not overindulge or 'lose form'. Confucius himself would not touch wine or meat directly bought from the market, as they were not initially offered to gods or ancestors as part of a ritual. In daily life, wine should be used as tonic for the elders and medicine for the sick. While Confucianism warned against neglected governance as a result of excess of wine, it did not view banning wine as an effective means of enforcing social stability, but recommended that laws should be clearly defined to regulate drinking habits. We can clearly detect echoes of the Duke of Zhou's teachings in Confucian philosophies on wine.

The Confucian–Taoist reality/spirituality and rational/romantic dualities both contradict and complement each other. Beyond wine culture, they have become a philosophy of life and part of the social consciousness of the Chinese. By and large, Confucianism provides guidance for living in terms of self-improvement and worldly aspirations, while Taoism offers opportunities for spiritual withdrawal and refuge at times of disillusionment and danger.

The far-reaching relevance of the Hundred Schools is alive and well today, and the philosophies can have a practical application within contemporary wine trade strategies.

Wine trade strategies inspired by the schools of Chinese philosophy

While visiting a wine fair in China, I had illuminating conversations with several merchants about business strategies based on the Hundred Schools of Thought. The topic we discussed was that, as the Chinese wine market tends to show weak sales during the months of June, July and August, what sort of strategies could a wine merchant adopt during these months?

According to the Taoist school of thought, it is natural to have business cycles with strong and weak months in sales. Around the Chinese New Year and Mid-Autumn Festival, sales will be naturally higher than in the summer months. A business should engage in activities that are natural to the business cycle and that will yield results in the most efficient way. It is ineffectual to invest extra effort and resources to boost sales when demand is weak. Instead, during these periods the business should focus on other essential activities, such as human resource management and training, improving the distribution network, meeting key suppliers and customers, and securing and renegotiating contracts. Executing these tasks well during the low season will enhance the smooth sales operations of the peak season. Identifying the most natural actions and non-actions suited to the season is the key to effectiveness.

The Legalists would argue that human behaviour can be guided by rules and incentives. During the months of weak demand the merchant could adopt more aggressive sales campaigns to entice consumers and boost demand through special offers, promotions, advertising and collaborations with stores and restaurants. Furthermore, the business should understand the fundamental reasons that led to the weak demand and address them. For example, if the weather is too hot for certain types of wine, such as a tannic red wine, to be desirable, then the wine merchant should target air-conditioned hotels and restaurants where the environment would make the wine more approachable or promote an alternative wine, such as an ice wine or sparkling wine, more suited to hot weather.

The Confucian approach would say that success is not just reflected in sales, but is also about relationships, goodwill and brand value. During periods of weak sales, the supplier should work towards increasing the total brand value by inspiring consumers to feel good and do good.

This could be achieved by setting aside budgets for wine education such as tasting events or food-and-wine matching competitions. The merchant should promote positivity about wine by spreading wine knowledge, showing how to practise responsible drinking in moderation with food, and use wine to bring the family closer as filial gifts to parents and in-laws.

A lesser known school of thought that has found relevance once more in our information age is the School of Small Talk, which advocates that successful businesses should recognise the importance of keeping abreast (or even better, ahead) of market trends. Gathering intelligence at the grassroots level to gauge consumer behaviour and sentiment is the most effective method to read market trends and future directions. In our connected digital age of social media, the School of Small Talk sounds remarkably modern and pertinent. For the wine trade, market research and analysis are important year round, but more time could be dedicated to this during the low-sales season.

As these varied business strategies show, the application and relevance of the Hundred Schools transcend time and space.

The relaxing of wine etiquette

As we have seen, during the Spring–Autumn and Warring State periods wine drinking became a less rigid affair, compared to the earlier Western Zhou period. The social aspect of wine came to the fore, while the strict formality of rites loosened. Now, a ruler might forego formalities to endear himself to his ministers and people, men and women were allowed to sit together for a casual drink and flirt, and drinking games flourished. Wine as pleasure seeped through society. To sterner moralists, this was like opening up Pandora's box. Confucius lamented that he wished to return to the Duke of Zhou's utopian epoch, and labelled his own time

Warring States period wine pot with bird-shaped lid. Bronze, height 32.6cm, diameter at mouth 6cm, weight 1.81kg. Found in Shaanxi province, 1967. Currently housed in Shaanxi History Museum

as the age of 'broken rites and wrecked music'. Among many wise sayings from Confucius, this one is atypical: 'This *gu* does not look like a *gu*. Is it a *gu*? Is it a *gu*?' Confucius was aghast at the sight of a ceremonial wine cup, known as a *gu*, that deviated from classical designs – it looked far too modern for his sensibilities.

Wine and patriotic metaphors

Early western Zhou ritual wine vessel, *gu*. Bronze, height 25.2cm, diameter at mouth 3.3cm. Excavated in Shaanxi province, 1976. Currently housed in Shaanxi Zhouyuan Museum

The loosening of decorum caused great anxiety for another hero of the era, Qu Yuan (*c.*340–278 BC), who lived in the latter part of the Warring States period. Qu Yuan was a native of Chu, a powerful and vast state that at one time was a likely contender to unify all of China. Qu Yuan served as state minister under two kings, but his talent and position attracted jealousy and slander and he was exiled twice. Qu Yuan was also one of China's most celebrated poets. His *Chu Ci* (*Songs of Chu*) and the aforementioned *Shi Jing* (*Book of Odes*) became the greatest legacies of ancient Chinese poetry. Qu Yuan's poems give us rare insights into the wine culture of his time and place, mixed with patriotic emotions of pride and pathos. He wrote about pressing wine, then filtering it to bring out the purest part of the wine. This would serve well as a metaphor for the kings who banished him, as the Chu court became increasingly muddied by self-serving officials appealing to the king's whims and clouding his judgement. Another verse describes a sweet wine from the state of Wu made with a white inducer which, when mixed with the wine of Chu and filtered, becomes special and clear. Cloudy sweet wine such as the Wu wine was considered inferior to the clear wine of Chu, due to the latter's extra filtering process. Qu Yuan hinted at Chu people's conscientiousness and connoisseurship, and perhaps also the desire to incorporate other realms into the fold of Chu to create an aspirational synthesis. His poems also mention fermentation repeated up to three or four times in order to produce higher quality wine with a mature and smoother mouthfeel, an allegorical endorsement for diligence and industry. Qu Yuan described the Chu people serving certain wines chilled in order to enhance their character, again indicating the Chu people's sophisticated taste. He recorded various types of wines for the first time, as well as their uses, for example mead and herbal wines with capsicum flowers and sweet osmanthus, which were used as tributes.

Unfortunately, his patriotic words could not turn around Chu's decline. From his helpless position of exile, he despaired at the complacency of the king and the court: 'All in the world is muddied and I alone clear; everyone is drunk and I alone sober,' he lamented. In 278 BC, seeing that the state of Qin was annihilating his beloved country, he jumped into the Miluo River and ended his life. To commemorate his death, the Double Fifth Festival, when people race dragon boats in search of him, is still widely practised today.

The Silk Road and the growth of commerce

As we will see below, the state of Qin brought the Warring States period to a close in 221 BC. This is an epic story of victory against all odds, but in our story of wine, the beginning of empire-building meant sacrifices that affected winemaking. The outlook for wine did not improve much for a century, until the emergence of the 'Silk Road', one of the world's oldest and most important trade routes. As a result, wine's star finally rose again, this time with an exotic grape flavour from the West. As wine became part of the social discourse, economy, technology and culture, its fortunes became forever linked with those of China itself.

Wine for 'All under Heaven'

The legalist politician Shang Yang (390–338 BC) irrevocably changed the fate of Qin, formerly a small and remote vassal state of Zhou. He pushed through stern reforms to increase productivity, strengthen military might, enforce social order, centralise power and promote merit-based social ranking until, by the time of the ambitious King Ying Zheng (259–210 BC), Qin was ready to eradicate the remaining warring states one by one: in 230 BC, Qin began a decade-long process of vanquishing the houses of Han, Zhao, Wei, Chu, Yan and Qi, thus ending the long and chaotic Warring States period and unifying China.

King Ying Zheng proclaimed his dynasty the First Empire of 'All under Heaven', and himself the First Emperor, Shi Huang Di, with his capital at Xian Yang, Shaanxi province. He enacted laws to consolidate power over his vast dominion, standardising currencies, measurements and written scripts to promote effective governance and commerce. To ensure a tight grip on power, Qin laws, based on the School of Legalism, were particularly harsh. Winemaking during this period was restricted. While the elite class continued to have access to wine, the peasant class were prohibited from making their own wine in order to conserve food crops. The Hundred Schools of Thought that had flourished during the Warring States period also met an abrupt end when free speech was curbed.

Shi Huang Di set in motion the building of the Great Wall of China, inspired by the defensive walls that had sporadically been built by various vassal states during the warring days. He is also famous for the Terracotta Army he had prepared to protect himself in the afterlife. Both projects are astounding additions to world heritage, but were achieved at great expense and the suffering of his people. His dream of a glorious and perpetual lineage was to end shortly after his own untimely death, with his ill-fated successors cut down amid power struggles and rebellion.

Eventually, peasant revolts and rebel factions gave way to two remaining contenders for the Mandate of Heaven: Liu Bang and Xiang Yu. Their epic struggles, known to posterity as the battles of Chu-Han, left us many enthralling tales.

One such story, the Banquet of Hongmen, has become a popular idiom in Chinese to mean hidden (often malicious) intentions disguised by friendly pretexts. It demonstrates the use of wine, usually a symbol of camaraderie and hospitality, for evil intent. It also illustrates a common 'weapon' used by the Chinese in hostile or uncertain social contexts: that of feigning drunkenness to lower the enemy's guard, to excuse an action or to protect oneself. The narrative still plays out metaphorically on the battlefield of business, especially when trust is lacking between parties. On the one hand, wining and dining is an effective means to deepen understanding, but on the other, it can serve up intrigues and conspiracies.

THE BANQUET OF HONGMEN

In 206 BC, after defeating the Qin forces, Xiang Yu stationed his 400,000-strong army at Hongmen, on the outskirts of the capital Xian Yang, which had recently been conquered by Liu Bang. Upon hearing that Liu Bang wanted to proclaim himself emperor, Xiang Yu was furious and wanted to attack. Liu Bang, though he held the gate of the heartland, had an army of only 100,000 men. Xiang Yu's uncle, Xiang Bo, was a friend of Liu Bang's chief minister, Zhang Liang, and was anxious to pacify the two sides.

Heeding Xiang Bo's advice, Xiang Yu gave a banquet at Hongmen in order for Liu Bang to explain himself. According to traditional banquet etiquette, the highest-ranking person is seated facing east, the second-ranked facing south and the lower-ranked facing north, while attendants are placed facing west. The arrogant Xiang Yu placed himself prominently facing east, while Liu Bang was given the third-ranking seat. Observing this arrangement, Liu Bang made an apologetic toast to Xiang Yu: 'General, you and myself had both the same aim of defeating Qin. You fought north of the river, while I took the south. By chance I was

A 'sword dance' under the influence of alcohol is sure to unnerve
any banquet guests

the first to enter the capital. Today the two of us meet at last. Please do
not listen to rumours and misunderstand my intentions.' Xiang Yu, upon
hearing this, sheepishly replied, 'Well, if it wasn't for your own people
spreading the rumours, I would have disregarded them. Why would I be
angry otherwise?'

The men sat down and toasted each other with more wine. Xiang
Yu's army chief, Fan Zeng, was aghast that Xiang Yu seemed to be sat-
isfied with a mere ego massage. Alarmed that the wily Liu Bang was
able to diffuse the tension so quickly, Fan Zeng decided that Liu Bang
must be eliminated now to avoid future uncertainties. He tried to sig-
nal to Xiang Yu numerous times but was ignored. Undeterred, Fan Zeng
then went to his subordinate, General Xiang Zhuang, and instructed:
'Go forth to offer a performance of sword dance and kill Liu Bang in an
accidental drunken manoeuvre.' Since we have all had much to drink,
we could make an excuse of it. We must get rid of him here and now, or
we will all be his prisoners one day.' Xiang Zhuang obeyed and proposed
to showcase his sword skills for entertainment. Xiang Bo saw through
his tricks, however, and stood up to join him, saying: 'What is one for

swordplay! Let me pair with you.' The two men began their 'play', one for the kill and the other to defend. Zhang Liang, seeing this, was petrified for Liu Bang's life and went outside to call for back-up. He told Liu Bang's general Fan Kuai what was going on. Fan Kuai wasted no time and marched into the banquet holding sword and shield. Xiang Yu was startled, and asked who this man was. Zhang Liang replied, 'He is one of our men.' Hearing this, Xiang Yu yelled: 'Hero, would you dare drink wine with us?' Fan Kuai shouted back: 'I fear not even death, what of a bowl of wine!'

Later, Liu Bang excused himself from the banquet and called Fan Kuai out with him. He wanted to leave but was afraid to appear discourteous for not bidding farewell. Fan Kuai remarked, 'They are the butcher's knife and chopping board, we are the fish and the meat. Under such circumstances, what courtesy is to be paid!' Liu Bang asked Zhang Liang to wait until after he had left and pay respects on his behalf with gifts of jade, and slipped away through a side road back to his camp.

Upon learning, eventually, of Liu Bang's departure, Xiang Yu casually tossed away his gift of jade. Fan Zeng, out of frustration, hacked his gift of jade with his sword, and sighed, 'He slipped away! Liu Bang will seize our lord's claim! We are all doomed!' His words would prove prophetic.

In 202 BC, after a series of tactical manoeuvres, Liu Bang's army surrounded Xiang Yu at Gai Xia, trapping him with few provisions and men. Seeing that all was lost, Xiang Yu bade farewell to his beloved in a tear-jerking story rendered as 'farewell my concubine' which became immortalised in popular culture, and ended his own life by the Wujiang River.

Liu Bang founded the Han dynasty, known in history as Western Han, in 202 BC. The new dynasty faced forbidding challenges of power consolidation and a country traumatised by years of war. During periods of socioeconomic uncertainty, wine was once more prohibited in order to conserve crops and prevent social unrest, and the prohibition of 'drinking gatherings' was introduced again during the early part of the Han dynasty. A gathering of three or more people drinking together attracted a penalty of four *liang* (64g) of gold.

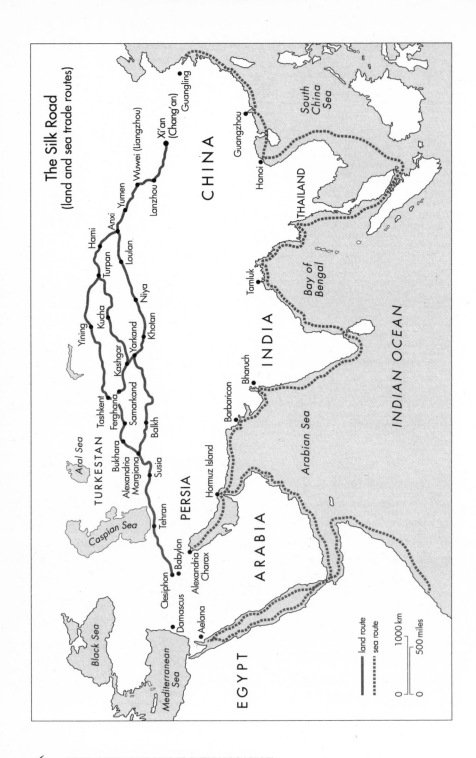

The Silk Road
(land and sea trade routes)

Grape vines on the Silk Road

By the time Emperor Han Wudi came to the throne in 141 BC, social and economic conditions in the country had markedly improved. Wudi's distinguished reign propelled China into a golden age of prosperity in which wine culture was able to flourish once more. In 139 BC, Wudi sent a military officer and diplomat named Zhang Qian (164–114 BC) with a delegation of over a hundred people on a mission to the areas west of China's borders to seek allies against the Xiongnu forces (nomadic peoples of the Eurasian Steppe, sometimes referred to as the Huns). Eventually, after much struggle, Zhang Qian reached the Central Asian plain, visiting Dayuan (Ferghana, Uzbekistan), Kangju (Syr Darya, Kazakhstan), Daxia (Bactria, Afghanistan) and Yuandu (the Indian subcontinent), among other places. From then on, the Han court had frequent contact with the Western Regions.

Zhang Qian brought back valuable accounts of the outside world to a largely introspective China and opened China up to the world, making cultural and commercial exchanges possible. He also introduced foreign technologies and products to China, among them grape vines, grape wine and winemaking techniques. Along the route that Zhang Qian had discovered trade relations began to flourish, creating what we now know as the Silk Road. The Silk Road, at its peak, stretched approximately 7,000km from Chang'an (present-day Xi'an) westwards to the eastern shores of the Mediterranean and the Roman Empire (*see* the map of the Silk Road opposite). A seaborne Silk Route also developed: a passage from the coast of Canton (Guangdong) in southern China to India and Thailand, which required a sea journey of ten months. The Han court also established a maritime relationship with the Roman Empire and managed to reach the eastern shore of Africa.

Although wild native grape varieties may have been used to make wine in Chinese antiquity, grape wines were rare, often the preserve of royalty. It is generally believed that Western grape varieties, along with Western winemaking techniques and even winemakers, were formally introduced to China as a result of Zhang Qian's westward journeys during the Western Han dynasty. One of the most authoritative Chinese histories, *Shi Ji* (*Records of the Grand Historian*), which was completed by Sima Qian in the first century BC and covered 3,000 years of history, noted how 'the Han envoy took samples, and so the Emperor planted ... grapes'. Emperor Wudi showed a keen interest in vine cultivation and tended vines within his palace grounds. The *Records of the Gand Historian* also mention grape wine:

> *Around the dominion of Dayuan [Ferghana, eastern Uzbekistan], grapes are used to make wine. The wealthy would store in excess of 10,000 dan [1 dan was around 20 litres during the Han dynasty]; some could last over ten years without deterioration.*

Wine commerce comes of age

The wine trade matured considerably during the Han dynasty. Wine houses served food that complemented their wine, and large restaurants began to emerge. As a result, taste profiles for wine became more complex: in addition to the mostly sweet and mild wines recorded since Zhou times, new wine styles took on more prominent acidity and spicy characteristics, opening them up to wider possibilities for food and wine combinations. Alcohol levels, however, remained fairly subdued. The so-called 'strong' wine at this time was no more than 10 per cent alcohol by volume.

Although wine houses and merchants had existed since at least the Zhou dynasty, the first named Chinese wine merchants to make an appearance in historical records are found in a love story from the Han dynasty.

SIMA XIANGRU AND ZHUO WENJUN

Sima Xiangru was a talented man: prolific in music and prose and an excellent swordsman. His early career at court was unsuccessful, however, and he returned home impoverished. One day he went to a banquet hosted by a wealthy local man, Zhuo Wangsun, who had a beautiful and clever daughter named Zhuo Wenjun. She was 17 years of age but recently widowed. After a few cups of wine, a guest approached Xiangru and said: 'I hear you are a man of music, pray perform a song for us.' Xiangru obliged, and composed a song called 'Phoenix Love', with lyrics of courtship intended for Wenjun. The girl heard the exquisite music and peered from behind a screen to see who was performing. She was immediately taken by the handsome Sima Xiangru and his brilliance. After the banquet, Xiangru bribed Wenjun's maid to deliver a love note reiterating his admiration. Wenjun was smitten and eloped in the night with Xiangru.

When Zhuo Wangsun learned of his daughter's elopement he was outraged with shame. He disapproved of Sima Xiangru's poverty and the disgraceful behaviour of his daughter, and disinherited her immediately. The lovers, however, were unrepentant. Wenjun sold off all her personal belongings and opened a wine house to make a living. The elopement became hot gossip for miles and business proved swift for the young couple. Zhuo Wangsun felt even more embarrassed, knowing his precious daughter was now wearing coarse clothes and serving customers. Eventually, he accepted the match and reinstated his daughter and son-in-law, and the couple were able to enjoy a wealthy lifestyle again.

After some time, Sima Xiangru's skills were recognised in court and he obtained titles and positions worthy of his talents. With his rise in position came the temptations of other beautiful women, and he began to contemplate taking a concubine. Wenjun was heartbroken and decided to leave her husband. She wrote a heart-wrenching poem titled 'Song of White Heads' to Sima Xiangru, which included the line 'I wish for one-hearted love, white heads that never part'. Sima Xiangru read the poem, and was so moved by her love, grace and accomplishment that he dismissed the thought of another woman and renewed his undying vow to Wenjun.

Wenjun is much admired in popular culture for her boldness of spirit, her passion in love, her willingness to endure hardship and her good eye in choosing a husband. (At a time when Chinese men often took as many concubines as they could afford, Wenjun's uncompromising stance and her triumph over her husband's resolve were truly commendable!)

State controls on the wine trade

As trade flourished along the Silk Road, many foreign traders came to the capital Chang'an to set up wine shops and seek their fortunes. Often their shopfronts were run by women, whose exotic looks and intoxicating wines caused quite a stir in the capital. Willing customers flocked to them and business thrived, creating a vibrant scene in the metropolis. Wine commerce was incredibly profitable for the traders. A large-scale wine merchant could earn a thousand times the annual income of an official. From Emperor Wudi's time onwards, the ruling class was increasingly aware of wine commerce as a source of lucrative treasury income. In 98 BC Wudi decreed that all wine sales would be taken under state control through official channels. This provided an important source of income to fund expensive border defence programmes. Only the sales channel, not the stages of production, was monopolised, as Wudi recognised that this was where most value was added. To put it into perspective, the sales of iron and salt were also monopolised in a similar way, as they were considered essential and valuable commodities, which underlines the significance of wine trade at the time. The monopolisation of the most profitable part of the chain, however, had adverse effects on producers, who could no longer benefit from the large mark-up at the point of retail. To realign incentives for all parties along the chain, Wudi's son, Emperor Han Zhaodi (94–74 BC) abolished state-controlled wine sales in 81 BC in favour of a wine tax. Subsequent rulers experimented with various models of monopoly and taxation to extract income from wine while maintaining the health of the industry, with varying degrees of success.

After the reign of Wudi, the Han dynasty experienced a series of political crises. In just 93 years, from 87 BC to 5 AD, the dynasty was to see seven emperors – several young, who died without heirs, and several weak, who were incapable of ruling. The empire was opened up to power struggles, usurpers, border unrest and uprisings. The prohibition of wine, which formed a barometer of social health, was again in place, but although it was frequently decreed, it was poorly implemented. Certain regions even banned wine for marriage ceremonies, which was met with fierce resistance.

In 25 AD, after years of turmoil and civil wars, a victor named Liu Xiu (6 BC–57 AD) emerged and re-established the Han dynasty, known as the Eastern Han (25–220 AD). The dynasty enjoyed a period of relative stability, but was to face a similar fate to that of the Western Han. It went through eleven young and short-lived emperors between AD 88 and 220, during which time various power groups – dowager empresses, imperial guardians and court eunuchs – grew stronger and systemically more corrupt. Wine, too, played its part in scandal. We can gauge the value of grape wine during this time from the 'Biography of Zhang Rang', part of the historical record *Hou Han Shu* (*Book of Later Han*): Zhang Rang was a powerful and corrupt eunuch of the late Eastern Han who commanded the appointment and dismissal of officials. It was said that he accepted a gift of around 20 litres of grape wine from a rich merchant called Meng Tuo. In return, Zhang awarded Meng Tuo the ministerial post of Liang-zhou (parts of present-day Gansu, Ningxia and Inner Mongolia).

Technical progress and changing tastes in wine

The near-contemporary chronicle *Han Shu* (*Book of Han*) described wine as 'heaven's bounty', a term that has been in popular usage ever since. This is an apt description, since the varieties of wine available at the time fully utilised nature's bounty: in addition to grape wine, others were made with jujube dates, cypress leaves, osmanthus flowers, chrysanthemums and 'hundred powdered flowers', which, as the name suggests, contained the ground powder of a hundred types of flower.

Technical advancement in fermentation inducers (*jiu qu*) allowed for more styles and increased alcohol strength as winemakers became more adept at using inducers to control the degrees of fermentation. Inducer making became highly specialised, and it was common for some winemakers to purchase inducers from specialist *jiu qu* producers. As a result, inducers compressed into balls or bricks for ease of handling began to appear. As inducers became more effective, the weak, thin and one-dimensionally sweet styles gradually went out of fashion, including *li*. Weightier wines with a more rounded mouthfeel associated with higher alcohol levels were favoured. Balanced characteristics were deemed to be good qualities in a wine, while prominent sour or bitter notes were signs of a poorly made wine.

The Han dynasty saw some significant contributions towards Chinese medicine and an increased repertoire of wine-based remedies. Several famous doctors and medical books came from this period. For example, Sima Qian's *Shi Ji* (*Records of the Grand Historian*) detailed medical cases of the famous Western Han physician Chun Yuyi, which included wine-based treatments for chest complaints and even difficulties during childbirth. Another celebrated physician, Zhang Zhongjing of the Eastern Han, recorded his remedial wines and techniques involving wine to enhance the efficacy of medicinal ingredients. The legendary doctor Hua Tuo, of the late Eastern Han, was famous for his wine-based general anaesthetics called *ma fei san*, one of the earliest forms of general anaesthetic in the world.

Drunkenness becomes an art: artistes and *garagistes*

Chinese civilisation had arrived at a golden age during the Han dynasty, and wine became associated with learning and sophistication. An era of connoisseurship and artisan '*garagistes*' (small-scale home winemakers) beckoned.

The Han dynasty was to meet a similar end to that of the great Zhou dynasty before it: regional powerhouses rose and consolidated power, rendering the central government redundant. The Three Kingdoms period that ensued is particularly memorable for its abundance of captivating stories and colourful characters, much like the Spring–Autumn and Warring States periods that followed the Zhou dynasty.

Wine, again, strengthened the hand of power brokers. The roles wine played were multifaceted: gestures of loyalty and camaraderie were expressed through wine; across-table political wrangling still required the courtesy of wine; bluffing and counter-bluffing in military espionage often deployed the feigning of intoxication, with wine as the essential prop; while the start of a military campaign and victory in battle were marked by offerings of wine to heaven, earth and the warriors.

Grape wine continued to be relished by the elite. Cao Pi (187–226), the self-proclaimed Emperor of Wei, was among the most articulate in his enthusiasm for it. In his *Edict to All Medics*, a proclamation to his court officials, he remarked that China is bountiful in fine fruits, yet the grape is particularly commendable: 'sweet but not sugary, acidic but not sharp, cooling but not cold, long in taste and abundant in juice, eliminates anxiety and relieves thirst'. Grape wine allows one to 'inebriate well yet sober up easily'.

As winemaking techniques improved, age-worthiness in wine became better understood and a desirable quality. Medicinal wines and seasonal wines catered for well-being, while the poetic wine names, such as the 'Thousand-day Inebriator', 'Beauty Preserver' and 'White Fall Spring Wake', reflected the sentiments of the age. China remained tumultuous for a large part of the first millennium AD. Over time, wine also became an essential means by which political outcasts and nonconformists sought self-preservation and the abandonment of reality. The state of drunkenness became desirable, fashionable, even noble.

Political turmoil and the Three Kingdoms

As the Han emperor's power hollowed, three overlords established strongholds during a period commonly known as the Three Kingdoms. Cao Cao (155–220), a mighty warlord and politician, established the House of Wei. Liu Bei (161–223) founded the House of Shu. Sun Quan (182–252) headed the House of Wu.

In 280 China was reunited under the precarious Jin dynasty, yet ceaseless warfare and political struggles continued, states appeared and were swallowed up. Between 420 and 589, China entered a period known as the Southern and Northern dynasties, which saw the rise and demise of several short-lived regimes: Liu Song, Qi, Liang and Chen in the south; and the Northern Wei, Eastern Wei, Western Wei, Northern Qi and Northern Zhou in the north.

This tempestuous period is one of the most notorious eras in Chinese history, largely thanks to the famous historical novel *San Guo Yan Yi* (*The Three Kingdoms*), written by Luo Guanzhong in the fourteenth century. It opens with the oft-quoted line: 'The Empire, long divided, must unite; long united, must divide.' This novel has had a major influence on the culture and politics of China, from the phrases and references it has lent to the Chinese language to the case studies in human conditions and war tactics that still influence the Chinese psyche today. The tumultuous historical backdrop yielded colourful characters and stories: heroes and beauties, villains and traitors, sages and warriors, triumphs and pathos. An epic novel of 120 chapters, it contains over 300 references to wine. As ever, wine is used to forge alliances, strengthen friendships, inspire loyalty, establish relationships, honour guests, reward success, convey sympathy and raise military morale, and was a prop in military tactics to influence and persuade, to provoke opponents, to beguile foes, to bluff spies and to poison enemies.

A brotherhood sealed by wine

The first chapter of *The Three Kingdoms* tells the story of a historical union of brotherhood. It narrates Liu Bei's chance meeting with his future left- and right-arm warrior brothers – Guan Yu and Zhang Fei. Over a conversation with the two strangers, Liu Bei speaks of his visions so touchingly that the three decide to become sworn brothers under the blossoms of a peach garden, pledging life-long loyalty to the common cause of restoring the royal house of Han. They offer sacrifices and provide a feast of wine and food for 300 young recruits who have joined their campaign. This fated meeting books their places in history forever.

In China, the concept of sworn brotherhood is well embedded in culture and drenched in wine. It is the bond between people who share

An illustration of 'in peach garden three brothers unite' from
The Three Kingdoms story

the same visions and principles, who swear absolute and life-long loyalty to each other, and this story of Liu Bei, Guan Yu and Zhang Fei is the most loved. To this day, temples are found thick with incense dedicated to their worship, unaffected by the passage of time. Traditionally, the rituals of sworn brotherhood would involve the brothers swearing an oath, kowtow-ing (*kou tou*) to heaven, to earth and to each other, as well as toasting one another, emptying three bowls of wine (in some cases containing drops of each other's blood to symbolise a blood bond) to pay respects to heaven, earth and one another. In modern China, the act of toasting and emptying cups of wine to represent friendship, good wishes, loyalty and trust still carries echoes of the kinship demonstrated by these beloved heroes.

One of the epic battles of *The Three Kingdoms* is the Battle of *Chibi* (Red Cliff) in 208, fought between the northern force of Cao Cao and the southern alliance of Liu Bei and Sun Quan. The Yangtze River was the dividing line that Cao Cao had to cross.

CAO CAO OFFERS WINE TO THE RIVER

The scene was set for the greatest showdown between the North and South. On the night of 10 December 208, Cao Cao rode to the river bank, boarded one of his large warships and surveyed his navy. He cast his eyes afar to take in the beauty of the southern landscape: wherever he looked, the view stretched to infinity. Filled with confidence and eagerness, he felt on the verge of grasping his lifetime's ambition. He ordered wine to be sent round to his troops and hosted a great feast by the river. He offered wine to the river, then drank three full goblets himself and remarked to his men: 'I rode the length and breadth of All under Heaven. I have not forsaken my ambition to be a giant of a man. Now the scene before us fills my heart with passion. I shall perform an ode, and you must all join me!'

> *I sing before the wine, how many chances does one have in a lifetime?*
> *Like the dew of daybreak, a man's days are swiftly gone …*
> *What could relieve us of sorrows? Only the creation of Du Kang [wine].*

These words were to immortalise Cao Cao's ambitions, and rank among the most recited lines in Chinese poetry.

Unfortunately for Cao Cao, however, his defeat was determined before the battle had even begun: the Sun–Liu alliance had already trapped him in an intricate web of premeditated tactical manoeuvres, full of deception and counter-intelligence played out between toasts of wine and make-believe intoxication. Here it will suffice to borrow a line from *The Three Kingdoms*: If you want to know what happened, read on.

The rulers and the ruled: double standards in wine

Many of the heroes of the Three Kingdoms period were ardent wine lovers, with the wily Cao Cao, handsome Zhou Yu and formidable Zhang Fei among the most colourful drinkers. During this time of turmoil, however, wine was a precious commodity. While the armies enjoyed their share of 'morale wine' and the nobles enjoyed it as a privilege, the rulers were wary of wine consumption among the common people, regarding it as wasteful of resources. Cao Cao wrote poetry in praise of wine but attempted to enforce prohibition, which was met with fierce opposition by some of his ministers, most notably the famous scholar and Confucius's twentieth-generation descendent, Kong Rong (153–208). Liu Bei also imposed a brief ban on winemaking, including a ban on the private possession of winemaking tools. On one occasion, Liu Bei's minister Jian

Zhuge Liang, the '*garagiste*'

Yong found an opportunity to demonstrate the absurdity of the law by requesting Liu Bei to arrest a man walking down the street with a woman, declaring: 'The man possesses the tool for rape, so please arrest him – just like the man you arrested for having the tools for making wine.' Hearing this, Liu Bei laughed and scrapped the prohibition law.

Over time, the ruling class came to realise that prohibition was rarely enforceable or effective. On the contrary, the opposition aroused by such restrictions could undermine the regime. Furthermore, the prohibition of wine directly translated into the loss of significant tax income. Subsequent dynasties were more cautious about imposing prohibition laws. Bans tended to be occasional, regional, short-lived and imposed only as a drastic measure when agricultural, economic and political conditions were hazardous.

As state interference softened, private winemaking gradually blossomed in all areas of society. Cao Cao and Zhuge Liang, Liu Bei's chief strategist, were both accomplished winemakers, and said to have produced high-quality grain-based wines. Unsurprisingly, their winemaking activities were geared towards their political aims: Cao Cao made wine to pay artificial piety to the Han emperor, while Zhuge Liang's wines were used in war rituals and as tribute and reward.

Wine escapism in troubled times

During the turbulent period of the two Jin and the Southern and Northern dynasties, warfare was rife, politics were treacherous and life was hard. People longed for spiritual escapism. Religion, literature, arts and wine culture took on newfound prominence. Numerous history books and genealogies appeared, innovative poetry, calligraphy and songs flourished, and drunkenness became fashionable as symbolic of disgruntled scholars. The 'Seven Sages of the Bamboo Grove' were among the most renowned of these: the men were said to enjoy unconstrained drinking and merrymaking among bamboo groves, out of which were composed stunning poetry, essays and songs rich in metaphors and satire critiquing the contemporary regime. Ruan Ji, one of these 'seven sages', inflicted 60 days of drunken unconsciousness upon himself in order to avoid a powerful and corrupt suitor to his beautiful daughter.

After thousands of autumns and tenfold as many years,
who would care for your glory and shame?
I only regret this life is too brief,
to drink wine to my heart's content.

Tao Yuanming (c.352–427, one of the 'Seven
Sages of the Bamboo Grove')

During these periods, many learned men felt threatened by the perilous political climate and opted for obscure lives in secluded locations. Their unused talents and unfulfilled ambitions, however, caused them immense frustration. Many turned to wine to while away the time, to escape their heavy hearts and to express their feelings freely under the pretext of inebriation. Wine drinking represented a desirable state of freedom, release, creativity and elated spirituality. Household winemaking for private consumption became a widespread phenomenon among working people and the scholar class. Homemade wines often contained seasonal flowers

Seven disillusioned men who while away their time drinking heavily – quite acceptable if you are called the 'Seven Sages of the Bamboo Grove' and come up with writings for posterity

or produce, such as rice wines steamed or steeped with peach flowers, plum juice, pear flowers, pomegranate flowers or jaggery (cane sugar). Wine drinking was often accompanied by song, dance and poetry-making, affiliating wine with discernment, accomplishment and style.

In 353, 42 members of the literati gathered on the occasion of the Shang Si festival (the third day of the third lunar month) at a place called Lanting (Orchid Pavilion) near Shaoxing, Zhejiang province. This ancient festival was celebrated with outings by the water to enjoy picnics, wine and orchids. On this occasion, the learned gentlemen played a popular drinking game: they floated a wine cup down a small creek and, whenever the cup stopped, the man closest to the cup would drink the wine and compose a poem. Thirty-seven poems were composed that day, for which the famous calligrapher Wang Xizhi wrote the 'Preface to the Orchid Pavilion Poems'. Wang Xizhi is one of the most celebrated calligraphy masters in history and is honoured as the 'calligraphy saint'. The 'Preface to the Orchid Pavilion Poems', written in the semi-cursive style, is his most venerated work. It was copied incessantly by subsequent admirers – emperors and scholars alike. It was thanks to a drinking game that this extraordinary work came into being.

The 'Preface to the Orchid Pavilion Poems' has attained unassailable cult status among Chinese calligraphy works. The original is lost but it has been fervently imitated by many later masters of calligraphy

An encyclopaedia for winemakers

Qi Min Yao Shu (*Essential Techniques for the Peasantry*) is the most comprehensive Chinese agricultural text still extant. It was written by Jia Sixie around 533–44, during the Southern and Northern dynasties. From its first publication, *Qi Min Yao Shu* was highly esteemed. It may have even influenced people further afield: when Charles Darwin, the pioneering nineteenth-century British naturalist, mentioned an ancient Chinese encyclopaedia as a source of inspiration he was probably referring to *Qi Min Yao Shu*.

The book provides a wealth of insights into the history of wine-making in China. It informs us that, traditionally, the most productive wine regions were in the northern plains of China. Fermentation induction is treated as a subject in its own right, separate from the techniques of making wine. Ten types of inducer are recorded, along with their ingredients, production methods, potency and required dosages. For example, the most potent inducer needs to be only one-thirtieth of the total ingredients used in wine production. A lesser one, in contrast, might account for around 15 per cent. The high-potency inducers recorded in *Qi Min Yao Shu* are remarkable even by modern-day standards: inducers typically make up 10 per cent of grain wine ingredients nowadays.

The book indicated that compacted inducers are by and large more effective than their loose counterparts. Since the time of the Han dynasty, inducer-makers had realised the advantages of manually compressing it into bricks or balls, and the book lists hand-kneading and foot-stamping among ways of manual compaction, and also recorded the invention of moulds for more efficient and uniformly compacted inducers. The addition of medicinal ingredients such as mulberry leaves, Chinese mugwort and cornel flowers to the inducer is given thorough treatment, while the suitability and cleanliness of the environment for inducer making is also emphasised. A total of 43 types of inducer, mostly for grain-based wine and wine infused with medicinal materials, are listed. The book also gives detailed coverage of the choice of inducer, the proportions of ingredients, the importance of seasonality, the timing of every step of the winemaking process, and the quality and temperature of the water used – all factors that determined the type and quality of the resulting wine.

On the subject of seasonality, *Qi Min Yao Shu* states: 'Wines made in spring or autumn, are greater than that made in summer. Yet the wines made after the fall of mulberry leaves, are greater than that of spring.' Chinese classic literature often makes references to 'spring wine', 'autumn wine', 'winter wine' and even 'mulberry fall wine'. Not only do these terms mark the seasonal characteristics of the wines, they are also often loaded with sentimental feelings about the seasons. On the subject of spring wine, *Qi Min Yao Shu* notes that 'south of the river the terrain is warm ... make [spring wine] in the second [lunar] month. North of the river the terrain is cold ... make in the third month'.

For good-quality water, an important factor in winemaking, *Qi Min Yao Shu* recommends that 'when freezing just arrives, nearing year end, the pulse of the water becomes still; take the water and it is good to use'. The 'pulse' of the water refers to all the substances that may be found floating in the water, including microbial organisms and impurities. Furthermore, the water should be boiled for sterilisation, but cooled before the inducers can be added so as not to kill the active microbiota in the inducers.

The book also covers the 'official methods' of winemaking: the procedures recommended to make wine of a certain standard. Some winemakers preferred to adhere to these methods in order to procure the exact amount of ingredients required and produce wine of a predictable nature and quality.

Nine-stage spring wine

Qi Min Yao Shu records a tribute wine made by Cao Cao for the Han emperor, Xiandi in AD 196. The wine was named *jiu yun chun jiu* ('nine-stage spring wine') and was based on traditional techniques known in Cao Cao's hometown of Bozhou in Anhui province. He had started making the wine in early spring, on the second day of the twelfth lunar month. Nine rounds of quality rice were added during the fermentation period, and each addition was made three days apart. The book comments that adding more inducer would make the wine drier (more bitter), while adding more rice would make the wine sweeter.

The emphasis on nine rounds of fermentation was not only to create a good wine worthy as an imperial tribute, but also to play on the symbolisms of the number nine. The words for 'nine' (九 *jiu*), 'wine' (酒 *jiu*) and 'long-lasting' (久 *jiu*) are homophones in Chinese. Chinese emperors revered the number nine as an auspicious sign for their long reign and the persistence of their lineage. Indeed, nine is the supreme number in Chinese culture, the largest single digit, which represents the dragon and hence the emperor. Its pre-eminence can be seen in the nine-by-nine golden door nails on the gates of the Forbidden Palace, the Nine Dragon Screen in Imperial Beihai Park, and the multiples of nine stone plates that form the concentric nine-by-nine Circular Mound Altar at the Temple of Heaven, to name just a few imperial ciphers.

The golden age of empire and wine culture

Sui dynasty glazed porcelain wine jug from the famous Shouzhou kiln. Currently housed in Anhui Museum

During the Sui and Tang dynasties in the sixth to ninth centuries, wine culture mingled with high fashion, poetry and art. Grape wine, in particular, reached its apogee as the Tang dynasty's influence and borders pushed further westwards, and interactions with the Western Regions flourished. Vines were cultivated in the northwest and even the Central Plain of China.

The Sui and Tang dynasties

After four centuries of trials and tribulations, in 581 Yang Jian, the powerful minister of Northern Zhou, forced his child-emperor nephew to abdicate and established a new dynasty, Sui. Like the Qin dynasty of the third century BC, the Sui dynasty (581–618) achieved the great feat of unifying a chaotic, divided China. And, similarly, Sui was to end with the second generation. From 611 onwards, peasant revolts erupted across the country and in 618 the Sui emperor and his heir were killed. The dynasty fell, but left far-reaching legacies that echoed those of the Qin dynasty before it. Qin had realised the concept of unification – not just of territories, but of language, writing, measurements, currencies and defensive walls that became the Great Wall. The Sui dynasty established China's internal waterways, now known as the Grand Canal, which transformed China's transportation and trade capabilities. It also championed ambitious policy reforms, most notably the meritocratic Imperial Examination System, which would be further strengthened during the Tang dynasty (618–907).

The Tang dynasty was founded by an aristocrat-turned-rebel-leader, Li Yuan, aided by his second son, Li Shiming, who later became the celebrated Emperor Taizong, hailed by many to be the most exemplary of emperors. At the peak of the Tang dynasty, China was one of the greatest empires the world had ever seen.

Wine culture during the Tang dynasty flourished alongside economic vitality. From nobles to scholars, artisans to commoners, wine was

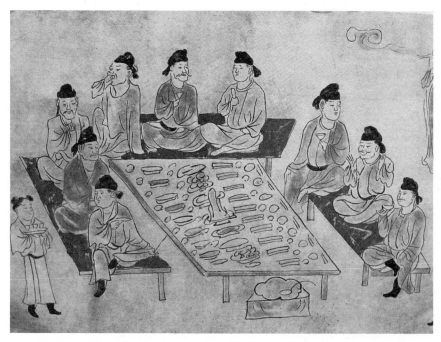

Wall mural of a banquet scene from the Tang dynasty. Height 180cm, width 235cm. Currently housed in Shaanxi History Museum

enjoyed by all levels of society. The ruling class saw the thriving wine industry as a sign of social strength and was benevolent towards its prosperity. Poems of the time remarked that people in every corner of the capital, Chang'an, were making wine and finding pleasure in wine, while, away from the headiness of the capital, wine houses could be found in the remotest of places. There were also vignettes about grape wine being part of a girl's dowry, or people carrying wine flasks on their belts when they were out and about, lest they were caught unprepared when a scenic spot or a fated encounter called for a tipple.

The health-giving properties of wine were particularly important to Tang drinkers, and herbal ingredients were used more widely. Chrysanthemum, lotus, cinnamon and wormwood (comparable to an early version of absinthe) were among the favourites. A type of pine wine was also fashionable, made with the resin, foliage and nuts of the pine tree, and possibly comparable with retsina, a resinated wine popular in Greece. The pine tree's evergreen quality was immensely appealing as a symbol of steadiness and longevity for the health conscious as well as the poetically inclined.

Grain-based winemaking, too, continued to develop and evolve. Innovation in more potent fermentation inducers upped the achievable alcohol levels. According to contemporary writings, grain wines at the time tended to display tinges of green, while some had yellow or red hues. These colours were due to the types of inducer being used.

Higher quality wines tended to have a longer production and ageing period, which indicates better control of the fermentation process. They were mostly clarified, using pressing or filtering methods. Although sweet and off-dry (subtly sweet) profiles were widely considered desirable in a wine, overtly sweet wines were by now considered average or even inferior, as the Tang poet Bai Juyi eloquently puts it: 'the grand household snorts at syrupy wine; the exalted scholar laughs at petty poetry'.

Wine drinking was an important social skill. Intoxication accompanied by song and poetry was the order of the day, and the movers and shakers of society frequented wine houses almost daily for business and pleasure. Wine houses were places to see and be seen in. As a result of this demand, wine houses were valuable real estate and popular business investments among the rich. The savvy money brokers accepted various forms of payments at their establishments: cash, barter, pawning or a credit account, effectively offering financial services around the lucrative commodity that was wine. Wine houses and shops were sophisticated in marketing and operations too: 'wine flags' and banners developed into an art form in their own right, sometimes accompanied by rhyming couplets from eminent patron poets (such as 'with today's wine let today be fuddled, with tomorrow's woe let tomorrow be troubled'). Food that complemented wine or was prepared using wine propelled Chinese culinary culture to new heights. 'Taste before you buy' was often an enticing clincher in a competitive market. Special attention was paid to the décor and ambiance of venues. A final trump card was the presence of pretty young girls skilled in singing and dancing, deployed to 'persuade wine' on their already-willing customers.

Various ways to tax the wine industry had been experimented with down the ages, but tax evasion was a perennial problem faced by every government: not even capital punishment could deter die-hard dodgers. Wang Zhongshu, an eminent contemporary scholar, recorded that countless people every year were put to death for evading wine tax, and that often one offender would implicate many others along the chain. In 846, a tax was established on inducers with the following logic: since the fermentation inducer was a key component to winemaking, the state would take over all production and sales of inducers. Wine sales, on the other hand, were not state controlled at the time, but were subject to sales tax. By recording the purchases of inducers, wine production volume could be inferred, and so the government could deduce whether the tax paid by the wine producers was proportionate to the amount of inducers purchased through the official channels. This legislation was one of the more effective among various combinations of state monopoly and taxation laws. Of course, it was not entirely fool-proof: soon enough the state was clamping down on the illegal activities of inducer-making and smuggling. Tang dynasty winemakers would perhaps laugh nervously at the joke about tax and death being the only certainties in life.

Over-indulgence in wine nourished creativity. Wine-induced impromptu performances of music, lyrics, poetry, painting and calligraphy proliferated. In particular, Tang poetry is considered one of the greatest legacies of the dynasty, and many distinguished poets of the time were fervent wine lovers. Poems were often set to music and were popularised by wine-house girls. A story recounts how three eminent poets gathered incognito in a wine house and wagered that whoever among them could have the most poems set to music by the singing girls that evening would be declared the superior poet.

Around 50,000 Tang poems survive to this day. Unsurprisingly, numerous took inspiration from the singing girls of the wine houses and the exotic foreign tavern ladies. Popular romantic references to blossoms, spring time, willows, the moon and so on in Chinese literature may well be the result of wine-infused fantasies. These colourful snippets of poetry bring back a bygone era of drinking.

> *Exotic girl with complexion of a flower; she runs the wine shop with a smile like the spring breeze.*
>
> *I have been to them all – the flowers are falling; where next on my outing? Gladly with a smile, I enter the wine house of the exotic beauty.*

Li Bai (701–62)

Many poets found inspiration in the company of beautiful and accomplished girls in wine houses

The immortal saint of poetry and wine: Li Bai

Li Bai, cherished as the poetry and wine saint by contemporaries and posterity alike, ranks among the most well-known and influential names in Chinese history. Tang poetry is one of the most revered literary forms in China, in large part thanks to Li Bai's elegant, romantic and innovative contributions. His love for wine is as legendary as his flair for poetry. 'In pours wine, out pours poetry' was his work ethic, which served well in obtaining him a drink wherever he went, and he certainly lived up to this reputation. Emperor Xuanzong (685–762) was an ardent admirer of his talent and intended to give him a prominent role in court. Alas, Li Bai was notorious for his 'haughty bones' – an attitude of disregard in the face of authority – which became more outrageous after a few drinks. A contemporary luminary, Du Fu, described Li Bai refusing to embark upon the royal barge at the emperor's

'In pours wine, out pours poetry': the wine saint Li Bai

summons and proclaiming himself the god of wine (god status is a reserve for the emperor – what a thing to say in the presence of the son
of Heaven!). Wine was his lifeline, but also his downfall. History has
looked kindly upon him, putting his unfulfilled political dream down
to an artistic temperament, a quality usually more admired than ridi-
culed. Legend has it that Li Bai died while chasing after a bright full
moon's reflection in the river in a state of drunken jollity.

> Drinking Alone by Moonlight (Opus 1)
> *Among the flowers a pot of wine;*
> *I drink alone with no companion.*
> *Raising my cup, I invite the bright moon to join me;*
> *She brings along my shadow, and makes us a party of three.*
> *Alas, the Moon does not care to drink;*
> *And my shadow tags along but vacantly.*
> *Yet for now they make good friends;*
> *Let us find cheer while spring time is still here.*
> *I sang, the moon swayed with me;*
> *I danced, my shadow tumbled along with me.*
> *While we are conscious, we find joy together;*
> *After we are drunk, we go our separate ways.*
> *O an eternal bond free from mortal bindings,*
> *To meet such a companion,*
> *I would journey through the River of the Sky.*

Du Fu (712–70), another celebrated and prolific Tang dynasty poet,
toasted eight of his eminent contemporaries in a light-hearted yet vivid
poem. (In order of appearance in the poem, the 'eight immortals of wine'
are: He Zhizhang, a famous scholar, poet and bureaucrat; Li Jin, the fief
duke of Ruyang; Li Shizhi, great-grandson of Emperor Taizong and prime
minister to Emperor Xuanzong; Cui Zongzhi, a noble and high-ranking
official; Su Jin, a poet and scholar; Li Bai, the most famous Tang dynasty
poet; Zhang Xu, a celebrated calligrapher famous for his cursive style;
Jiao Sui, known for his love for drink and outrageous speech.)

The Eight Immortals of Wine
Zhizhang rides on his horse as if rocking on a boat,
his vision flowers,
should he fall into a well, he would sleep soundly at the bottom.
Duke Ruyang drinks three jugfuls before facing the emperor,
en-route a winemaker's cart causes profuse salivation.
Alas, why not grant him the fiefdom of the Wine Spring.
Our Prime Minister spends tens of thousands for daily pleasures,
he drinks like a whale and sucks up the rivers of a hundred mountains.
Keep the wine close and politics distant, he's giving other talents a chance.
Zongzhi is a handsome youth,
he raises the cup to face the heavens with a haughty gaze.
What a striking stature, the silhouette of jade tree bracing wind.
Su Jin has long been fasting before the Buddha's portrait,
yet even he, is not immune to inebriated truancy.
Li Bai inputs a jug and outpours a hundred poems.
He is likely to be found drowsing in a tavern in Chang'an city.
The emperor summons him to board the royal barge, yet he refused,
your humble servant, he proclaimed, is the god of wine.
Zhang Xu drinks three cups and becomes the cursive legend.
Off goes his hat and out with exposed head, no matter the presence of princes.
His swerving brush descends on paper like clouds and smoke.
Jiao Sui after five jugs finds his true spirit.
His bold speeches and zealous opinion
send shockwaves to four corners of any banquet table.

Drunken dressage

In the heyday of the Tang dynasty, even dressage horses were called upon to celebrate with wine. Emperor Xuanzong loved rare-breed war horses and in the early part of his reign, spectacular dressage

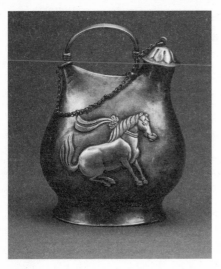

Wine pot with motif of dancing horse with a wine cup in its mouth, gilt silver, Tang dynasty. Height 14.8cm, diameter at mouth 2.3cm, weight 0.549kg. Excavated in Shaanxi province, 1970. Currently housed in Shaanxi History Museum

performances were put on for his birthdays. Handsome young trainers conducted the horses to dance to music. The most famous dance, set to the 'Tending Cup Song', was a marvellous choreographed banquet finale in which the horses picked up cups brimming with wine with their mouths and knelt to toast before the emperor. The horses then tossed back the wine in one gulp and fell to the ground in simulated drunken glee. Xuanzong's prime minister, Zhang Yue, captured the scene and the playful horses with these words: *'More the wondrous, the banquet ends with song for the wine cup; bowed heads and lowered tails, drunk like mud.'*

Lady Yang and the decline of Tang

Yang Yuhuan (719–56), popularly known as Yang Gui Fei, the Noble Consort, was one of the most celebrated Chinese beauties. She was beloved imperial consort of Emperor Xuanzong, who bestowed her with 'the passion for three thousand upon one': the reference to the numerous concubines kept within the emperor's harem only served to emphasise that Lady Yang was unrivalled in her beauty and the emperor's favour.

Wine was one of Lady Yang's indulgences. Her flushed complexion after drinking was said to be remarkably alluring, and Xuanzong affectionately compared her intoxicated red face and dishevelled make-up to a 'sleepy begonia flower'. This gave rise to a fashion phenomenon that is evident from Tang dynasty paintings of court ladies – so desirable was the 'intoxication look' that it was widely simulated by ladies with

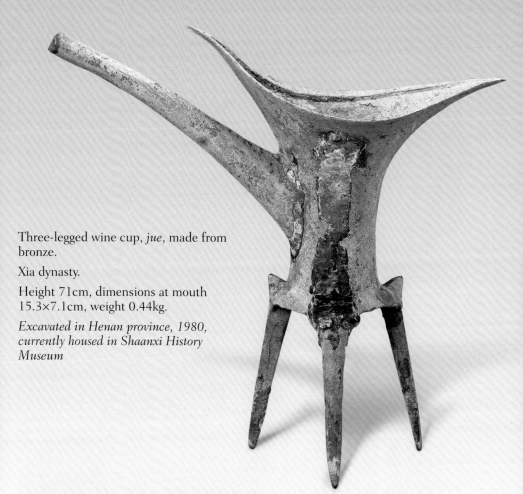

Three-legged wine cup, *jue*, made from bronze.

Xia dynasty.

Height 71cm, dimensions at mouth 15.3×7.1cm, weight 0.44kg.

Excavated in Henan province, 1980, currently housed in Shaanxi History Museum

Ritual wine vessel, *zun*, with *taotie* (a mythical beast) motif, made from bronze.

Shang dynasty.

Height 47cm, mouth diameter 39.3cm.

Excavated in Anhui province, 1957, currently housed in Anhui Museum

Ritual wine container with lid and top handle, *you*, used to hold a specific type of fragrant tribute wine, *Chang*, made with black millet and turmeric; made from bronze.

Western Zhou dynasty.

Height 36.4cm, dimensions at mouth 14.8×11.6cm, depth 19.6cm, weight 6.5kg.

Excavated in Shaanxi province, 1966, currently housed in Shaanxi History Museum

Bull-shaped wine container, *zun*, made from bronze.

Mid-Western Zhou dynasty.

Height 24cm, length 38cm, depth 10.7cm, weight 6.75kg.

Excavated in Shaanxi province, 1976, currently housed in Shaanxi History Museum

Ritual wine container, *yi*, made from bronze.
Mid-Western Zhou dynasty.
Height 38.4cm, dimensions at mouth 20×17cm, depth 16.4cm, weight 12.78kg.
Excavated in Shaanxi province, 1963, currently housed in Shaanxi History Museum

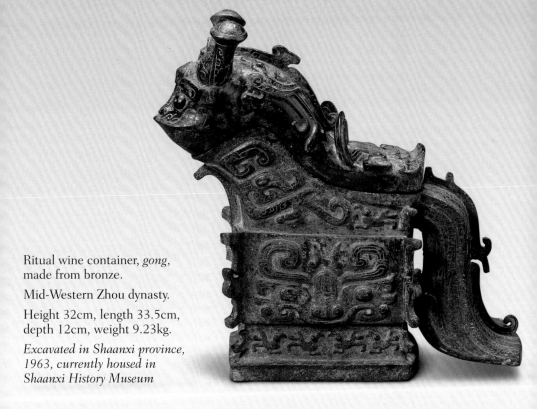

Ritual wine container, *gong*, made from bronze.

Mid-Western Zhou dynasty.

Height 32cm, length 33.5cm, depth 12cm, weight 9.23kg.

Excavated in Shaanxi province, 1963, currently housed in Shaanxi History Museum

Drinking pot, *hu*, made from bronze.
Mid-Western Zhou dynasty.
Height 17.2cm, mouth diameter 16.6cm,
depth 10cm, weight 2.66kg.
*Excavated in Shaanxi province, 1975, currently
housed in Shaanxi History Museum*

Wine pot for blending wine, *he*, with dragon handle, made from bronze.
Eastern Zhou dynasty (Spring–Autumn period).
Height 17cm, mouth diameter 14.4cm.
Excavated in Anhui province, 1978, currently housed in Anhui Museum

Set of wine cups with 'gentleman offers wine' inscriptions, made from lacquered wood.

Western Han dynasty.

Height 10.7cm, dimensions at mouth 18.5×15.7cm.

Excavated in Hunan province, 1973, currently housed in Hunan Museum

Wine pot with Buddhist motifs, made from green glaze porcelain.

Southern dynasty.

Height 22.5cm, mouth diameter 11cm, diameter at widest 21.8cm.

Excavated in Anhui province, 1982, currently housed in Anhui Museum

Persian wine goblet imported via the Silk Road, made from gilt bronze.

5th century AD.

Height 10.3cm, mouth diameter 9.2cm.

Excavated in Shanxi province, 1970, currently housed in Datong Museum

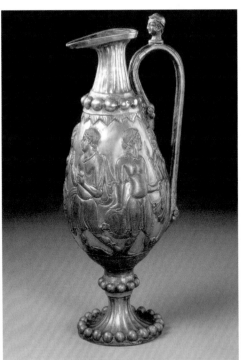

Wine pitcher with foreign figures, made from gilt silver.

5–6th century AD.

Height 37.5cm, diameter at widest 12.8cm.

Excavated in Ningxia province, 1983, currently housed in the Guyuan Museum of Ningxia

Persian wine pitcher, made from silver.

No later than 8th century AD.

Height 28cm, diameter at widest 15.6cm.

Excavated in Inner Mongolia, 1975, currently housed in Aohan Qi Museum, Inner Mongolia

Dragon head rhyton, made from three-colour glaze ceramic.

Tang dynasty.

Height 8cm, width 5.5–7cm.

Excavated in Shaanxi province, 1982, currently housed in Shaanxi History Museum

Horned beast rhyton with gold cap, made from agate.

Tang dynasty.

Height 6.5cm, length 15.6cm, mouth diameter 5.6cm.

Excavated in Shaanxi province, 1970, currently housed in Shaanxi History Museum

Wine cup with flower and bird motifs, made from gilt silver.

Tang dynasty.

Height 6.1cm, mouth diameter 7.6cm, weight 0.95kg.

Excavated in Shaanxi province, 1982, currently housed in Shaanxi History Museum

Wine pot with flower motifs, made from gold.

Tang dynasty.

Height 21.3cm, mouth diameter 6.6cm, base diameter 6.6cm.

Excavated in Shaanxi province, 1969, currently housed in Xianyang Museum

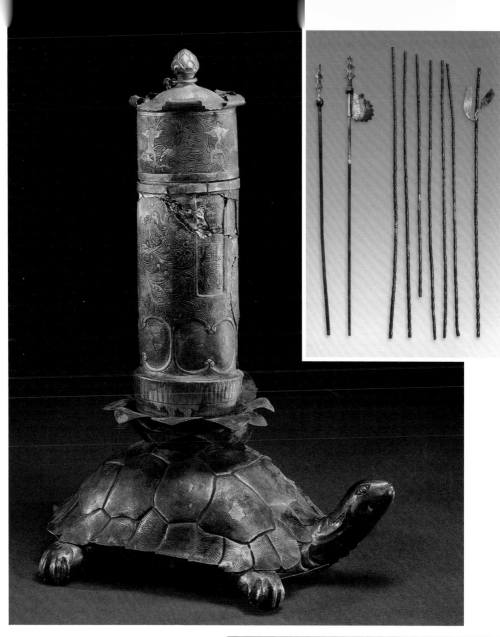

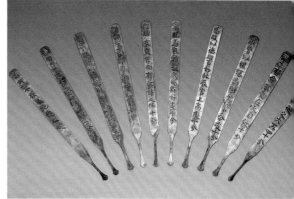

Drinking game set, made from gilt silver. The candle-shaped tube on the tortoise base contains game rules, forfeits and tokens (*right and inset above*). Game rules are based on the Confucian Analects.

Tang dynasty.

Height 34.2cm, body length of tortoise 20.4cm.

Excavated in Jiangsu province, 1982, currently housed in Zhenjiang Museum

Wine cup with base, made from polished natural shells.

These cups may have been used in drinking games as their sizes and shapes are variable and thus amusing for drinking a forfeit. They are frequently mentioned in literature but are rare finds in archaeology.

Northern Song dynasty.

Height 10cm, length 17.5cm, width 11cm.

Excavated in Shaanxi province, 2006, currently housed in Shaanxi History Museum

Wine cup with hornless dragon motif, made from silver.

Song dynasty.

Height 6.9cm, mouth diameter 8.6cm, base diameter 4cm, weight 0.117kg.

Excavated in Sichuan province, 1996, currently housed in Pengzhou City Museum

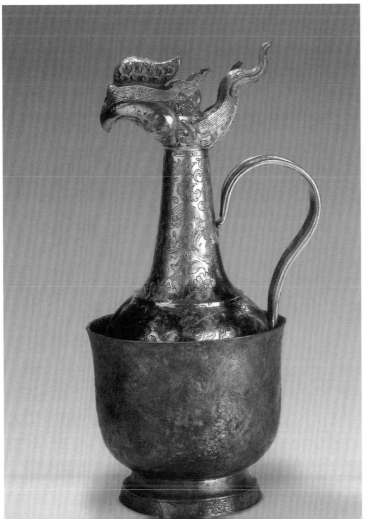

Wine ewer and warming bowl set with flower motifs and phoenix head topper, made from silver.

Song dynasty.

Ewer height 31.8cm, mouth diameter 5.2cm, weight 0.64kg.

Warming bowl height 10.5cm, mouth diameter 15.6cm, depth 7.4cm, weight 0.257kg.

Excavated in Sichuan province, 1996, currently housed in Pengzhou City Museum

Wine cup in a sunflower design, made from gold.

Southern Song dynasty.

Height 5cm, mouth diameter 10.6cm, base diameter 4.4cm.

Excavated in Anhui Province, 1952, currently housed in Anhui Museum

Tomb wall mural depicting wine preparation.

Liao dynasty (rival regime to the Song dynasty).

Height 140cm, width 80cm.

In situ, excavated in Hebei province, Zhang Shiqing (d. 1116) tomb, 1974

Tomb wall mural depicting wine preparation.

Yuan dynasty.

Height 159cm, width 176cm.

Excavated in Shanxi province, 2004, currently housed in Changzhi Museum

Depiction of grape wine and chrysanthemum winemaking.
Illustrations from *Shiwu bencao* (*Materia dietetica*), a dietetic herbal in
four volumes dating from the Ming dynasty.

Apricot leaf wine ewer, made from gold.

Ming dynasty.

Height 26.4cm, mouth diameter 6.4cm, weight 0.868kg.

Excavated in Hubei province, 2001, currently housed in Hubei Provincial Museum

Peach-shaped wine cup with dragon motif, made from jade.

Qing dynasty.

Height 4cm, length 11.2cm, mouth diameter 7cm.

Currently housed in Shaanxi History Museum

A cart for carrying wine, pulled by seven horses. A man with a whip drives the team forward.
Painted by Zhou Peichun (active c. 1880–1910)

此車是裝酒
大車之圖

generous application of rouge powder. Many works of literature and art down the ages have been dedicated to Lady Yang, in particular a famous Peking opera entitled *The Noble Consort's Intoxication*.

While Emperor Xuanzong and Lady Yang were cocooned in love and pleasure, trouble was brewing at the core of the Tang court. In 755, one of the emperor's most trusted generals, An Lushan (703–57), who was Lady Yang's adopted son, launched a rebellion and declared himself Emperor of Yan. The rebellion took eight years to quell and left an open wound in the mighty Tang dynasty that would lead to its decline and eventual downfall.

THE NOBLE CONSORT'S INTOXICATION

Early one evening, Lady Yang and Emperor Xuanzong arranged to meet at the Hundred Blossoms Pavilion to enjoy wine and flowers. Lady Yang

The Noble Consort's intoxication is immortalised in Chinese opera

arrived early with her entourage to wait upon Xuanzong. But, after a long and patient wait, Xuanzong was still nowhere to be seen. Lady Yang drank by herself to while away time. The beauty of the surroundings and the wine were arousing, and Lady Yang looked lovelier than ever. Eventually, a servant arrived with word that Xuanzong had changed his plans and had gone to the palace of another consort for the night. Hearing this, Lady Yang was bewildered by his sudden change of heart and enraged with jealousy. Fuelled by the flames of the wine and her unappeasable desire for her beloved, she loosened her silk robes and danced provocatively in front of her ladies-in-waiting and the eunuchs, chanting songs of sullen disappointment. Her entourage was at a loss, yet could not help but secretly admire the 'intoxicating beauty and the beauty intoxicated' before their eyes.

The peak of grape wine

During the Tang dynasty, the western frontier was extended and grape vines and winemaking techniques became increasingly accessible. After Emperor Taizong's 641 conquest of Gaochang (near Turpan in present-day Xinjiang province), wine made with the local white grape variety known as *maru* ('mare's teat'), due to its elongate shape, became popular in the Tang capital Chang'an. Taizong personally oversaw viticulture activities and made grape wines of 'eight different hues'. New regions such as Taiyuan and Liangzhou (present-day Wuwei) along the eastern and western corridors of the Yellow River also cultivated vines and produced good-quality grape wines.

Grape wine, a coveted rarity since the time of the Han royalty, had finally come of age. It could now be found in restaurants and wine shops in Tang cities. We know that both red and white wines were available because literary references exist for both 'red' and 'green' grape wines. Some grape wines were made by natural fermentation, as per the imported practice from the Western Regions, and these wines would be quite recognisable to a modern drinker. But others were made with fermentation inducers, and some were even mixed with grains, in line with Central Plain winemaking habits – an indication of the grape wine going native. Fruit wines in general were more common as agriculture and transportation improved. Lychee wine, for example, was much relished at the time.

Grape wine's reverence mirrored the empire's prosperity and an age of multiculturalism. Many grape wine merchants at the time were foreigners who travelled to China via the Silk Road. Their exotic shop girls, novel foods and delicious wines were all the rage. Grape wine continued to expand its celebrity fanbase, notably Li Bai and Lady Yang. It was also a source of comfort for frontier soldiers, as this poem suggests (*pipa* is a lute with four strings).

> Lyrics for the Liangzhou Melody
> *Fine grape wine glistens in the cup of evening light,*
> *I wish to enjoy the wine, alas the sound of pipa summons for battle.*
> *If I should lie drunken on the battlefield,*
> *Pray, sir, do not mock me,*
> *For since the time of old, how many do return from the frontiers of war?*
>
> Wang Han (687–726)

The poem is particularly illustrative of its time. The area of Liangzhou, a western region in present-day Wuwei, Gansu province, began grape-wine production during the Tang dynasty. The numerous literary endorsements of Liangzhou wine and accounts of it being enjoyed by the extravagant Lady Yang suggest the wine was of high quality. Grape wine was highly coveted and frontier soldiers were rewarded with it to boost morale.

The height of private winemaking and a sophisticated wine market

By 884 the Tang empire was carved up by local factions scrambling for power and the dynasty existed only in name. In 907 the Emperor Zhaoxuan was forced to abdicate by his disingenuous protector, Zhu Quanzhong. Alas, even the great Tang dynasty could not escape a mortal end.

While the Mandate of Heaven continued to change hands, by the turn of the first millennium, China was already a fully fledged, venerable civilisation, wielding and absorbing influences far and wide. It had become accustomed to the 'long united must divide, long divided must unite' cycles of harmony and discord. For half a century after the fall of the Tang dynasty, China had experienced a period known as the Five Dynasties and Ten Kingdoms (907–60) characterised by short-lived regimes and regional ruling houses. In 960 a military commander named Zhao Kuangyin (927–76) led a revolt and, opportunistically, his subordinates placed a yellow robe upon him (yellow was the colour of the emperor) and declared him emperor. The Song dynasty (known as Northern Song in history) was thus founded, and Zhao Kuangyin became known as the dynastic progenitor Emperor Taizu.

By now, society and wine culture were sophisticated, and the general level of wine connoisseurship was high. An age of innovation and an exuberant private winemaking scene encouraged people to learn, experiment, share and adopt ideas. The varieties and styles of wine had become truly innumerable, with professional and amateur winemakers all eager to hallmark creations to match their own taste. A contemporary compilation entitled 'Record of Wine Names' recorded over 100 famous wines produced by royalty, nobles, mandarins, wine merchants, taverns, restaurants and peasants. Grain wines still accounted for the vast majority of wines, some of which were made into aromatic wines that incorporated traditional or experimental herbs, flowers, plants or spices, with the age-old emphasis on the medicinal qualities of the ingredients.

Fruit wines were also popular, such as those made with plums, dates, apricots, pears, lychee, tangerine, coconut, but the grape still reigned supreme in this category.

EMPEROR SONG TAIZU'S WINE TRUMPS MILITARY MIGHT

Song Taizu, the new dynasty's founding emperor, was a usurper who was acutely aware of the precarious nature of his power. One evening in the autumn of 961 Song Taizu hosted a banquet and invited his most powerful generals. Over cups of wine, the party was joyous and full of camaraderie. Once everyone had been relaxed by the wine, the emperor dismissed all the attendants and announced that his most trusted generals must speak freely among close friends. The emperor, apparently inebriated, poured his heart out over the wine, tearfully thanking his comrades for their support, but complaining that the role as emperor filled him with anxiety. 'I could not have been emperor without you all, yet now that I have power, I can no longer sleep. I trust you, my brothers, but what of your subordinates? They are undoubtedly more loyal to you as masters than me as emperor. Can you really resist power and fortune, if it is right before you within grasp?' He questioned them rhetorically, 'If your subordinates were to enrobe you in imperial yellow, how could you possibly refuse, even if you had no such intention yourself?' Suddenly the mood in the room changed, as the generals detected

Song dynasty 'plum blossom vase'-shaped porcelain, popular as a wine service, from the famous Jizhou kiln. Currently housed in Anhui Museum

the dangerous undertone of the emperor's words. They begged Taizu to point out how they could prove their loyalty. 'You have fought hard all your lives, why not enjoy life now? Is it not better to accumulate wealth, land, children and live without trouble and danger?' The generals thanked the emperor profusely for his 'thoughtfulness towards their well-being'. The next day, all at the banquet sent letters of resignation on the grounds of ebbing health. Taizu wasted no time in accepting their requests and paid them off handsomely. Thus the new emperor, using wine-cup diplomacy instead of bloodshed that had all too often tainted the founding of new dynasties, removed in one clean sweep all of his most powerful military threats and earned the respect of his subjects.

Innovation and technology

Although the Song dynasty experienced almost ceaseless border unrest, by and large it is remembered as a period of vibrancy, prosperity and enlightenment, with innovation and learning pushing new frontiers. The invention of block and movable-type printing accelerated the spread of ideas and technology – it is no coincidence that several important wine books and many more complete records of wine ingredients and processes come to us from the Song dynasty, such as *Jiu Pu* (*The Purview of Wine*) and *Bei Shan Jiu Jing* (*The North Mountain Wine Folio*). Progress was made in many fields, including agriculture, irrigation, medicine, mathematics, astronomy (the circumference of the earth was estimated to an accuracy of several metres), navigation (the magnetic compass used for divination was now applied to orientation), warfare (the offensive capabilities of gunpowder were exploited) and finance (the world's first paper currency began circulation). Productivity increased, the population multiplied, commerce flourished and trade beyond the borders expanded.

Scores of texts on wine propagated knowledge about a diverse range of wine- and inducer-making methods. Clarified yellow wine, achieved by pressing followed by filtering towards the end of the winemaking process, was by now common. The finished product was usually heated to destroy bacteria, to improve longevity and to kill leftover yeasts that might cause continued fermentation. The conditions, temperature and timing of this heating process were exacting. Some historians believe that distillation techniques were already used in Chinese winemaking by this time, as several wines thought to be distilled liquors were named in contemporary writing. Some had even been known ever since the Tang dynasty.

With a flurry of innovative practices, wine became more colourful and the flavours more eclectic. Colours ranged from clear through white, green, yellow, red to black, with anything in between, and were often determined by the characteristics of the inducers used. In terms of taste, sweetness remained the dominant trait in many wines, but dry or even bitter profiles grew in popularity. With increased dryness and alcohol levels, words like 'vigorous', 'powerful', 'spicy' and 'zealous' appeared as praise for high-quality and stronger wines. The overall impression and mouthfeel of wine were also widely commented upon: clarity, smoothness, fragrance and spiciness were all desirable qualities. Aromatic wines (often grain wines infused with essences from plants, herbs and flowers, such as cinnamon, chrysanthemum, lotus flower, pine and bamboo), fruit wines (for example grape, lychee, citrus and pear), fermented honey or milk also made popular drinks. Song dynasty grain wines reached high levels of sophistication and quality, and it serves as an exemplary era of gold standards that still inspires today's yellow wine industry.

Wine in the bottle is warmed by immersing in a bowl of hot water. This fine set of porcelain comes from the famous kiln at Jingdezhen, with a lotus-flower shaped bowl and decorative top. Currently housed in Anhui Museum

Wine bottles in various standard sizes became a popular way to package and measure wine. Rare and quality wines were sometimes sold in silver bottles, but the majority were contained in ceramic bottles. Empty bottles would be collected and reused by the vendor. Grain wine was usually served warm in a two-piece service that consisted of an outer warming bowl (*zhu wan*) and an inner wine bottle (*zhu zi*). Hot water was poured in the outer bowl to warm the wine inside the inner bottle.

Homemade wines and commercial wines: an age of exuberance

Advances and expansion in agriculture, in particular in rice cultivation, spurred on an age of prosperity and population growth. Thanks to an abundance of grain crops, winemaking among private households flourished during this time. The general atmosphere of learning and progress greatly influenced homemade wines of the era – many amateur wine-makers took their task seriously and strived for quality, character and consistency in their unique creations. Some ordinary folks attained celebrity status through their wines, while some wines were venerated because of the celebrity of their producers. Notable among the latter was Su Shi (also known as Su Dongpo, 1037–1101), one of the most influential writers and politicians of the Song dynasty, and a connoisseur of gastronomy and wine. He is credited with creating a pork belly dish braised in rice wine – *Dongpo rou* – which is still one of the most famous Chinese dishes worldwide. His poetically named wines were much admired, Among them was a rice wine named 'The True One Wine', a medicinal wine using the plant 'Heavenly Gate Winter' (*Asparagus cochinchinensis*, or Chinese asparagus), and a mead-like wine styled as 'Spring for Ten-thousand Households'. Such names make it clear that Su Shi took great pride in his winemaking.

As homemade wines were limited in quantity and made just for private consumption, like-minded *garagistes* often organised tastings and exchanged their wines. Homemade wines became powerful social tools, used as special tokens for friends and family or to engage the attention of a useful official. The exchange of wine as gifts among the literati was often accompanied by poetry, calligraphy, painting or musical composition by way of a tasting or thank-you note.

Commercial wine enterprises, too, were extremely active and lucrative during the Song dynasty, in spite of, and perhaps as a result of, heavy-handed state control. Government permits and taxation were strictly enforced along each part of the production and sales chain. As a result of the government's ability to extract a large amount of treasury income from wine, wine consumption was encouraged during this time by the ruling class. The innumerable and competitive wine houses were particularly romanticised by the patronage of the literati, beauties and wandering free spirits.

Rhapsodies and drunken fists

Poetry prospered in another form: as lyrics set to song rhythms, known as *ci*. Wine and nature were popular backdrops in *ci*, as lyrical metaphors for joy, sorrow, escapism, meeting, parting or longing. A famous

The 'drunken fist' is a notorious Chinese martial arts style

piece composed by Su Shi at the Mid-Autumn Festival includes the oft-quoted lines:

> *How often does a bright moon grace the sky?*
> *Raising my wine cup to the heavens, I asked...*
> *Why should the moon begrudge us so,*
> *to be full and complete when people are apart?*

Song culture celebrated, on the one hand, delicacy and refinement, epitomised by lyrics and poetry that observe elegance of forms, and on the other, the valour and candour of *jiang hu* spirits – *kung fu* masters roaming freely as they please, unbridled. Yet these seemingly opposing philosophies and styles are steeped in a common passion: wine.

The notion of *jiang hu* is an elusive one. In its most literal sense, the phrase refers to 'rivers and lakes'. Yet *jiang hu* encompasses a wider realm, physically and philosophically, that has captured the imagination through the ages: the far corners of the earth, the turbulent and treacherous world, the unpredictable journeys through life, the romance of adventure and freedom. The concept of *jiang hu* in popular culture has been spread globally by martial arts literature, movies and games, most of which have at their core the themes of loyalty, honour, sacrifice for one's ideals and, of course, plenty of thrilling adventures, swashbuckling fights and unrestrained drinking!

An important example of the genre is the historical novel *Shui Hu Zhuan* (*Outlaws of the Marsh*, also known as *Water Margin*), attributed to Shi Nai'an (*c.* 1296–1372). It is set against the backdrop of the latter part of the Northern Song dynasty, but was written and compiled in the fourteenth century. The story concerns Song Jiang, the head of 108 outlaws based on Mount Liang, who were superior in martial arts, each with unique strengths and skills, and bonded by loyalty towards each other and their common ideal of carrying out their own brand of justice, righting the wrongs of the world, standing up for the weak and challenging the powerful and the corrupt.

Many of the most beloved *jiang hu* heroes share a common passion and weakness for wine, as is vividly demonstrated by the many instances of wine-drinking – over 600 – portrayed in *Shui Hu Zhuan*, which bring to life the rich wine culture of the Song dynasty. We see the popularity of wine houses even in the remotest places and the array of services they offered, including food, lodgings, sometimes as a den for hiding and plotting. We also observe the leading role of wine and drinking games in festivities; the symbolism of wine in ceremonies such as alliances, memorials, welcomes and send-offs; the etiquette of wine in matters such as the drinking order at feasts and political gestures of peace (the emperor's gift of royal reserve); and its place as a tool of enmity (the emperor's 'gift of death' by way of poisoned wine).

Some of the most memorable episodes in *Shui Hu Zhuan*, which have made a valuable contribution to the heritage of Chinese martial arts, are the scintillating performances of *Zui Quan*, the Drunken Fist, a highly skilled martial art form in which the opponent is deceived by the feigning of a drunkard's uncoordinated and unbalanced movements, using staggered and diverting manoeuvres to confuse the opponent as to the position, direction and timing of the strikes. High degrees of balance and control and excellent reactions are required. In the novel, the Drunken Fists were swung out while the heroes were indeed intoxicated. In one breath-taking episode, the opponent is a bloodthirsty tiger and the fight can only be to the death. As a real-life discipline of martial arts, however, real inebriation would be detrimental to the execution of this extremely difficult style.

The lyrical life of Li Qingzhao

The Song dynasty poet Li Qingzhao (1084–1151) was one of the most distinguished ladies of letters in Chinese history. Her lyrics, and her life, tell a fateful personal story and reflect the turbulence of the late Northern Song dynasty. Her use of simple yet original language and her ability to capture moments and moods touch a universal emotional chord. She was also an avid wine lover. In her poems, wine could represent fond memories of mischief, young lovers' bliss or an ineffective cure for heartache.

At 18 she married Zhao Mingcheng, a 21-year-old scholar and avid antique collector. The union was idyllic, as the pair shared the same passion for literature and art. They found great joy in collecting and cataloguing ancient bronzes, manuscripts, paintings and calligraphy, often pawning clothes in order to acquire precious pieces. Over time they built up a vast collection, and Zhao was on course to fulfil his life's ambition of compiling the most comprehensive account of important bronze and stone inscriptions. Li's poetry of this period reflected her feeling of immense marital bliss and, when Zhao was away on official duty, her intense longing for him.

> *The snow already knows of spring's coming,*
> *seeing the sprinkle of plum blossom dress up the white branches.*
> *Her fragrant face half showing,*
> *she emerges in the courtyard,*
> *a jade beauty, fresh out of her bath, and newly made up.*
> *Nature seems to have showed her special favour,*
> *indulging her beauty in splendid moonlight.*
> *Let us enjoy our golden chalice with emerald liquor,*
> *don't resist the intoxication!*
> *Of all the flowers, this is the one beyond compare.*

The happiness that she treasured did not last. In 1127, the Northern Song regime was overpowered by the invading Jurchen army. War and chaos descended, and the couple were forced to flee. They suffered great hardship but, most unbearably, large portions of their collection, lovingly acquired over many years, were left behind, destroyed or lost as they moved from one place to another. Further catastrophe was to befall: in 1129 Zhao died suddenly of typhoid. Li was inconsolable, and drifted as a refugee for years. Her later poems convey a great sense of pathos and loss, both for herself and for her country. Among them are some of her most haunting legacies.

> *Year after year in the snow we used to drink wine,*
> *plum blossoms for my hair,*
> *we were intoxicated.*
> *Now here I am rolling the fallen petals in my hand,*
> *for no good purpose,*
> *only drenching my clothes with tears.*
> *This year I am at the ocean's corner, the land's end.*

My temples are showing white.
Judging by the evening wind gathering force,
I shall be hard put to see the plum blossoms again.

A new claim to the Mandate of Heaven

Throughout the Song dynasty, China was constantly alternating between conflict and truce, with various ethnic factions on its northern border. In particular, the regimes of the Liao (also known as the Khitans), Xia (Tanguts) and Jin (Jurchens) were increasingly powerful. In 1127 the Northern Song dynasty lost control of its capital, Kaifeng, to the Jurchens and the Song court fled southward, moving its capital to Lin'an (modern-day Hangzhou), thus giving rise to the Southern Song dynasty. Despite its relocation, the Song court continued to be on the defensive against the invading Jurchens until, in 1141, a treaty ceded territories north of the Huai River to the Jurchen Jin dynasty (1115–1234, not to be confused with the Western and Eastern Jin dynasties, 265–420). The northern ethnic peoples were characterised by their bold and unbridled spirit and their astounding capacity for drink. They were excellent horsemen and archers: racing, hunting and archery tournaments were popular and prestigious, with wine as the prize to honour the victors. On one memorable occasion 'the Dowager Empress shot a bear, and the entourage presented her with wine, in honour of her health'.

The fusion of cultures between the ethnic and Central Plain people was inevitable, and enriched wine drinking for all. The Jurchens incorporated elements of Chinese culture and technology, added traditional Chinese festivals to their own, thus creating more occasions to drink and feast.

'Ode to Grape Wine'

Yuan Haowen (1190–1257) was a poet who lived through the turbulent later Song dynasty and the Jurchen Jin dynasty. In the preface to his 'Ode to Grape Wine', Yuan wrote about the loss of winemaking traditions to warfare, and his joy in a chance rediscovery courtesy of his friend, Liu Guangfu, whose hometown Anyi, in Shanxi province was a region abundant in grapes but where winemaking knowledge had been lost. He relates how a neighbour, who had returned home after fleeing from bandits, found some grapes left in a bamboo container. The bamboo container happened to have been sitting on top of a pot, and the grape juice had drained into the pot. There was a distinct wine aroma and the liquid tasted like delicious wine. They had discovered that grapes, if covered for a while, could produce wine through natural fermentation. The lost secret was finally rediscovered. Yuan observed: 'it had been a long time since wine like this had existed. I have only heard of it from travellers from the Western Regions who told of people taking grape juice and burying it to make wine. The wine gets better the longer it is kept. Some families would seal up tens of thousands of litres of wine ... The natural winemaking technique, lost for a hundred years, is now found, and it matches the evidence from thousands of miles away.' He considered the discovery remarkable enough to warrant the writing of the 'Ode'.

Wine during the Mongol Yuan dynasty

While China was battling with expansionary ethnic powers, one power in particular, of a type that had never been seen before in human history, was waiting in the wings: a nomadic people turned empire-builder that laid claim to more than one-fifth of the earth's land area and ruled over a quarter of the world's population at its zenith. It was an empire that would change the face of not only China, but the world. Cue the Mongol empire.

In 1227 the Tanguts submitted to the Mongols and in 1234 the Jurchens also folded, leaving no buffer to prevent the Mongols' push into inner China. As they conquered, the Mongols sought to secure their position by integrating, rather than overhauling, the deep-rooted and sophisticated cultures of the Han Chinese. In 1271, the fifth khan, Kublai Khan (1215–94) chose a Chinese dynastic name, the Yuan dynasty, in his bid for the Mandate of Heaven, which he obtained in 1279 by overpowering the Southern Song dynasty and unifying China.

Wine was a particularly good example of cultural and political integration. Elements of Mongol and Han drinking customs merged: the ritualistic aspects now aspired to greater drinking capacity. The Mongols' favoured wine, *kumis*, made from fermented horse milk, was elevated to court wine status and its production was in turn refined by Chinese winemaking skills. *Kumis* had long been well known among Asiatic nomads and travellers. It could be made quite simply by mixing fresh and soured horse milk, usually in a container made of horse skin, followed by vigorous stirring, shaking, beating or kneading by hand to speed up fermentation. *Kumis* is usually ready in three to four days. It is famed for its unique pungency and is certainly an acquired taste for those unaccustomed to it.

William of Rubruck was a thirteenth-century Flemish explorer sent by Louis IX of France as a missionary to the East. In *The journey of William of Rubruck to the eastern parts of the world*, Rubruck recalled tasting the Mongols' *kumis*, mead, grape wine and rice wine. He described *kumis* as a very pungent and potent drink with a pleasant and lingering taste, somewhat almond-like, while rice wine was comparable to the best wine in Auxerre, except that it did not have the perfume of grape wine.

The Yuan dynasty made its capital, Dadu – the 'great capital' – in modern-day Beijing. The Mongol empire and the Yuan dynasty brought about a large-scale cultural exchange and the fusion of multitudes of ethnic groups. As a result, wine culture took on multicultural dimensions, with even more varieties

Silver wine bottle, Yuan dynasty. Height 35.2cm, diameter at mouth 6.4cm, diameter at base 11cm. Excavated in Anhui province, Confucius Temple complex cellar, 1955. Currently housed in Anhui Museum

appearing. The expansionary Mongol empire amassed more land areas in the Western Regions, and the areas from which tributes of grape wine were sent to Beijing extended further westwards. The high alcohol content achievable by distillation was in vogue, and gave rise to *shao jiu* (meaning 'burnt wine'), more commonly known today as *bai jiu*.

Wine houses continued to use large banners and flags to attract patrons. By now, celebrity endorsement was common practice, and portraits of well-known figures were exploited for advertising. Wine vessels became rather large during the time of Yuan, reflecting the superior drinking abilities of which the Mongols boasted. One of the best-preserved vessels from this time measures 182cm in length, 135cm in width and 55cm in depth, and even larger ones have been recorded. A large capacity for drink was equated with manhood and commanded respect, and the Mongol rulers were quick to associate their drinking prowess with power. Marco Polo, the famous Italian explorer, described great banquets at Kublai Khan's court at which pure gold vessels filled with wine and *kumis* from a herd of 10,000 pure white horses were prepared for the khan exclusively. When the khan drank, all his subjects knelt and flattened themselves on the floor and an orchestra played a fanfare in unison. Once the emperor had finished, the orchestra stopped and people rose to resume their activities. Incidentally, the oft-heard 'chin-chin' when we clink our glasses derives from the Italian equivalent of 'cheers', but it is said that its true origin lies in Marco Polo's observation of Chinese drinking etiquette, in which it is customary for the host and guests to chorus the word *qing* ('please') before drinking.

Wine-drinking etiquette became rougher around the edges under the Mongols. Social drinking with 'forceful persuasion' came to the fore. Kublai Khan was known to force his ministers to drink. Anyone who could no longer oblige was stripped of their headpiece and robe as punishment – a mock stripping of power for being a lightweight. Mongol hosts liked to see their guests incapacitated by wine to demonstrate generosity. 'Forceful persuasion' is still common today, in which people pour wine for each other and say *ganbei* (dry the cup) insistently. One is obliged to empty the cup or be regarded as having not shown respect to the proposer. This can continue until one is reduced to beg for leniency!

By the time of the Yuan dynasty, grape wine consumption had reached a historical peak in China. Tributes and production from the enlarged Western Regions and the Central Plain reached unprecedented volumes. Marco Polo recorded that the area of Taiyuan (Shanxi province) had vast vineyards and produced great quantities of wine that were distributed to many parts of China.

Vinification had been gradually indigenised since the time of the Han dynasty, and, with the Mongol empire opening up the western frontiers to an unrivalled degree, Western grape wine and winemaking styles made fresh inroads into China. The main difference in vinification was between natural fermentation (the Western Regions method) versus the use of fermentation inducers (the Central Plain method). We know from literature that both white (often referred to as green) and red (sometimes referred to as purple) wines were made in China. Distilled grape wine – brandy, in other words – was also popularised.

A detailed note, describing how grape wine was made in the extreme Western Regions using natural fermentation, was written by Xiong Mengxiang, a Yuan dynasty bureaucrat. The grapes would be brought in before they were completely ripe. The fermentation vat was a large, clean, stone container lodged in the ground that could hold several hundred litres. Innumerable grapes, stacked like a mountain, would be spread out and flattened by stamping with the feet. Then the whole lot would be pressed down and sealed into the vat with a large piece of wood, and a further layer of sheepskin or carpet-like material was added to complete the seal. No addition of fermentation inducers was required. Then the room would be closed and, after 10–15 days, several men would remove the carpet and wooden lid to reveal the vat already filled with wine. The clear part of the wine was taken out and placed in a separate container to make the 'head' wine. The remaining sediments would be pressed again by stamping, and the process repeated. Several days later, another batch of wine would be taken. This would be done three times altogether to produce three wines: head wine, second wine and third wine.

Grape wine made in the Central Plain of China often used fermentation inducers, as in traditional grain wine methods. As the Chinese had long relied on the use of inducers to control fermentation, this approach to grape wine was a logical extension of traditional practices. For this reason, grape wine made this way was listed as 'controlled wine' in official manuals that gave instruction on how to make a quality-assured wine to a state-approved standard.

The popularity of grape wine during Yuan is attributable to another factor: a preferential tax rate was applied to grape wine, probably to wine made without inducers. According to the *New History of Yuan* (an official history of the Yuan dynasty written in the twentieth century), grain wine was taxed at 25 per cent, whereas grape wine was taxed at only 6 per cent. In 1273 a debate was held at court to consider increasing the tax on grape wine to the same level as that of grain wine. The idea was rejected, however, on the basis that grape wine did not use up food crops in the way that grain wine and inducers did, and therefore it was argued that it should not incur the higher tax rate. This suggests that the Yuan court was consciously promoting grape wine.

The Yuan dynasty produced an official manual on agricultural practices, *Nong Sang Ji Yao*. In its description of grape vines, it mentioned that vines cannot survive the cold, and will die if not buried. This indicates that the practice of burying vines (*see* page 26) had a long history in Chinese viticulture thanks to the severe winters in the north, where many vineyards were located.

Decadence and decline

During the Yuan dynasty, musical drama was performed in vernacular tongues for the first time, thus becoming accessible to the masses. Musicals and theatre became a phenomenon, infiltrating all levels of society and incorporating multiethnic influences and artistry. The refinement of poetry and lyrical styles combined with acrobatics, dancing, costumes and set designs created an extravaganza for all. Wine featured heavily in the plays, as well as on the tables of the audiences. Accomplished actresses and singers attained celebrity status and were frequently invited to accompany eminent men for drinks, songs and dancing. Many poems dedicated to fine wine and fine ladies by their admirers portrayed a seductive lifestyle that tantalised the senses, with the exquisite sight of beauty and fashion, the rapturous sound of music and songs, and the fragrant nose and satisfying taste of wine and food. Wine culture was heaven on earth.

Towards the end of the Yuan dynasty, the Mongol empire began to fracture. There was a loss of influence beyond China's borders and internal conflicts intensified at court. The populace fell into discontent and unrest flared up across the land. In 1368 a peasant-born Han leader named Zhu Yuanzhang (1328–98) took control of the capital and declared himself Emperor Hongwu, the first emperor of the Ming dynasty.

An identity crisis for wine and empire

From the fourteenth to the seventeenth centuries, the Ming dynasty rulers restored ethnic Han rule over China, and began a series of political, intellectual and social reforms to reinforce traditional Chinese values. After a prolonged period of ethnic rule, the empire felt an unprecedented sense of identity crisis and the ruling class attempted to emulate the past glories of the Zhou, Han and Tang dynasties by adopting aspects of their policies and moral codes.

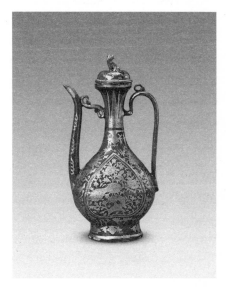

Ming dynasty wine ewer with golden peacock and peony patterns. Height 29cm, diameter at mouth 5.9cm, diameter at base 8.8cm. Excavated in Shaanxi province, 1959. Currently housed in Shaanxi History Museum

A return to Confucian roots

The Ming rulers sought to retrace and reinvent traditional Chinese education, particularly the Confucian schools. They believed that the weakness and demise of the Yuan dynasty was partly due to the innate barbarity of the rulers' nature, which had spread ignorance and a lack of decorum throughout society. These attempts were reflected, too, in early Ming wine culture: there was a renaissance of strict drinking etiquette according to rites and protocols, with the varieties and qualities of wine and the types of wine vessels being meticulously classified and ranked according to social function and social status. This, however, proved difficult to maintain. Chinese wine culture had been through dynasties of pleasure-seeking, and was quick to find revelry again in reviving indulgent, exuberant and excessive ways of drinking. Wine's identity could no longer be dictated by the ruling class or be restricted to the ancient orders of ritualistic decorum.

Ming was a momentous period of urbanisation in China and enjoyed one of the most productive and socially stable periods in Chinese history. As great strides were made in industry and commerce, Ming society became more capitalist than feudal in nature. Winemaking was by now considered an industry in its own right, rather than a practice ancillary to agriculture. Innumerable small wine producers sprang up across the land, creating a vibrant, innovative, competitive landscape for the wine scene.

Wine in Ming art and literature

In literature, Ming was an important dynasty that produced some of the most well-known Chinese novels, including *The Three Kingdoms*, *Outlaws of the Marsh*, *Journey to the West* and *The Plum in the Golden Vase* (or *The Golden Lotus*), each of them drenched in wine culture. We have already come across *The Three Kingdoms* and *Outlaws of the Marsh* in the context of their historical settings. *The Plum in the Golden Vase*, whose authorship remains a mystery, borrows an episode from the *Outlaws of the Marsh* in which a corrupt and lustful local tycoon named Ximen Qing seduces a married woman, Pan Jinlian (Golden Lotus), and persuades her to poison her husband so that he can take her as a concubine. From there the book weaves its own tale of intrigue, recounting the domestic and sexual politics and the downfall of the Ximen household, and casting a critical eye over moral corruption through its depiction of Ximen's indulgent lifestyle and the sexual and material desires of the characters. An important novel of manners that stirringly dissects society and the human condition, its sexually explicit content made it infamous and it was banned for centuries. Wine is a frequent feature in the backdrop to the narratives and a recurrent accomplice to misdeeds. In the dramatic episode relating Ximen Qing's seduction of Pan Jinlian, wine was the conspirator in the act:

The Monkey King riding the clouds to steal the heavenly nectar

'Tea is the stirrer for fancy; wine is the matchmaker for desire'. Quite the match for 'Would you like to come up for coffee?'

In sharp contrast, *Journey to the West*, written by Wu Cheng'en (*c*.1500–82), tells of the arduous endeavours of the Tang dynasty monk Tang Seng and his four disciples to obtain Buddhist scripture and enlightenment. Despite the sombre subject matter, wine makes more than 100 appearances: apart from the repeated emphasis that monks should not succumb to the lure of wine, there are lavish descriptions of wine rituals in the heavenly realm, complete with exquisite wine vessels made of gold, jade, crystal, coral and other precious materials, and dazzling arrays of wines: grape wine, coconut wine, medicinal wine and other heavenly creations. In one episode, the rebellious Monkey King is displeased to find the gods hogging all the alcohol for themselves. He retaliates by running around drinking the wines as they are being laid out for a heavenly banquet to which he is not invited. Going from one jar to another, he tastes all the heavenly creations that he has never known. His monkey subjects produce their own coconut wine to welcome him home, but he declares it inferior to the wines he has just tasted, and insists on returning to the banquet to steal more. When he brings back the heavenly nectars, the monkeys throw a feast of their own in honour of their heaven-realm bounty. All hail the Monkey King! All are in ecstasy!

Playing cards were known as 'wine cards' because they were designed for drinking games. Although playing cards existed in China during the time of the Han and Tang dynasties, they acquired artistic value and unprecedented popularity during the Ming dynasty. Ming wine cards were illustrated with artwork, writing and game rules and were exquisite collectables, with many famous artists and calligraphers involved in their creation. Historical wine legends, led by Li Bai, were favourite portrait subjects, as were the heroes of Mount Liang, the so-called *Outlaws of the Marsh*.

Among the most eminent artists of the day, Tang Yin (1470–1523) and Zhu Da (1626–1705) were colourful characters and hopeless wine lovers. Their paintings and writings were highly prized and difficult to obtain, yet it was said that they were easily persuaded by the lure of wine and would produce an outpouring of wondrous artworks while intoxicated, not knowing or caring that their art was preyed upon by the cunning wine pourer.

BEN CAO GANG MU (THE COMPENDIUM OF MATERIA MEDICA)

This encyclopaedia of Chinese medicine was compiled and written in the sixteenth century by the renowned Ming doctor Li Shizhen (1518–93). This colossal book, which classifies 1,892 substances believed to have medicinal properties and records 11,096 prescriptions, is the most comprehensive and credible record of Chinese medical knowledge at that time. While writing *Ben Cao Gang Mu*, Li Shizhen consulted over 800 medical books and added his own extensive knowledge and experience as a medical practitioner. His work addressed the often erroneous, inconsistent and scattered nature of many medical journals that had come before.

The book contains vast numbers of entries related to wine. It attributes the origin of wine to the Yellow Emperor and identifies many different types of wine, fermentation inducer and winemaking technique. For example, he gives particular praise to the health-giving benefits of a red fermentation inducer made with *Monascus purpureus* (red yeast rice), in which modern medical science is interested for its cholesterol-reducing properties, among other benefits. For grape wine, Li outlined three production methods: natural fermentation, fermentation with inducer and distillation. On natural fermentation he noted that 'grapes stored for a while will produce wine on their own. It is fragrant, sweet, fierce and bold,

First edition of *Ben Cao Gang Mu*, 1590

this is the true grape wine.' Alternatively, 'by mixing grape juice with inducer, wine can be made as per the usual rice wine method.' Whereas to make brandy:

> *Take some ten catties [around 6kg] of grapes, add wine inducer to make wine. After fermentation, pour it into a cauldron to be steamed, and collect the condensation. The rouge colour is particularly appealing.*

He further noted that the quality of the grapes would impact the character of the wine, observing that thin-skinned grapes tended to produce finer wine while thick-skinned grapes added bitterness. Li also understood that even when water freezes, alcohol does not. He commented: 'there will be one part [of the wine], while, even in extreme cold, all the other parts are frozen, but this part is not. That is the wine's alcohol.' On wine's properties, Li observed that grape wine is 'warming for the kidneys' and can 'enhance the colour of the complexion', while brandy can 'regulate *chi*' and is 'anti-inflammatory'.

Li made distinctions between the social and medical aspects of wine, warning that not all wines are suitable for medicinal purposes and that any medicine can be effective only if the dosage is carefully considered. Although his compendium records numerous health benefits of wine ('in moderation, aids circulation and the flow of *chi*'), it also warns of excess drinking ('harms the stomach and bile, burdens the heart and lessens the years'), unsuitable pairings (wine and tea) and bad drinking habits (taking a cold shower while under the influence of alcohol), and offers several antidotes to excess consumption ('use cold water, mung bean powder and broad bean shoots to make soup', or 'chew dried Chinese bayberries').

'Only wine and wool': why the Chinese did not discover Europe

Emperor Yongle's reign (1403–24) is deemed the zenith of the Ming dynasty. He had a vision of maritime might that would showcase China's grandeur to the outside world and spread China's influence far and wide. He sent a capable eunuch, Zheng He (1371–1433), on sea expeditions to what was then known as the Western Ocean (now the Indian Ocean) and, between 1405 and 1433, Zheng He made seven sea voyages, visiting 36 countries and regions in South-east Asia, the Middle East, Somalia and the Swahili coast.

The explorations of Zheng He greatly enhanced the reputation of the Chinese empire. He pacified notorious pirates en route, but most of his journeys were about peaceful diplomacy and ritualised displays of magnificence. Zheng He took with him gifts of porcelain, silk, gold and silver. In return he received gemstones, medicinal ingredients, precious wood, spices and many novelties, including zebras, ostriches and a giraffe. In a typical voyage, around two years in duration, over 27,000 men travelled in 100–300 ships. Around 60 of these were enormous 'treasure ships' bearing Chinese products and precious gifts, the largest of which were over 130m in length and over 50m wide, which would comfortably accommodate a football pitch. These were the largest ships in the world at the time, no less than 20 times the capacity of Christopher Columbus's ships, which sailed 87 years later.

With the passing of Emperor Yongle, however, his successors decreed a U-turn on Chinese maritime activities. Sea expeditions were stopped and nautical technology was neglected. The sudden change of attitude was astounding. What brought it about?

By now, China had known several periods of great prosperity. It prided itself on its self-reliance and believed itself to be the centre of the world, calling itself the Central Kingdom or Middle Kingdom. Influence was not about colonisation, but rather an aura of superiority that would radiate from its centre and draw others to admire it and aspire to its riches. Towards the end of Emperor Yongle's reign, an ongoing struggle for influence between the eunuchs and the scholar-bureaucrats intensified and the debate over the security of China's identity resurfaced. Should outward communication and discovery, as represented by Zheng He's adventures, be the way to promote China, or should China close in to preserve its civilisation and emit but not admit influence? In the end, it was the conservative faction that gained favour. The scholar-bureaucrats promoted an introspective and puritanical view of empire. They argued that China was self-sufficient and superior in terms of its own economy, culture and spirituality, and that China's resources were better deployed inwardly, so as not to be 'tainted' by 'barbaric' influences.

Anecdotes and hearsay reflected the general attitude that 'Europe had only wine and wool, nothing that China could not produce'. Despite China's superior size, power, economic strength and techno-logical advances at the time, it abandoned its peerless maritime head start. Wine and wool, the assets that had embroiled France and England in the Hundred Years War, seemed to have had the opposite effect on the Chinese appetite for expansion. In fact, grape wine appeared to have entered a lull during the Ming dynasty. There are several possible explanations: grape wine no longer enjoyed the tax benefits of the Yuan dynasty and was now taxed in the same way as other wines. Meanwhile, distilled liquors had become much more popular as people acquired the taste for strong, fiery alcohol. Of course, it would be a gross simplification to suggest that a lack of interest in European grape wine dulled China's desire to rule the waves. Nevertheless, the fate of the last imperial dynasty, Qing (1644–1912), had already been set in motion by the Ming rulers' introspection. For it was Europe's maritime advancement, which began around the same time that the Ming rulers abandoned theirs, that shaped the subsequent empires of the world and exposed China to centuries of foreign plunder. An identity crisis was about to set sail towards the Middle Kingdom.

A new wine age beckons

By 1644, the Mandate of Heaven passed to the Qing dynasty, which was founded by the northern ethnic Manchus, descendants of the

Qing dynasty wine vessel, with eight auspicious motifs. Height 49.5cm, diameter at mouth 19.7cm, diameter at base 21.5cm. Currently housed in Anhui Museum

Jurchens. Imported grape wines from the Old World, as we know it today, had reached China via Christian missionaries and traders. Some of these wines came from European countries as tributes to the Qing court, given in return for the privilege of trading rights with China. They were revered by royalty and the elite – such foreign imports were rare and arguably represented the best in grape wine at the time. Yet for all the fine wines and state-of-the-art Western goods presented to the Qing court, nothing could rival the West's desire for Chinese produce such as tea, porcelain and silk.

Many of the wines made during the Qing dynasty would still be recognisable and appreciated today. In addition to high-quality grain wines, distilled liquors had matured in technique and repertoire. Sorghum was the most popular ingredient, although rice, barley and wheat were also common. Cocktails and blended liquors, made by mixing distilled liquor with fruit juice, sugars, natural flavourings and medicinal ingredients, or by blending the ingredients before the distillation stage, also thrived.

Three Emperors and the Thousand Elders banquet

Towards the end of the sixteenth century, a Jurchen leader named Nurhachi (1559–1626) began to consolidate various Jurchen tribes in north-eastern China. By 1616 Nurhachi had more or less unified all Jurchen people and declared himself khan of the Later Jin dynasty. His son Huang Taiji (1592–1643) continued his ambition. To avoid negative associations with the twelfth-century Jurchen Jin, in 1636 the new khan changed the Jin dynasty name to Qing and the Jurchen ethnicity to Manchu. During a lifetime dedicated to conquest, Huang Taiji's power expanded beyond what was later known as Manchuria into Korea, Mongolia and Ming China. The 277-year-old Ming dynasty came to an end when, in 1644, the peasant leader Li Zicheng sacked the capital, Beijing. In the ensuing bid for power between the peasant army and the Qing forces, Qing emerged as the ultimate winner, seizing Beijing and establishing a hold on all China.

The Mandate of Heaven generously bestowed upon the Qing dynasty three highly regarded emperors in succession: Kangxi (1654–1722), Yongzheng (1678–1735) and Qianlong (1711–99). Their reigns spanned from 1661 to 1796, during which time China once again displayed unmatched might and prosperity. All three emperors had in their counsel a distinguished advisor named Sun Jiagan (1683–1753), who was highly learned and forthright in his opinions, notably his view on the prohibition of wine. Earlier in his career he had been in favour of prohibition, but later he decided this position had the 'irrationality of

a bookworm'. Having spent time among the common people and observed their livelihoods, he concluded that 'wine is essential to life'.
Without wine, people could not conduct rituals, socialise or attend to
the elderly, since wine was both tonic and medicine. If the law inter-
fered too much with winemaking or the wine trade, then a large part of
the population would inevitably break the law, but prohibition would
remain ineffective.

Regarding the competition for agricultural resources between people's need to eat and winemaking, Sun Jiagan noted that grain wine and
distilled liquor made use of many agricultural by-products, such as crop
stalks, peels and shells. Therefore, wine could create value out of waste
material and enhance productivity during periods of comfort and abundance. Furthermore, Sun noted that market dynamics would regulate

Wine and feast at a winter ritual to honour ancestors.
Brush drawing by Chinese artist, c. 1850

wine prices: if the supply of wine was plentiful then prices would be low, and vice versa. Prohibition would have the adverse effect of reducing supply but not demand. This would push up the price of wine and encourage illegal production and trading, causing more harm than good to people's livelihoods and the economy.

Sun Jiagan's well-argued opinion was based on his genuine interest in, and observation of, real lives, and reflected his sharp intellect and analytical mind. No wonder all three of the most illustrious Qing emperors consulted him.

In 1713, on the occasion of Emperor Kangxi's sixtieth birthday, the emperor gave a famous banquet in the Garden of Perpetual Spring at the royal palace within the walls of the Forbidden City. Kangxi wished to honour the wisdom of age and to reflect on his own long and illustrious reign. The royal invitation extended from the emperor's elderly kinsmen to veteran generals, long-serving mandarins and distinguished scholars, and all the way down to community elders and regional 'longevity stars' across the land. In fact, men above the age of 65 were all invited. At the banquet, all the young princes between 10 and 20 years of age were summoned to honour the elders and pour wine for them, despite the princes' higher status. It is estimated that no fewer than 7,000 elders participated in the celebrations, which lasted several days. Another such banquet was held in 1722 in preparation for Kangxi's seventieth birthday, for which Kangxi composed a poem entitled 'The Thousand Elders Banquet', and the name caught on.

Emperor Qianlong, Kangxi's grandson, continued this tradition, giving an Elders Banquet in 1785 to mark his fiftieth year on the throne. On this occasion he personally poured wine for elders above the age of 90, and summoned all his sons, grandsons and great-grandsons to pour wines for the guests. He hosted another Elders Banquet in 1796, the year of his abdication in favour of his fifteenth son, a move intended to ensure that the length of his reign would not surpass that of his grandfather Kangxi. This, he believed, was the ultimate act of filial piety and show of respect to his grandfather.

Claret – the emperor's tonic of choice

Emperor Kangxi was peerless in his all-round abilities: he possessed a superior intellect, great political instincts and leadership skills backed up by military capabilities. By nature, he was curious and thirsty for knowledge. Born with the blood of a Manchurian father, a Han mother and a Mongolian grandmother, and raised under an equally diverse range of teachings, Kangxi was arguably the most cultured and culturally open-minded ruler of China. He took a great interest in Western technology, and was particularly impressed by a group of French Jesuit missionaries sent by Louis XIV of France, who brought Western astronomical equipment, medicine and studies in geometry and arithmetic. Kangxi employed several of them in his court, and commissioned scientific research and translations of Western books into Manchu and Chinese. The emperor also showed special favour by allowing these missionaries the freedom to preach and practise Catholicism in China. In turn, the missionaries reported back vivid accounts of the life and culture of China to the French court, inflaming the *chinoiserie* fervour in Europe. Louis XIV of France and Emperor Kangxi of China, both patrons of learning and culture, began, out of mutual curiosity, to bridge the immense geographical and cultural gap between them via the exchange of gifts and travels undertaken by the Jesuit missionaries and through the priests' writings.

Kangxi was known to be fond of grape wine. Following a bout of illness, he accepted a recommendation from the Jesuit mathematician Louis le Comte to drink a few glasses of red wine every day with his meals. Louis le Comte was born in Bordeaux to a noble family and had most likely prescribed claret as the choice tonic for the Emperor. Kangxi adopted this habit for the rest of his life and went on to rule for 61 years – the longest reigning sovereign in the history of China. Grape wine again found the loftiest of endorsement and favour among the royal and elite circles.

A Dream of Red Mansions

One of the greatest marvels of Chinese literature was circulated during Emperor Qianlong's reign. *Hong Lou Meng* (*A Dream of Red Mansions*) by Cao Xueqin (c.1715–c.1763) is part autobiographical, part meta-physical, and narrates the prosperity and decline of a prominent Qing household. The novel is a masterpiece on many levels: it interweaves reality and illusion in its intriguing plot, portrays colourful characters, narrates heart-wrenching love stories and combines beautiful poetry and detailed accounts of many aspects of Chinese culture and lifestyle at the time. The book is one of the most difficult Chinese works to translate, as it harnesses many levels of meaning and incorporates a great deal of classical poetry and puns.

Hong Lou Meng is a treasure trove of vivid depictions of wine culture. It recounts in great detail the rich variety of wines stocked in a wealthy Qing household, including various types of liquor, medicinal wine, spiced wine, grain wine and imported grape wine. The author seems to be an advocate for drinking warm wine, as there are numerous descriptions of warming wine before serving. In one scene, the protagonist, Baoyu, hints to his host that the goose feet and duck tongue pickled with distiller's grain would taste even better with wine, rather than the tea that he has been offered to drink. The host immediately orders some wine to be heated. Baoyu remarks, 'don't bother to warm it, I prefer drinking it cold', but he is immediately persuaded to the contrary. 'Don't you know that warm wine will dissipate quickly in the body? If you drink it cold, it will stay stuck inside your system and you'd be warming it up with your internal organs. How could the organs not be damaged?'

The plot incorporates many festivities and feasts at which wine was essential, along with the associated customs and etiquette. It describes around 20 days of feasting and drinking during Chinese New Year, with Chinese opera and performances by dancing girls staged at banquets. There were days for viewing the snow, the moon, lanterns and blossom, which would be accompanied by wine, drinking games, musical performances and poetry-making. A huge variety of drinking games, both highbrow and silly, ranging from the composition of poetry, song, rhyming verses and riddles to games of dice, cards and thumb wars, are all vividly depicted.

A crab feast is among the many memorable scenes in the novel: steamed crabs, a seasonal delicacy enjoyed in autumn, are washed down with piping-hot yellow wine and accompanied by poetry on the subject of the chrysanthemum, a flower in full autumnal glory. The delicate heroine, Daiyu, complains of indigestion after eating some crab, and remarks that she would like a mouthful of 'hot spirits'. Her attentive love interest, Baoyu, immediately orders some liquor to be heated and steeped with acacia flowers.

The crab feast, seemingly an innocent banquet organised on a whim to inspire poetry-making within the walls of a grand household, was a stark reminder of the wealth gap that was fracturing Qing society. As Granny Liu, a poor distant relative, later calculates, 'crabs of that size ... together with the wine and snacks ... altogether cost more than twenty taels of silver! My Amita Buddha! That's what we country folks live on for a whole year!'

A rude awakening for the Central Kingdom

Towards the end of Qianlong's reign, the seeds of trouble began to sprout. Years of prosperity had made the royal family increasingly extravagant and complacent. Corruption was rife, the discipline of the armies was lax, internal conflicts intensified. At the same time, European states were competing for territories, resources and trade, and became bolder and more aggressive as their wealth and discoveries accumulated. The Qing court treated foreign emissaries and traders with disdain. Foreign trade was conducted under the Canton System, which permitted very limited port access around the southern province of Canton. Trade terms were also conducted under the Tributary System, in which the superiority of the emperor of China must be acknowledged by foreign states and tributes were paid in exchange for gifts and favour from the Qing court. This was, by and large, accepted by the Europeans on the grounds of practicality, since competition for access to trade was strong and they received much more valuable gifts than the tributes they paid.

Frustratingly for the Europeans, though, China continued to be self-reliant and uninterested in exploring trading relationships, while Chinese tea, silk and porcelain were in huge demand in the West. The Europeans tried to tickle the Chinese fancy with many items, such as wine, food, spices, textiles, pocket watches and clocks, scientific instruments, even curiosities such as a hot-air balloon, but any subsequent interest could not match the insatiable Western demand for Chinese goods. Although trade with China was very lucrative for the foreign traders and their political patrons at home, the trade imbalance with China and the infuriating trade conditions were bitter pills to swallow.

In the latter part of the eighteenth century, British traders began to route opium from the British-controlled poppy fields of India into China and introduced opium mixed with tobacco to the populace – a means of earning silver to pay for the goods they wanted from China. Opium addiction soon soared among the Chinese population, extending to the poor, who could not afford the habit, and army personnel, which threatened the defensive capability of the realm. The Qing government protested and banned opium trading, but to no avail. Significant weakening of the economy, treasury, defence and health of the people from widespread opium addiction eventually led to the First Opium War in 1839. Chinese naval capabilities were no match for the British maritime might, with their ships equipped with the latest technology and weaponry: the British blasted havoc along the coasts, extending further inland and northwards. In 1842 the Qing government conceded the Treaty of Nanking (Nanjing), in which an indemnity of 21 million silver dollars (the Mexican silver dollar was a dominant trade currency due to the Spanish colonial legacy; the sum converts to roughly 48,000 tonnes of pure silver) was paid to Britain. Hong Kong Island was given to the British empire and five trade ports were opened up to British merchants, along with extraterritorial privileges. Other aggressors followed suit with the threat of force and, in 1844, the Treaty of Wanghia (with the US) and the Treaty of Whampoa (with France) were conceded by the Qing government.

After signing these 'Unequal Treaties', China entered a partially colonised state, with import and export dynamics largely dictated by Western powers to serve their own interests. China – the Central Kingdom, which had prided itself as the 'celestial empire', and which firmly believed that All under Heaven were drawn to bow before her wondrous civilisation and treasures – was now given the rudest awakening of all.

As a result of the opening up of seaports to foreign countries, imported wines increased in volume and variety. According to *Qing Bai Lei Chao* (*Anthology of Petty Matters of Qing*), a scrapbook-style compilation of observations and records from the Qing dynasty:

> *Grape wine is made from grape juice, foreign imports are abundant, and have several varieties. Ones made with the grape skin are red in colour and called red grape wine, which can alleviate intestinal ailments. Ones made without the skin are white or slightly yellow in colour, called white grape wine, which can aid bowel movements. There is also another grape, from Spain, which is very high in sugar. The resulting wine is clear and colourless, and is called a sweet grape wine. This is the best for a patient, it can bring about a fast recovery.*

This sweet grape wine is certainly a reference to a Muscatel wine. Even with foreign wines, the Chinese were keen to assign health benefits to them. As the power balance tipped towards the foreigners, foreign goods, including European wines, attained greater prestige. European wines were consumed by high society and served the ever-growing expatriate communities.

The Qing dynasty's position deteriorated further under the strain of external aggressors and internal uprisings. Between the 1860s and 1890s a 'Westernisation Movement', aimed at promoting, learning and adopting Western technology in order to bolster defence and industrial production, gained traction, but the devastating burdens of ceaseless conflict shortened the lifetime of the movement, and it was ultimately unable to achieve its aim of 'strength and prosperity' sufficiently to save the Qing dynasty.

From 1861 onwards the Qing throne was occupied by puppet emperors, while the Dowager Empress Cixi (1835–1908) ruled from behind the screens. In response to a rebellion in 1900, an alliance of eight Western forces ransacked the capital Beijing, forcing the imperial family to flee. In 1912 the Qing dynasty was finally extinguished with the abdication of the last emperor, Puyi (1906–67), giving way to the birth of the Republic of China, led by its first president, Sun Yat-Sen (1866–1925).

As imperial China bowed out after almost four millennia, however, a new age of winemaking in China was just beginning.

Wine's changing fortunes as imperialism ends

Even during the tumultuous times of the late Qing period, wine culture was not entirely forsaken. Encouraged by the Westernisation Movement of the late nineteenth century, an emigrant Chinese patriot named Zhang Bishi (1840–1916) returned to China and established the first large-scale industrialised Chinese winery, Changyu, in 1892. He lobbied and impressed people in high places, including the leader of the Westernisation Movement, Li Hongzhang, who signed the licence of incorporation for the company. Emperor Guangxu's tutor, the famous calligrapher Weng Chenghe, took up his brush to create the company logo.

The inspiration for Zhang Bishi's plan to industrialise grape wine production in China came from a chance conversation with a French diplomat at an embassy wine tasting. Over a glass of exceptional Bordeaux, the diplomat claimed that Yantai, in China's Shandong province, could probably produce wine of a similar quality. He told Zhang Bishi that, while serving the Franco-British alliance during the Second Opium War (1856–60), his men were stationed at Yantai, and the nearby hills were abundant with wild grapes. The troop had made wine from these grapes and found that the taste was surprisingly good. The French soldiers had even joked that they might start new lives as winemakers in China.

Zhang Bishi took note and visited Yantai. He examined the local terrain and climate and was delighted to find it well suited to a winery. After Changyu was established, he imported European grape vines, Western winemakers and oak barrels. He also built Asia's largest cellar at that time, which was 1,976m² in area and 7m in depth – a feat that took 11 years and three attempts to complete.

Since its establishment, important figures on different sides of the political spectrum have found common ground in their support for the Changyu winery. After the fall of imperial China in 1912, President Sun Yat-Sen of the Republic of China visited the winery and gifted his calligraphy to the company. In 1954 Changyu brandy accompanied Prime Minister Zhou Enlai of the People's Republic of China on his diplomatic mission to the Geneva Convention. In 1956 Chairman Mao Zedong, on examining a report from Changyu on the state of grape wine production, indicated that 'Grape wine production should be greatly promoted. Let the people drink more grape wine.'

Today, Changyu Pioneer Wine Co. is still a market leader in China and one of the largest wine companies in the world. Its vast range extends across the spectrum from basic to mid-tier to premium wines covering red wine, white wine, ice wine, sparkling wine, brandy, vermouth and tonic wine, with wineries in Shandong, Beijing, Liaoning, Shaanxi, Ningxia and Xinjiang. It is also venturing beyond China's borders, starting with acquisitions in Cognac and Bordeaux. Changyu wines are now sold internationally, and the UK was its first export market.

The modern era

During the twentieth century, China experienced an arduous journey of self-rediscovery. The epoch was landmarked by numerous events, such as the establishment of the Communist Party (1920); the Chinese Civil War, which led to the stalemate between the mainland and Taiwan (1927–49); the Long March of the Red Army (1934–5); the Founding of the People's Republic of China by Mao Zedong (1949); the campaign of collectivisation and industrialisation known as the 'Great Leap Forward' (1958–61); the persecution of cultural heritage, free thinking and free speech that occurred during the Cultural Revolution (1966–76); Deng Xiaoping's economic Reform and Opening Up since 1978; entry to the World Trade Organization (WTO) since 2001; the first Chinese manned space mission in 2003; the Beijing Olympics in 2008; and the (re)emergence of China as a global economic superpower at the dawn of the twenty-first century. Much of modern and contemporary Chinese history still inflames wounds, incites controversy and ignites heated debates, and it is perhaps too soon to judge, or even properly to narrate, the last century of Chinese history.

Let us return to the subject of wine in the People's Republic of China. Mao Zedong declared the birth of this New China on 1 October 1949.

The country has come a long way since its early period under a Communist regime of planned economy (1949–78). These decades were characterised by various experiments with agricultural collectivism, centrally set wages and productivity targets, allocated skills, labour, industrial inputs and outputs, and goods rationing. Yet even during these years, which are mostly remembered for unsuccessful, even disastrous economic misadventures and the traumatic Cultural Revolution, foundations were quietly being laid for China's wine industry. State-run research and cultivation centres were established to investigate China's wine-production resources and potential. Extensive categorisation of native grape species, wine-grape breeding programmes and experiments with imported varieties have been continuing since the 1950s. The first wave of imported European grape varieties came from the Eastern bloc, due to China's political alignment with the region at the time. French, Italian and American wine grapes were only brought into New China during the 1970s.

China's vast land area is home to over half of the world's grape-vine species. Some display high resistance to cold and diseases, which are desirable qualities for winegrowing. Cross breeding between native-grown varieties, such as *Vitis amurensis* and *Vitis quinquangularis Rehd* with European vine varieties, for example Muscat, Merlot, Cabernet Sauvignon, Chenin Blanc, Riesling and Vidal, can result in cultivars that combine the best qualities of their parents, such as Chinese cold hardiness and disease resistance, with European sweetness. China's breeding programmes have by now produced over 200 cultivars and planted several thousands of hectares of vineyards, and these figures are sure to increase.

During the early decades of New China, domestically produced wines were often blended with juice, sugar and flavourings to reduce costs. They would not qualify as wine by today's standards. In any case, wine consumption among the masses was negligible. This 'half juice' practice was gradually phased out but only officially abolished in 2004, as China endeavoured to conform to international standards across various industries after joining the WTO in 2001. Even today, some domestic Chinese wines are labelled as 'full juice' to reassure consumers that the wine is 100 per cent grape.

In 1979, China was about to experiment with the market economy and, as if to mark this watershed moment and the end of the old economic regime, the Great Wall Wine Company produced China's first dry white wine made with a native-grown grape variety called *longyan* (Dragon's Eye). The wine itself was unremarkable in quality, but it symbolised a first step. Around the same time, China began the Reform and Opening Up of its economy, starting with the decollectivisation of agriculture and the opening up to foreign investments. From the late 1980s, protectionist policies and price controls gradually gave way to market-like dynamics accompanied by increasing privatisation and the contracting out of state-owned industries, thus spurring on a first generation of entrepreneurs and wealth.

The 'made in China' label, ubiquitous in the twentieth-century as a label for labour-intensive but low-cost mass production, is being reinvented in the twenty-first century in an effort to associate it with high-end, high-tech and creative industries. Or rather, there is an endeavour to *restore* its historical reputation as epitomising skill, innovation and quality. We only need to visit a museum to be reminded of what 'made in China' used to mean: the wonders of human ingenuity. Chinese wine is part of the new 'made in China' phenomenon, with ambition to become a leading producer of the world.

The renaissance of wine in China

Regimes have come and gone, dynasties have risen and fallen, but thousands of years of history have attested to the inextinguishable spirit of the Dragon's Descendants, who always find the will and the way to restore glory. During difficult times, prohibition was frequent in order to prioritise food production and reduce the non-essential use of agricultural land. During periods of political fragility, drinking gatherings were often curbed to avoid antisocial and riotous behaviour. When the country was prosperous and stable, however, wine was relished by all levels of society. Time and again in history we have observed the intertwining of wine, politics and living standards. And now, as China prospers once again, the taste for the good life inevitably returns. We have seen that Western-style grape wine, in particular, is enjoying a new age of rapid growth in China. This is not, as many believe, merely the result of fashion and a new taste for Western things and lifestyle brought about by globalisation, but a revival of an age-old drink of choice, updated for the modern age.

Its success is also in no small part due to the current political stance that is encouraging it. Unlike grain-based wine production, which competes with food resources and fertile agricultural land, grape vines can produce superior wine from less fertile soils and thrive in terrains unsuitable for traditional farming. This opens up new frontiers in land preservation, particularly the fight against desertification. It also invigorates employment and the economy. Furthermore, grape wine's perceived health benefits, and its comparatively lower alcohol level versus traditional high strength liquor, *bai jiu*, are met with both official and public approval.

The huge potential for the wine industry in China is indisputable. What are the key ingredients in fulfilling that potential? We only need to look back in history to know: the continued strength of the Chinese economy, a stable and benevolent political climate and, of course, the interest, cultural participation and collective wisdom of the people.

Drink a cup of wine, the road ahead is long.

Li Bai (701–62)

APPENDICES

Where to buy Chinese wines

In recent years, Chinese wines have been exhibited prominently at international fairs, where their tasting sessions are often over-subscribed. I have tasted memorable Chinese wines at fairs, such as Vinexpo and Decanter Fine Wine Encounter, but for the curious wine-lover outside of China, opportunities to taste good-quality Chinese wines remain hard to find. In the USA this is already changing, with Chinese wine sales reaching $700 million in 2016. In particular, Dragon's Hollow from Ningxia was a well-received range of wines.

In the UK, the British fine-wine specialist Berry Bros. & Rudd began stocking a selection of Changyu wines in 2013 and supermarket chains have since followed suit. In 2017, Sainsbury's unveiled Changyu's Noble Dragon Red, a fruity and full-bodied Cabernet Gernischt (Carménère) blend with Cabernet Sauvignon and Cabernet Franc produced in Yantai, Shandong province, as well as the Changyu Noble Dragon Riesling from the same area. Tesco opted for the aforementioned Château Changyu Moser XV Cabernet Sauvignon as its introductory Chinese wine, a classic Bordeaux-style red produced in Ningxia. These entry-level wines are priced around £8.50 to £10. Other high-profile wine merchants, such as Liberty Wines and Fine+Rare, have opted to showcase mid- to high-end Chinese wines. Panda Fine Wine, the first specialist trade supplier of Chinese wines in the UK, began operation in 2018 and has a well-chosen selection of boutique wines. Private members clubs, such as London's 67 Pall Mall, and luxury retailers, such as Harrods, Selfridges and Hedonism Wines, are also introducing Chinese wines, sometimes with exclusive tastings events. The list of stockists is expanding.

We shall watch this space with interest, not least to see whether the restaurant trade will play a more prominent role in enhancing the international reputation of Chinese wines and liquors. Some top-end London restaurants and bars are leading the charge, for example, Hakkasan, Sexy Fish, Hutong at the Shard, China Tang at the Dorchester and Dinner by Heston Blumenthal at the Mandarin Oriental. But nothing beats a trip to China, of course. Wine tours and specialist operators have been on the rise in recent years, and most wineries in China have been built with tourism in mind from the outset, with plenty of opportunities to taste and purchase the wines.

Wine tourism in China

China's oldest and largest wine producer, Changyu, is leading the wine trail in China. It has tourist-friendly vineyards with European-style châteaux in six different wine regions. Its Wine Culture Museum in Yantai, Shandong province, opened in 1992 and covers an area of 10,000m². It showcases Changyu's winemaking history since 1892 and boasts a large underground cellar, built in 1894 and more than 7m deep. It was once the largest underground cellar in Asia.

Changyu's various châteaux experiences offer vineyard and cellar tours and tastings as well as workshops where participants can pick grapes during the harvest season and make their own wines. Visitors can also get creative by making their own wine labels or buy wine-based skincare products.

Yantai Changyu Wine City is another ambitious project, and combines research, winemaking and tourism. It spans over 1,000 acres and has enlisted help from Disney designers, with two gothic-style castles and a 19-storey wine institute shaped like a wine barrel surrounded by champagne flutes. Visitors can wine and dine in the castles and marvel at one of the largest wine and brandy production centres in the world, including an impressive production line with a daily bottling capacity of 2.1 million bottles.

If you enjoy a bit of golf by the coast with your wine tour, Château Junding, south-east of Penglai in Shandong province, could be your calling. It boasts an 8,000m² underground cellar, which is now the largest in Asia. There are all the comforts of a luxury hotel as well as an 18-hole golf course close to the vineyards.

If you want to visit vineyards close to the capital city Beijing, the up-and-coming region of Yan Huai River Valley, which borders Beijing and Hebei province, would be a good choice. Huai Lai Amethyst is an award-winning premium estate. From there you can even make a quick detour to an ancient stretch of the Great Wall, which was originally built around the second century BC.

For an unlikely stay in a Scottish-style castle in China built by a Yorkshireman, the Treaty Port Vineyard and Castle in Penglai, near the Domaines Barons de Rothschild vineyard in Shandong province, will serve up a unique experience with plenty of stories about all that is weird and wonderful in the modern wine industry in China. The estate's owner Chris Ruffle even wrote a book, *A Decent Bottle of Wine in China*, about it.

For a distinctly Chinese vineyard experience, Jade Valley Wine & Resort is a worthy contender. It is situated 35km east of the historical capital city, Xi'an (the starting point of the ancient Silk Road and home to the Terracotta Warriors), in a valley of the Qinlin Mountains, surrounded by rural scenery. The estate was built by an acclaimed architect, Qingyun Ma. It stands out among Chinese wineries as an excellent example of harmony between the traditional and the modern, East and West, local landscape and vineyard topography. The property offers luxury accommodation, a winery and cellar tour, wine tastings with local cuisine and snacks, and a chance to see the famous shadow-puppetry, a local form of theatre that is included on UNESCO's 'Representative List of the Intangible Cultural Heritage of Humanity'.

Ningxia is fast becoming a destination wine-tour region. There are numerous highly acclaimed wineries worthy of a comprehensive itinerary, including the likes of Kanaan, Silver Heights, Helan Qingxue, Xi Xia King and Lux Regis. There are organised wine tour operators in this area.

Another worthy mention goes to Grace Vineyard, located 40km south of Taiyuan in Shanxi province. The estate produces remarkable wines and offers accommodation and wine and local food tasting.

For a tasting experience of other types of Chinese wines, and an invaluable educational trip, visit the China Huang Jiu Museum, which showcases the history and culture of Chinese grain-based wines. It is located in Shaoxing, Zhejiang province, where the most famous Shaoxing *huang jiu* brand is produced. The Chinese Wine Culture City in Renhuai City, Guizhou province, is a colossal complex built by the Kweichow Moutai wine company. There are also numerous *bai jiu* museums built by various *bai jiu* brands.

This is by no means a comprehensive list of China's visitor-friendly wine destinations, but rather a few seeds of curiosity to plant in your mind, which may lead to a future adventure.

High-profile vineyard acquisitions

Bordeaux is the most coveted destination for vineyard acquisition among Chinese tycoons and state-backed enterprises. Approximately 150 Bordeaux vineyards are currently under Chinese ownership.

Hong Kong billionaire Peter Kwok was the first Chinese investor in Bordeaux with the purchase of Château Haut-Brisson in 1997. Twenty years on he has accumulated a portfolio of eight vineyards in the region.

High-profile public figures such as actress Zhao Wei (owner of Château Monlot and Château Patarabet) and Alibaba founder Jack Ma (owner of Château de Sours and Château Perenne) have joined forces to form a Bordeaux club of Chinese château owners, sharing technical knowledge and routes to market. The two also have interests in the Bordeaux *négociant* Cellar Privilege, which boasts an underground storage big enough for one million bottles, with a view to serving Chinese clients.

In 2016, Jack Ma launched an annual online wine and spirits festival, showcasing over 100,000 wines on his e-commerce platform Tmall.

In contrast to Bordeaux's fairly relaxed attitude towards foreign ownership of vineyards, the sale of Château de Gevrey-Chambertin to Louis Ng Chi Sing in 2012 caused uproar in Burgundy. The Chinese gambling tycoon's €8 million bid beat a local syndicate's €5 million effort to prevent it going to foreign hands, and local winemakers expressed dismay at the lack of government intervention and support. Louis Ng Chi Sing, however, was not the first Chinese buyer in Burgundy. That title goes to a then 28-year-old businessman, Shi Yi, who purchased two hectares in Vosne-Romanée earlier the same year.

Across the pond, former NBA basketball star Yao Ming has established himself as a serious wine brand in Napa Valley, California. Yao Family Wines produces a Yao Ming Cabernet Sauvignon and a Napa Crest blend of Cabernet Sauvignon, Merlot and Petit Verdot. In keeping with Napa Valley's established tourism tradition, Yao Family Wines boasts a hospitality centre and an exclusive wine club. Robert Parker, the single most influential wine critic before his retirement in 2016, said of Yao Family Wines, 'These are high-class wines. The two Cabernets are actually brilliant, and the Reserve bottling ranks alongside just about anything made in Napa.'

KEY DYNASTIES AND DATES

Three Sovereigns and Five Emperors (pre-history–*c*.2070 BC)

Age of legends and semi-divine leaders of unassailable virtue. It spans from the emergence of primitive human settlements to the Neolithic period. Iconic artefacts from this period include bone flute, painted pottery, carved jade and stone tools.

Xia dynasty (*c*.2070–*c*.1600 BC)

A quasi-legendary dynasty whose existence is still contested due to the lack of contemporary written records. Conventionally acknowledged by archaeological evidence as the Erlitou culture found in the Central Yellow River valley, but no definitive items hallmarking the dynasty have been found so far. It marks the early Bronze Age in China. Iconic artefacts from this period include early bronze ritual vessels, metalwork, glazed ceramic, ivory carving and early lacquerware.

Shang dynasty (*c*.1600–*c*.1046 BC)

The first recorded Chinese dynasty for which both written and archae-ological records exist. The realm spanned the North China Plain and centred on a series of different capitals, the last of which was probably at Anyang. Iconic artefacts from this period include bronze vessels, pottery, oracle bones with inscriptions, carved jade figurines and ceremonial weapons, musical instruments and carved ivory cups with inlay.

Zhou dynasty (Western Zhou *c.*1046–771 BC; Eastern Zhou 770–256 BC)

The most influential ancient dynasty, which established political, philosophical and cultural frameworks that guided all subsequent dynasties. Its concept of the Mandate of Heaven – the sacred and unique right to rule, which is bestowed on one virtuous ruler at a time and withdrawn from a tyrannical one and reassigned – was the central doctrine of imperial China. Western Zhou's capital was at Hao (near present-day Xi'an). In 770 BC the court was forced to flee eastwards from enemy onslaught and moved its capital to Luoyi (present-day Luoyang), which marked the start of Eastern Zhou. Eastern Zhou is further divided into the Spring–Autumn period (770–476 BC) and the Warring States period (475–221 BC), during which time regional factions fought each other for land and power, and over time consolidated into larger states that rendered the Zhou government irrelevant. By 475 BC, seven remaining states vied to become the overlord of all China. Iconic artefacts from this period include bronze vessels, weapons, coins and musical instruments, lacquerware with gold and silver inlays, mural painting, painted silk, bamboo scrolls with writing, calligraphy on silk, crystal ware and jade ornaments.

Qin dynasty (221–207 BC)

The first Chinese empire founded by the victor of the warring states: Qin. Its capital was at Xianyang. A short but significant dynasty during which many efforts towards unification and standardisation, such as in systems of measurement, written script and currency, were made. It is responsible for two UNESCO world heritage sites: early sections of the Great Wall and the Terracotta Army at the First Emperor (Shi Huang Di)'s tomb site.

Iconic artefacts from this period include life-size armies of terracotta warriors and chariots at Xi'an, stone carvings and inscriptions and coinage.

Han dynasty (Western Han 202 BC–AD 8; Eastern Han AD 25–220)

The battles of Chu-Han after Qin's demise raged on between 207 and 202 BC, until Han emerged the victor. The Han dynasty was a golden age of prosperity comparable to the near-contemporary Roman empire, which was rising in the West. The Silk Road was established in the second century BC, starting from the capital city Chang'an (present-day Xi'an) and extending westwards into Central Asia and Eastern Europe, totalling 6,400km. The dynasty was interrupted by the usurper Wang Mang's Xin dynasty in AD 8–23, and reconstituted in AD 25, when it became the Eastern Han, with its capital relocated to Luoyang. Iconic artefacts from this period include jade 'mummy' suits with gold threads, lacquerware, bronze sculpture, porcelain, gold imperial seals, calligraphy on silk, large mural paintings or calligraphy, brick art and marriage brick (to commemorate marriage between a Han princess and an ethnic chieftain, a frequent manoeuvre to underline a political alliance).

Three Kingdoms (220–80)

Towards the end of Eastern Han, three regional factions became powerful and rendered the Han emperor a puppet. After a period of stalemate, the trio were self-proclaimed as emperors of three kingdoms: Wei (220–65), Shu (221–63) and Wu (229–80). Iconic artefacts from this period include green-glazed pottery, ornamental jade, embroidered silk, bronze 'money trees', textiles, lacquerware and lacquer shoes.

Jin (Western Jin 265–316; Eastern Jin 317–420)

A turbulent period following the Three Kingdoms. The Jin rulers never secured their grasp on power. Ceaseless warfare and political struggles continued, states appeared and were swallowed: 16 kingdoms came into being between 304 and 409 during the period of Jin. Western Jin's capital was at Luoyang, while Eastern Jin's capital was Jiankang (present-day Nanjing). Iconic artefacts from this period include glassware, gold ornaments, jade and calligraphy.

Southern and Northern dynasties (420–589)

China remained divided during this period, which saw the rise and demise of nine short-lived regimes. During this time, military and related technologies notably advanced. After the end of the Han dynasty, the fertile south of China became increasingly powerful and resourceful, and thus increasingly contested. Iconic artefacts from this period include mural or stone paintings, Buddhist figurines, carving and calligraphy, and carved jet (lignite).

Sui dynasty (581–618)

China was reunified under Sui after nearly four centuries of division. A short but pivotal dynasty that left us with a UNESCO World Heritage site, the Grand Canal, a vast system of waterways that connected strategic centres along the north-eastern and central-eastern plains, including connections between Sui's first capital Daxing (present-day Xi'an) in the central-west and its second capital Luoyang (after 605) to the central-east, as well as present-day Beijing in the north-east and Hang Zhou in the south-east. The Grand Canal was tasked with transporting grains from the fertile river valleys to the capital and frontier garrisons in the north. It was transformational for China's internal trade and communication capabilities, and is still in use today. Iconic artefacts from this period include stone sculpture and white-glaze pottery.

Tang dynasty (618–907)

Building on the administrative and cultural frameworks of the Sui dynasty before it, Tang reached an age of prosperity and sophistication that was unparalleled and unprecedented. Its capital Chang'an (present-day Xi'an) was the greatest metropolis in the world at the time. The reputation of the Chinese empire also reached its zenith. The period produced two unmatched emperors, one revered as the model for all emperors (Taizong), and the other the only woman who ruled China, not as a meddling empress or dowager regent, but under the title of emperor (Wu Zetian). Iconic artefacts from this period include tricolour glaze ceramics, gold and silverware, agate ware, large bronze temple bells, Buddhist statues and relics, large mural painting or banner painting on silk and textiles, typically with a Buddhist theme.

Song dynasty (Northern Song 960–1127; Southern Song 1127–1279)

After the fall of Tang, factional fighting plunged China into chaos for a period known as the Five Dynasties and Ten Kingdoms (907–60). Once the Song dynasty has unified China as the legitimate inheritor of the Mandate of Heaven, science, technology, culture and commerce flourished once more. The Song dynasty was an age of enlightenment and prosperity. The northern borders, however, were ceaselessly infringed by ethnic steppe tribes. Eventually the Song defences were breached and the capital Kaifeng was overrun in 1127 by the ethnic Jurchens who had set up the Jurchen Jin dynasty (1115–1234). The Song court fled south, relocating the capital to Lin'an (present-day Hangzhou), and ruled what was left of the hinterland, known in history as the Southern Song. Yet the threat of invasion never stopped. For the first time, a Chinese dynasty of 'legitimate lineage' faced existential threats from non-Han ethnic aggressors. Iconic artefacts from this period include porcelain from the 'five great kilns': Ru, Guan, Jun, Ding, Ge (for example, monochrome-glaze and crackle-glaze porcelain), celadon-glaze porcelain, Buddhist statues, jade, scroll paintings and calligraphy.

Yuan dynasty (1279–1368)

The Mongol empire swallowed up the squabbling ethnic Tanguts and Jurchens along with the Han Chinese and founded the Yuan dynasty, acknowledged in Chinese official history as a foreign-ruled Chinese dynasty in which a Chinese-style administrative system was largely maintained. It set up capital at Dadu, present-day Beijing. This was an age of unprecedented interaction and trade between the different peoples under Mongol rule. Vernacular language began to emerge in literature. Iconic artefacts from this period include monochrome-glaze porcelain (for example eggshell, crimson, light blue) and multicolour-glaze porcelain ('blue-and-white' or 'blue-and-white-with-red').

Ming dynasty (1368–1644)

A restoration to Han Chinese rule brought about a mass revival of neo-classical philosophies. During the early part of the fifteenth century, China's maritime capability reached its zenith and was unmatched in the world at the time, epitomised by seven awe-inspiring sea expeditions. Naval activities were abruptly abandoned after these expeditions, however, due to a heightened China-centric attitude that saw little need for active outward exploration. Although this would have detrimental implications for the subsequent dynasty, Ming was a socially stable period, during which time industry and commerce developed with a flavour of capitalism. The Forbidden City was laid out in the capital, Beijing. Iconic artefacts from this period include five-colour enamelware, blue-and-white ware, imperial seals, imperial head dresses, scroll painting and calligraphy.

Qing dynasty (1644–1912)

The Manchu-ruled final imperial dynasty, during which time China reached its maximum land area in terms of direct sovereignty, with its capital at Beijing. Until the mid-nineteenth century, China enjoyed an aura of the 'celestial empire' whose riches and produce were the wonders and desires of the world. China's naval technology, however, had been in decline while Europe's maritime advances had brought on ambitions for world dominance through missionary work, trade and colonisation. Foreign trade interests in China sparked trade wars and then full-blown war, initiated by the First Opium War with the English, who were followed by other foreign aggressors demanding unequal treaties that plunged China into a semi-colonised state. The Qing dynasty and imperial China ended with the abdication of the last emperor, Puyi. Iconic arte-facts from this period include blue-and-white ware, flambé-glaze ware, carved ivory, carved jade, gold imperial seals, goldware and silverware, agate ware, ornamental 'ruyi' sceptres, scroll painting and calligraphy, fan paintings, embroidered textiles and silks, bank notes, postal stamps and snuff bottles.

Timeline of dynastic China and selected world events

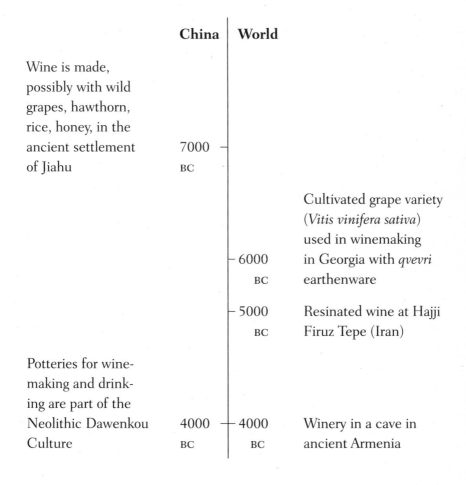

	China	World	
Wine is made, possibly with wild grapes, hawthorn, rice, honey, in the ancient settlement of Jiahu	7000 BC		
		6000 BC	Cultivated grape variety (*Vitis vinifera sativa*) used in winemaking in Georgia with *qvevri* earthenware
		5000 BC	Resinated wine at Hajji Firuz Tepe (Iran)
Potteries for wine-making and drinking are part of the Neolithic Dawenkou Culture	4000 BC	4000 BC	Winery in a cave in ancient Armenia

China	World
	Grape cultivation and winemaking is established around the Nile Delta, Egypt, possibly through contact with the Levant (Eastern Mediterranean). Viticulture spreads from the ancient civilisations of Mesopotamia to Indus Valley
Mythical age of the 'Three Sovereigns and Five Emperors' 3000 BC — 3000 BC	
Legendary winemaker Du Kang	
Legendary winemaker Yi Di	
— 2350 BC	Noah plants a vineyard on Mount Ararat in present-day Turkey, according to the Bible
— 2000 BC	The world's oldest known written story, *The Epic of Gilgamesh* from Mesopotamia, contains descriptions of wine
	Wine becomes known on the Greek peninsula
Xia dynasty 2070 BC	
Early Bronze Age wine jugs and ceremonial vessels epitomise the Erlitou Culture 1700 BC — 1700 BC	Wine cellar site in northern Israel

	China	World
Shang dynasty	1600 BC	
'Oracle bones' divination with earliest known pictograms for 'wine' and written records of wine used for ceremonies	1500 BC	*Vitis vinifera* (the common grape vine) begins to be spread across the Mediterranean by Phoenician traders
Western Zhou dynasty	1046 BC	
	1000 BC	Balché flavoured mead is favoured by the ancient Mayans
'*Admonition of Wine*' describes wine's role in virtues and vices, and sets out laws and moral codes around wine drinking	800 BC	Celts move into Britain; mead and beer are preferred drinks
Zhou court establishes a wine bureau and set numbers of wine officials and rankings, winemaking techniques and quality standards		Rise of city-states such as Sparta and Athens in Greece; Hellenic culture and conquests bring advanced winemaking to more Mediterranean regions, including southern Italy and Sicily

	China	World
The Book of Odes records many poems with wine themes		Greek god Dionysus is named in honour of wine
	776 BC	Wine is offered to Zeus at the first Olympic Games, Olympia
Spring–Autumn period	770 BC	
Rise of the 'Hundred Schools of Thought' where wine serves as a beverage as well as subject matter in symposiums	753 BC	Rome is founded
	500 BC	Wine plays an important role in Greek symposiums and the discourse of philosophy
		Height of the Persian empire; contemporary historian Herodotus writes that the Persians are very fond of wine and drink in large quantities

	China	World
Warring States period	475 BC	
King Goujian of Yue pours wine into the river to drink with his troops ahead of a decisive millitary campaign that ends the kingdom of Wu	473 BC	
Bian Que the 'miracle medic' applies medicinal wine beyond its use as tonics, such as to revive women from difficult birthing	460 BC	Hippocrates identifies medicinal benefits of wine
and as an anaesthetic prior to operations	375 BC	
	340 BC	Aristotle remarks on a wine that tastes of oregano and thyme
	303 BC	Chandragupta, founder of the Mauryan Empire, India, exchanges gifts including sweet wines with Seleucus, founder of the Hellenistic Seleucid Empire, following a peace alliance

	China	World
Qin dynasty – the first imperial dynasty of China	221 BC	
Winemaking is widely prohibited or heavily taxed in order to conserve food crops and establish social stability	218 BC	Hannibal's army crosses the Alps
Western Han dynasty	202 BC	
Compilations of ancient medicinal wines appear in 'Yellow Emperor's Canon of Internal Medicine'	200 BC	Cato the Elder writes about wine's medicinal values
Zhang Qian pioneers trade routes (the Silk Road) as envoy of Emperor Wudi and brings grape wine and vine stock from the West	119 BC	
Emperor Wudi establishes a precedence for government monopoly on wine sales to fund defence budget	98 BC	

	China	World
		100 BC — Phoenicians produce glass wine cups
		The rise of the Roman empire spreads wine culture and 27 BC — viticulture throughout Europe
Eastern Han dynasty AD 25 —		

Chinaware emerges
in drinking vessels as
the Bronze Age
reaches its tailend

Jesus shares wine as
AD symbol of his blood at
30 — the Last Supper

Roman invasion of
Britain introduces
vines and commercial
AD vineyards to
43 — Britain

First written record of
Bordeaux vineyards by
Pliny the Elder, who
also wrote 'In vino,
AD veritas' (In wine,
71 — truth)

	China	World

Meng Tuo bribes the prominent palace eunuch Zhang Rang with 20 litres of grape wine in exchange for a ministerial post at the corrupt court of Emperor Ling

AD 170

The Talmud, the compilation of Jewish teachings and laws, sets out wine's benefits and ceremonial purposes but warns of temptation and misuse

AD 200

Cao Cao offers wine to the river and composes a drinking ode ahead of the Battle of Red Cliff

AD 208

Romans promote the use of oak barrels for storing and transporting wine, replacing the amphoras; they noted the pleasant effect of oak on wine

The Three Kingdoms

AD 220

Cao Pi, an avid grape-wine lover, self proclaims as emperor of Wei

	China	World	
		AD 250	Rise of the kingdom of Aksum (present-day Eritrea and northern Ethiopia) as a significant political and trade centre, wine being a notable import
Western Jin dynasty	AD 265		
The 'Seven Sages of the Bamboo Groves' drink together and compose poetry, songs and calligraphy as escapism from the tumultuous political climate		AD 296	Britain is reinvaded by the Romans
Eastern Jin dynasty	AD 317		
		AD 330	Constantine the Great transfers the Roman empire capital from Rome to Byzantium
Wang Xizhi composes the 'Preface to the Orchid Pavilion Poems', arguably the most revered piece of Chinese calligraphy, after a day of drinking games with friends	AD 353		

China	World

Roman empire adopts Christianity; wine's central role in the Catholic Mass propels and propagates winemaking technology as Catholicism spreads across Europe

─ 380

Southern and Northern dynasties 420 ─

The Chinese agricultural encyclopaedia *Essential Techniques for the Peasantry* comprehensively details winemaking techniques

─ 476 Fall of the Western Roman empire

Anglo-Saxon Britain; the age of the legends of King Arthur

─ 500

Sui dynasty 581 ─

Construction begins on the Grand Canal, the world's longest man-made waterway (1,800km) 605 ─

Rise of the Islamic faith; alcohol consumption is generally forbidden among Muslims

─ 610

	China	World

Tang dynasty — 618

Li Bai, known as the 'poetry saint' and 'immortal of wine' of China, dedicates two poems to his contemporary and drinking partner Du Fu — 745

Du Fu, one of the most prominent Tang poets, writes a song dedicated to the 'Eight Immortals of Wine' – in praise of eminent contemporary wine lovers, among them Li Bai — 746

King Charlemagne gives the hill of Corton to the Abbey of Saulieu to grow grape vines; known today as the Corton-Charlemagne AOC, in Côte de Beaune — 775

Rise of the Viking age; there are archaeological suggestions that Vikings enjoy wine through Roman influences, in addition to mead and beer — 793

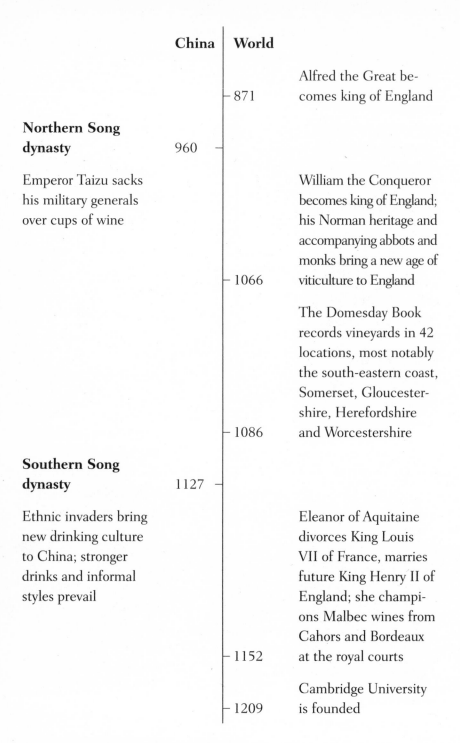

	China	World
		Alfred the Great becomes king of England
	— 871	
Northern Song dynasty	960 —	
Emperor Taizu sacks his military generals over cups of wine		William the Conqueror becomes king of England; his Norman heritage and accompanying abbots and monks bring a new age of viticulture to England
	— 1066	
		The Domesday Book records vineyards in 42 locations, most notably the south-eastern coast, Somerset, Gloucestershire, Herefordshire and Worcestershire
	— 1086	
Southern Song dynasty	1127 —	
Ethnic invaders bring new drinking culture to China; stronger drinks and informal styles prevail		Eleanor of Aquitaine divorces King Louis VII of France, marries future King Henry II of England; she champions Malbec wines from Cahors and Bordeaux at the royal courts
	— 1152	
		Cambridge University is founded
	— 1209	

	China	World
Yuan Haowen writes the 'Ode to Grape Wine' to commemorate a chance rediscovery of naturally fermented grape wine after a period of war	1215	
	1275	Marco Polo meets Kublai Khan in Dadu (present-day Beijing)
Yuan dynasty	1279	
Mongol rule brings further ethnic influences to the Central Plain; *kumis* (fermented horse milk), grape wine and strong liquors are in vogue		
	1337	Start of the Hundred Years War between England and France; trade of English wool and French wine are key catalysts
Ming dynasty	1368	
Zheng He's first naval expedition to the Indian Ocean to showcase China's maritime might under Emperor Yongle	1405	

	China	World
Zheng He dies on his seventh oceanic voyage; this marked an end to China's maritime advancement due to lack of political will and expansionist ambitions	1433 — 1434	Start of the Medici political dynasty in Florence and significant patronages during the Italian Renaissance
		Start of the Spanish conquistadors' journeys to the New World; wine and *Vitis vinifera* are later introduced to Mexico, Brazil, Peru and other parts of South America
	— 1500	
		Moctezuma II's reign begins, during which the Aztec empire reachs its largest size; fermented cocao is a sacred ceremonial wine in many Mesoamerican cultures
	— 1502	
		Portuguese Jesuit Saint Francis Xavier brings wine to Japan as a gift
	— 1549	
		Shakespeare writes in *Othello*: 'Good wine is a good familiar creature, if it be well used'
	— 1603	

	China	World

Qing dynasty — 1644

French Jesuit Louis le Comte arrives in China. He introduced Bordeaux wine to Emperor Kangxi, who drinks it daily with meals as a tonic — 1688

Height of the European age of exploration; Madeira is a key port of call due to its flourishing wine industry and wine style, first cultivated by the Portuguese

Emperor Kangxi invites 7,000 'longevitiy stars' to a palace banquet on his 60th birthday where royal princes serve wine to honour the elders — 1713

— 1700

Thomas Jefferson visits Bordeaux (a bottle of Lafite 1787 said to belong to him was sold for £105,000 in 1985, at Christie's in London)

A Dream of Red Mansions was first published; the semi-autobiographical novel describes the decline of a noble family and depicts the food and drinking culture of the period — 1791

— 1787

Great Britain's first diplomatic envoy to China, the Macartney Mission, visits the Qianlong emperor in Beijing

— 1793

China	World
	Bordeaux wine official
— 1855	classification begins
	First record of
	phylloxera killing vines
	in France; by the end
	of the century it would
	spread across Europe
— 1863	and North Africa
	European vines
	grafted onto rootstocks
	of American species
	offer resistance to
	phylloxera; the practice
	becomes widely
— 1870	adopted in Europe

Changyu winery is
founded in Yantai,
Shandong province,
as the first industrial-
ised winery in China   1892 —

The Last Emperor of
China abdicates; the
Republic of China is   The *Titanic* sinks on
founded   1912 — 1912   her maiden voyage

Notable Chinese festivals

Traditional Chinese festivals follow the Chinese agricultural calendar, which is based on a lunar system. Therefore the dates of the festivals map differently to the Gregorian (solar) calendar from one year to another, much like Easter falls on different dates from year to year. Chinese festivals are great occasions where friends and families gather and wines are gifted and drunk.

CHUN JIE (SPRING FESTIVAL – CHINESE NEW YEAR)

Chinese calendar: 1 January
Gregorian calendar: typically late January to mid-February

YUAN XIAO JIE (LANTERNS FESTIVAL)

Chinese calendar: 15 January
Gregorian calendar: typically mid-February to early March

QING MING (CLEAR BRIGHT FESTIVAL OR ANCESTOR DAY)

Chinese calendar: 15th day after the spring equinox
Gregorian calendar: typically around 5 April

DUAN WU (DOUBLE FIFTH OR THE DRAGON BOAT FESTIVAL)

Chinese calendar: 5 May
Gregorian calendar: typically late May to late June

QI XI (LOVERS' DAY, YOUNG GIRLS' DAY, CHINESE 'VALENTINE'S DAY')

Chinese calendar: 7 July
Gregorian calendar: typically August

ZHONG QIU (MID-AUTUMN FESTIVAL OR MOON FESTIVAL)

Chinese calendar: 15 August
Gregorian calendar: typically September to early October

CHONG YANG (CLIMBING DAY OR ELDERS' DAY)

Chinese calendar: 9 September
Gregorian calendar: typically October

XIAO NIAN (LITTLE NEW YEAR OR GOD OF THE STOVE DAY)

Chinese calendar: 23 December
Gregorian calendar: typically January to early February

Glossary of terms and historical figures

Terms

alcohol by volume/abv Standard measure of alcoholic strength expressed in percentage of how much ethanol is present in a given volume of an alcoholic beverage at a reference temperature of 20°C (68°F).

All under Heaven (*tian xia*) Chinese term and cultural concept that encompasses the entire geographical world or a political sovereignty, as well as the metaphysical realm of humanity.

appellation Geographical indication of where grapes for a wine were grown, or the regulated and protected designation of controlled viticulture and winemaking practices that define certain characters of a wine and its place of origin.

bai jiu/baijiu/baiju Clear-coloured Chinese liquor made from distilled, fermented grain, typically 40 to 60 per cent abv.

Cabernet Gernischt Common name for Carménère in China.

Central Kingdom/Middle Kingdom (*zhong guo*) Chinese term for China that in its literal meaning encapsulates a historical view that the country is the centre and middle ground of the world.

Central Plain (*zhong yuan*) Area of the lower reaches of the Yellow River that form part of the North China Plain. Often hailed as the cradle of Chinese civilisation.

château French word for castle (plural châteaux). In the context of wine, and in particular of Bordeaux, refers to a wine estate.

Confucianism (*ru jia* – School of Scholars) A system of social and political teaching centring on benevolence, ethics and self-improvement. The core teaching is that one should practice *Ren* (altruism and respect), *Yi* (morality and righteousness) and *Li* (manners and rites) as the principles of life and the basis for social harmony. *See also* Hundred Schools of Thought.

Da Hong Pao Highly prized tea grown on the cliffs of Wuyi Mountains in Fujian province. Its name means 'big red robe' and derives from a legend that an emperor sent big red robes to be wrapped around some cliffside tea bushes after the tea cured his mother of an illness. It is an Oolong tea (semi-fermented).

desertification Process of land degradation by which environments become more desert-like. It can be exacerbated by climate change, human activities and other factors.

diurnal temperature variation Daily temperature difference between day and night.

en primeur French term for wine sold as forward contract prior to being bottled.

fermentation inducer (*jiu qu/qu*) Cultured moulds, yeasts and grain complexes used to kick-start fermentation in Chinese grain-based and traditional winemaking.

ganbei Literally 'dry the cup' – similar to 'bottoms up' – a toast that is often taken literally to encourage each other to empty a cup of wine, usually *bai jiu*.

garagiste French term for small-scale winemakers. The term originally described small operators in Bordeaux's Right Bank.

glutinous rice Also known as sticky rice, it is mostly grown in South-east and East Asia.

hong jiu Chinese term literally meaning 'red wine'. It is also commonly used to mean Western-style grape wine irrespective of colour. *See also pu tao jiu*.

huadiao jiu Type of yellow wine from Shaoxing in Zhejiang province. It is made from fermented glutinous rice and wheat.

***huang jiu* (yellow wine)** Traditional grain-based Chinese wine typically 12–20 per cent abv.

Hundred Schools of Thought (*zhu zi bai jia*) Branches of philosophy and study that flourished during the Spring–Autumn and the Warring States periods (770–221 BC). *See also* Confucianism, Legalism, Taoism.

jiang hu Chinese expression literally meaning 'rivers and lakes'. It encompasses places typically occupied by outlaws or martial tribes, or metaphorical impressions of nomadic existence and freedom.

jiu qu See fermentation inducer.

Jurchen People who inhabited the region in today's north-eastern extremity of China bordering Russia. In 1127, the Jurchens gained control over much of north China and toppled the Northern Song dynasty to establish the Jin dynasty. In 1234 it was conquered by the Mongols. The Jurchens re-emerged as a significant powerhouse in the seventeenth century and founded the Qing dynasty.

kumis Fermented beverage made from horse milk. It is popular among peoples of the Central Asian steppes.

kung fu (gong fu) Form of martial arts but has wider applications in the Chinese language to encompass any endeavour that requires concentration, discipline and mettle.

Legalism (*fa jia* – School of Law) Philosophy that maintains that the only effective method of ensuring social order is through the imposition of discipline and law, because human nature is inherently self-serving. The legalists' stance favours the primacy of state welfare apparatus over the individual. *See also* Hundred Schools of Thought.

Mandate of Heaven (*tian ming*) Ancient and enduring Chinese belief system that a ruler's power comes from divine authority, and the deeds and behaviour of the ruler must meet with approval from Heaven or the privilege may be withdrawn and reassigned. Virtuous rule would increase the likelihood of the ruler retaining the Mandate, while an incompetent or cruel regime would be punished by disasters and uprisings, and the Mandate would ultimately change hands.

Marselan Cross of Cabernet Sauvignon and Grenache initially developed for the Languedoc region but in recent years has found success in China.

mead Alcoholic beverage made with fermented honey, typically 3 to 20 per cent abv. It has a long history and many variations exist throughout Europe, Africa and Asia.

Middle Kingdom *See* Central Kingdom.

millet Group of various grass crops among the oldest and most widely grown cereals in the world.

mouthfeel Wine-tasting term that refers to tactile sensations of a wine in the mouth.

négociant French term for merchant. In the wine trade, *négociants* are traditionally winemakers as well as traders.

oenology Study of wine and winemaking. Usually distinct from viticulture, which deals with the study of vine and grape growing.

osmanthus Genus of about 30 species of flowering plants belonging to the Oleaceae family, many native to East Asia. Very popular in China as a garden shrub, and used in cooking, drinks and Chinese medicine.

place de Bordeaux, La French term that describes the Bordeaux wine trade. In particular the intricate relationships between wine estates (châteaux), merchants (*négociants*) and brokers (*courtiers*).

provenance Record of origin and ownership that underpins authenticity, quality, condition and therefore value of an asset. In fine wine, the storage conditions are also important.

Pu'er tea Variety of fermented tea produced in Yunnan province; some age very well.

pu tao jiu Chinese term literally meaning 'grape wine'. *See also hong jiu.*

Reform and Opening Up (*gai ge kai fang*) Process of economic reform termed 'Socialism with Chinese characteristics', set in motion in 1978 by the reformist leader Deng Xiao Ping (1904–97).

saké Japanese rice wine.

shao jiu See *bai jiu*.

Shaoxing jiu Famous variety of yellow wine produced with high-grade glutinous rice and water from the Mirror Lake (Jian Hu) in Shaoxing, Zhejiang province. *See also huadiao jiu, huang jiu.*

shochu Japanese distilled grain-based spirit.

Silk Road Ancient network of trade routes that connected China and the West, first formalised during the Han dynasty in the second century BC. The term derives from the lucrative silk trade that flourished en route. Grape vines and wines are thought to have made inroads to China via the Silk Road. *See also* Han Wudi, Zhang Qian.

soju Korean distilled grain-based spirit.

sorghum Grass species cultivated for its grain, which is used for food and *bai jiu* production in China.

Taoism/Daoism (dao jia – School of the Way) Religious and philosophical approach to life known as the 'Way', which represents a mysterious, all-encompassing spirit of the universe that transcends space and time. The 'Way' points to the virtues of harmony between people and nature. *See also* Hundred Schools of Thought.

terroir French term that encompasses all the environmental factors of a place that impart unique characters to the wine produced on the site. It is a concept central to Old World winemaking philosophy.

tribute wine Since Chinese antiquity, wine's primary function was as an offering to honour gods and ancestors in rituals. Tribute wine must be of the highest quality and presented at ceremonies. Over time tribute wine also referred to wines made for the emperor or royal household.

vinification Process of turning grapes into wine.

viticulture Study and practice of grape culture.

Western Regions (*Xiyu*) Historical name for the regions west of Yumen Guan (the Jade Pass, the name of a gate of the Great Wall in today's Gansu province). The region was significant as a cultural and commercial passage between East Asia, the Indian subcontinent, the Middle East and Europe.

Yangtze River (*Yangzi Jiang, Chang Jiang*) Longest river in Asia and third longest river in the world. It runs for 6,300km from the Tibetan Plateau to the East China Sea, and drains an area of 1.8 million km².

Yellow River (*Huang He*) Second longest river in China, so-called due to the yellow sediment it carries to the sea. It runs for 5,464km from the Tibetan Plateau to the Yellow Sea, and drains an area of 750,000 km².

yellow wine See *huang jiu*.

Historical figures

Bai Juyi (772–846) Famous Tang Dynasty poet and high-ranking government official. He is self-styled as 'Mr Drunken Chanter' and is arguably the most prolific wine poet with an estimated 900 wine-related poems surviving to this day.

Cao Cao (155–220) Infamous warlord and influential chancellor of the late Eastern Han dynasty. A key figure of the Three Kingdoms period and founder of what was later the state of Cao Wei. He was an avid wine lover and winemaker.

Confucius (551–479 BC) China's most influential educator and philosopher. *See also* Confucianism.

Du Fu (712–70) Prominent Tang dynasty poet and a contemporary of Li Bai. Around 300 of his wine-related poems survive. *See also* Li Bai.

Du Kang Mythical pre-history figure often credited as the forefather of wine. *See also* Yi Di.

Duke of Zhou/Zhou Gong (11th century BC) One of the most revered legislators and philosophers in Chinese history. He is believed to have written the earliest code of conduct in China relating to wine drinking. He is also credited with classical works on rites and music, and the concept of the Mandate of Heaven.

Han Wudi/Emperor Wu (157–87 BC) Seventh emperor of the Han dynasty during whose reign the Silk Road was established and grape vines and wine were brought to China from the Western Regions. Han Wudi took a personal interest in vine cultivation and winemaking. *See also* Zhang Qian.

Huang Di (Yellow Emperor) Mythical leader in ancient China who is credited with numerous inventions, including wine, particularly medicinal wine.

Kangxi, Emperor (1654–1722) Fourth Qing dynasty emperor who is widely acknowledged as one of the greatest rulers in Chinese history. He reigned for 61 years and his longevity is said to be in part due to his daily habit of drinking a small glass of claret at meal times.

Li Bai (701–62) Hailed as the 'poetry saint' and 'god of wine' by his Tang dynasty contemporaries and posterity, Li Bai remains the most celebrated Chinese poet. Around 1,050 of his poems survive, of which around 170 relate to wine.

Li Qingzhao (*c.*1084–*c.*1155) China's most celebrated female poet. She was a wine lover and wrote numerous poems about wine – as elixir for joy or ineffective cure for heartache.

Liu Bang/Emperor Gaozu (256–195 BC) Founding emperor of the Han dynasty. He was the first peasant-born emperor of China and redefined the aristocratic order.

Liu Bei (161–223) Key figure in the late Eastern Han dynasty who founded the state of Shu Han during the Three Kingdoms period.

Qu Yuan (c.340–278 BC) Patriotic poet and minister of the state of Chu during the Warring States period. His poems contain some of the earliest written references to wine. The Dragons Boat festival is dedicated to his memory.

Shen Nong/Yan Di/Emperor Yan 'Divine Farmer' and mythical leader in antiquity. Credited with experimenting with farming methods and identifying many herbs and crops, including tea and medicinal wine ingredients.

Shi Huang Di/Qin Shi Hunag/Ying Zheng (259–210 BC) Founding emperor of the Qin dynasty and the first to unite 'All under Heaven' – the notion of a unified Chinese empire.

Shun, Emperor Legendary leader in ancient China who lived around the third millennium BC.

Su Shi/Su Dongpo (1037–1101) Famous Song dynasty poet and scholar. He was a connoisseur of many things including wine and food. He was a keen hobbyist winemaker.

Xiang Yu (232–202 BC) Chinese general and rebel leader who overthrew the Qin dynasty. He was subsequently defeated by Liu Bang, who founded the Han dynasty. *See also* Liu Bang.

Xuanzong, Emperor (685–762) Seventh emperor of the Tang dynasty and an admirer of Li Bai's poetry. He was a dynamic ruler who propelled Tang to its peak and reigned over one of the most illustrious periods in Chinese civilisation. Later in life he became extremely indulgent and arrogant. He underestimated a rebellion in 755, which set in motion the weakening and eventual demise of the dynasty. In popular culture his love for Lady Yang is much celebrated. *See also* Yang Gui Fei, Li Bai.

Yan Di *See* Shen Nong.

Yang Gui Fei/Yang Yu Huan/Lady Yang (719–56) Beloved Noble Consort of Emperor Xuanzong of Tang. Her rouged complexion after drinking wine was so alluring that court ladies tried to emulate the look with heavy applications of rouge powder – a fashion statement immortalised in Tang dynasty paintings of court ladies. In popular culture a famous Chinese opera is dedicated to the story of 'Lady Yang's intoxication'. *See also* Emperor Xuanzong.

Yellow Emperor *See* Huang Di.

Yi Di Mythical winemaker in antiquity. Often credited as the inventor of wine. *See also* Du Kang.

Yu the Great/Da Yu Semi-mythical leader and founder of the Xia dynasty *c*.2070 BC.

Zhang Qian (164–114 BC) Diplomat and explorer sent by Emperor Han Wudi to establish relations with Central Asian tribes. His adventures resulted in the trade routes that became known as the Silk Road. Western wines were among the goods that travelled to China along this route. *See also* Silk Road, Han Wudi.

Zheng He (1371–1433) Ming dynasty admiral, explorer and diplomat who commanded seven naval expeditions to South-east Asia, South Asia, Western Asia and East Africa in 1405–33.

Acknowledgements

I am grateful to my contributors, whom I am privileged to call friends. It is thanks to them that everything in this book feels so personal to me, including insights, discussions, images and calligraphies.

Li Demei: Associate Professor, Food Science and Technology College in Beijing University of Agriculture. Wine consultant to several wineries in China, including Jia Bei Lan, winner of the *Decanter* World Wine Awards International Trophy 2011. Contributor and columnist to several prestigious wine publications, including *Decanter China* and *The Oxford Companion to Wine* (4th edition). Li has won the 2012 Wine Intelligence 10-for-10 Business Award and was named in the *Decanter* Power List 2013, and Drinks Business Top 10 Most Influential Wine Consultants 2013.

Shen Qinyan: Researcher and curator at the Shaanxi History Museum in Xi'an, China, engaged in cultural relics management and protection. Research interests include the history and culture of the Sui and Tang dynasties, Tang dynasty gold- and silverware, and tomb murals. She has published 10 monographs and over 60 papers.

Wei Qiuping: Assistant researcher at the Shaanxi History Museum in Xi'an, China, engaged in cultural relics management and protection. Research focus: bronze, gold and silver, and tombstone inscriptions. She has contributed to four publications and over ten papers.

Lu Kuangsheng: Alias 'Stone Bull', he is a member of the Chinese Calligraphy Society, senior art consultant at the Xinxiang Calligraphy Research Centre, and vice chancellor of Henan Normal University Seniors Painting and Calligraphy Institute. He founded the 'Stone Bull' seal script, a style much admired by his peers. His calligraphy has been exhibited at home and abroad and won numerous accolades.

Mr Lu has developed Parkinson's disease and has taken to practising calligraphy with his left hand, as his right hand with which he normally writes is severely restricted by the condition. I would like to thank him especially for producing the excellent calligraphy works for this book using his left hand.

Fang Ruozhou: Zhengzhou Light Industry University, Eastern International Art College. He specialises in lacquer painting and Chinese painting, and has won numerous awards at provincial competitions.

Zhou Xiaojun: Henan Normal University College of Fine Arts. He has won numerous awards for his calligraphy, Chinese painting and oil painting. He was instrumental in the design and interpretation of Fang Ruozhou's contributions to the book.

Chengdu Youyuanfang Spirits Co. Ltd: Artisan winery based in Qionglai (historically Lin Qiong) in Sichuan province, which is the location of the love story of Zhuo Wenjun and Sima Xiangru (*see* page 162).

My heartfelt thanks to all who have inspired, supported and taught me in some way on my wine journey. In order of our first meeting:
2011: Jean-Charles Cazes (Château Lynch-Bages)
2012: Ludovic Bigo (Cuvelier-Fauvarque); Didier Cuvelier (Château Léoville Poyferré); Edouard Miailhe (Château Siran); Alexander Van Beek and Marc Verpaalen (Château Giscours, Château du Tertre); Véronique Sanders (Château Haut-Bailly); Philippe Blanc (Château Beychevelle); Jean-Hubert Delon and Pierre Graffeuille (Château Léoville-Las Cases, Domaines Delon); John Kolasa and Sandrine Bégaud (Château Rauzan-Segla); Jean-Paul Gardère (the late director of

Château Latour); Thomas Duroux (Château Palmer); Jean-Philippe Delmas (Château Haut-Brion, Domaine Clarence Dillon); Denis Dubourdieu (the late proprietor of Denis Dubourdieu Domaines); Claire Villars Lurton and Caroline Ruffié (Château Ferrière); Aline Baly (Château Coutet)

2013: Stéphanie de Boüard (Château Angélus); Andrew Henderson (Circle of Wine Writers, the Champagne Academy)

2014: Oz Clarke (Circle of Wine Writers)

2015: Miguel Torres Sr (Bodegas Torres); Edouard Moeuix (Établissements Jean-Pierre Moueix); Professor Li Demei (China Wine Association, Chinese Viticulture Society); Sarah Kemp (*Decanter*); Sylvia Wu (*Decanter China*), Richard Bampfield (Master of Wine)

2017: Lenz Moser (Château Changyu Moser XV)

2018: Huang Jianyong (Chengdu Youyuanfang Spirits Co. Ltd); Wang Fang (Kanaan Winery); Zhang Jing (Château Helan Qingxue); Michael Sun (Panda Fine Wine)

I am very grateful to Oz Clarke for his generous foreword, and delighted by it. I would like to thank Carey Smith, Samantha Crisp, Howard Watson, Marion Paull and everyone at Ebury Press who worked on this project – thank you all for guiding me through the whole process of realising my first book. Special thanks to Professor Li Demei and Rodney Paull for the excellent maps. Also my sincere gratitude to Laura Gladwin who helped me edit the early version of the manuscript and Emmanuel Nataf at Reedsy who made some crucial introductions that eventually led to the publication of this book. Of course I thank my family and friends for their indefatigable interest, support and patience. Anyone whom I have not mentioned but should have done, please get in touch and complain about it and I would be glad to go for a glass of Chinese wine with you.

INDEX

Fu Hao, 132
Fuchai, King of Wu, 148
Fujian (Hokkien) cuisine, 95

ganbei (dry the cup), 200
Gaozu, Emperor, *see* Liu Bang
Gardère, Jean-Paul, 82, 89
global economic crisis, 49, 56–7
God of the Stove Day, *see* Little New Year
     or God of the Stove Day
*Golden Lotus, The, see Plum in the Golden
     Vase, The*
Gong Niang No. 1 hybrid, 23
Goujian of Yue, King, 148, 241
grain crops, domestication of, 122, 125
grain-based wines (*bai jiu*), 18, 40–3,
     63–4, 69, 76, 93, 101, 134–5, 145,
     174, 178, 188, 191–2, 200, 211–12,
     255
     see also distilled liquors
Grand Canal, 177, 233, 246
Great Leap Forward, 220
Great Wall of China, 24–5, 156, 177, 231
Great Wall Wine Company, 222
Great Yu vessel, 135
gu (ceremonial wine cup), 154
Guan Yu, 168–9
Guangxu, Emperor, 219
gunpowder, 190

Han (state), 156–7
Han Chinese, 113, 124, 198, 203,
     234–5
Han dynasties, 21–2, 42, 75, 100, 159,
     161–2, 164–7, 174, 186, 201, 203,
     206, 232, 242–3
'happy wine', 99, 101
He Zhizhang, 182–3
'heaven–earth–people', 78–9, 81–2, 84
Heavenly Emperor, 112, 121
Hebei province, 28–9
Hong Kong, 50, 54, 217
Hongwu, Emperor, 203
hospitality, 99, 101, 113–14, 157
Hou Han Shu (Book of Late Han), 165
*Hong Lou Meng (A Dream of Red Man-
     sions)*, 214–15, 251

Hua Tuo, 166
Huang Di, *see* Yellow Emperor
huang jiu, see yellow wine
Huang Taiji, 211
Huaxia civilisation, 124
Hunan cuisine, 94
Hundred Schools of Thought, 149–53,
     156, 240, 257
Hundred Years War, 209

Imperial Examination System, 177
introspection, Chinese, 209–10
irrigation, 190

Jesuit missionaries, 214
Jia Sixie, 173
Jian Yong, 170–1
jiang hu spirits, 194
Jiang Tong, 124
Jiangsu cuisine, 95
Jiao Sui, 182–3
Jie, Emperor, 130
Jilin Institute of Pomology, 23
Jin dynasties, 167, 171, 197, 211, 232–3,
     245
Jin, *see* Jurchens
jiu (the word), 17–18, 99, 120
Jiu Gao (Admonition of Wine), 124, 136,
     144, 239
Jiu Pu (Purview of Wine), 190
jiu qu, see fermentation inducers
Journey to the West, 204–6
Jurchen Jin dynasty, 197, 234
Jurchens (Jin), 99, 196–7, 210–11, 234,
     258

Kangxi, Emperor, 75, 101–2, 211,
     213–14, 251, 262
Kolasa, John, 84
Kong Rong, 170
Korean ethnic group, 115
kowtowing, 169
Kublai Khan, 198, 200
kumis (fermented horse milk), 199, 249,
     258
kung fu, 88–9, 194, 258
Kwok, Peter, 228